First World War
and Army of Occupation
War Diary
France, Belgium and Germany

9 DIVISION
South African Brigade
3 South African Infantry Regiment
3 April 1916 - 25 April 1916

WO95/1782

The Naval & Military Press Ltd
www.nmarchive.com
Published in association with The National Archives

Published by

The Naval & Military Press Ltd

Unit 10 Ridgewood Industrial Park,

Uckfield, East Sussex,

TN22 5QE England

Tel: +44 (0) 1825 749494

www.naval-military-press.com

www.nmarchive.com

This diary has been reprinted in facsimile from the original. Any imperfections are inevitably reproduced and the quality may fall short of modern type and cartographic standards.

Contents

Document type	Place/Title	Date From	Date To
War Diary	Steenwerck	26/04/1916	28/04/1916
Miscellaneous	Headquarters. 1st S.A. Infantry Brigade. Sidi Bishr Camp. Alexandria, 6th April, 1916 App. 993	06/04/1916	06/04/1916
Miscellaneous	A Form. Messages And Signals.		
Miscellaneous	O.c. A. B.C & D Qr. M.G. Co. & To. O.C. Coy	06/04/1916	06/04/1916
Miscellaneous	Headquarters, 1st S.A. Infantry Brigade. Sidi Bishr Camp. Alexandria. 7th April. 1916. App 100.7	07/04/1916	07/04/1916
Miscellaneous	Headquarters, 1st S.A. Infantry Brigade. Sidi Bishr Camp. Alexandria. 11th April. 1916 App 101	11/04/1916	11/04/1916
Miscellaneous	Embarkation Order App 102		
Miscellaneous	Schedule "B".	18/04/1916	18/04/1916
Miscellaneous	Allotment Of Accommodation		
Miscellaneous	Embarkation Order G.-Col. E.F. Thackeray Cdg. 3rd. S.A.I. Sidi Bishr 12.4.16 App 103	12/04/1916	12/04/1916
Miscellaneous	Headquarters, 1st S.A. Infantry Brigade. App 134	17/06/1916	17/06/1916
Miscellaneous	Headquarters, 1st S.A. Infantry Brigade.	18/06/1916	18/06/1916
Miscellaneous	Copy No. 1		
Miscellaneous	Reference 9th Division No. X. 4/1274/ Para 10 Of 23rd April., App 104	28/04/1916	28/04/1916
War Diary	Steenwerck	02/05/1916	06/05/1916
War Diary	Le Bizet	06/05/1916	08/05/1916
War Diary	Trenches	08/05/1916	14/05/1916
War Diary	Lebizet	15/05/1916	20/05/1916
War Diary	Trenches	20/05/1916	26/05/1916
War Diary	Le Bizet	27/05/1916	28/05/1916
War Diary	Noote Boom	28/05/1916	29/05/1916
War Diary	Strazelle	29/05/1916	31/05/1916
Miscellaneous	Preliminary Move. App 108	07/05/1916	07/05/1916
Miscellaneous		22/05/1916	22/05/1916
Operation(al) Order(s)	The Officer Commanding, Company. Move Copy Of Operation Order No 30, 24th May 1916 App 123	24/05/1916	24/05/1916
Miscellaneous	Movements In Rear.		
Miscellaneous	Haystack.		
Miscellaneous	Intelligence Report.	12/05/1916	12/05/1916
Miscellaneous	O/c A Coy.	18/05/1916	18/05/1916
Miscellaneous	Machine Gun Rifle Fine.		
Operation(al) Order(s)	1st South African Infantry Brigade. Operation Order No. 31 App. 126	27/05/1916	27/05/1916
Miscellaneous	Intelligence Report Left Sector From 6. a.m 22/5/16 to 6.a.m 23/516	22/05/1916	22/05/1916
Operation(al) Order(s)	1st South African Infantry Brigade. Operation Order No. 28. App. 118	18/05/1916	18/05/1916
Miscellaneous	Intelligence Report From 6a.m. 9/5/16 To 6 a.m. 10/5/16	09/05/1916	09/05/1916
Miscellaneous	Messages And Signals. App. 116	13/05/1916	13/05/1916
Miscellaneous	Instructions		
Miscellaneous	Intelligence Report From 6 a.m. 25/5/16 To 26/5/16	25/05/1916	25/05/1916
Miscellaneous	O/c "A" Coy.	29/05/1918	29/05/1918
Operation(al) Order(s)	Enemy & Artillery Operation Into		

Operation(al) Order(s)	1st S.A. Infantry Brigade Operation Order No. 25. App. 108	07/05/1916	07/05/1916
Miscellaneous	Third South African Infantry.	04/05/1916	04/05/1916
Miscellaneous	Copy No 1		
Miscellaneous	War Diary. App 138		
Miscellaneous	Embarkation Orders (2)	11/04/1916	11/04/1916
Miscellaneous	Bde Hdqrs. S.A. Bde. 3rd Regt S A I		
Miscellaneous	Daily Intelligence Report	27/08/1916	27/08/1916
Operation(al) Order(s)	Operation Order No. 24		
Miscellaneous	Headquarters 1st Inf Bde.	04/05/1916	04/05/1916
Miscellaneous		20/08/1916	20/08/1916
Miscellaneous	Daily Intelligence Report Row Lock.	30/08/1916	30/08/1916
Miscellaneous	1st South African Infantry Brigade Annexure to Operation Order No. 50		
Miscellaneous	Secret.		
Miscellaneous	Headquarters 1st S.A. Infantry Brigade.	28/05/1916	28/05/1916
Miscellaneous	Reliefs Time Table	08/05/1916	08/05/1916
Operation(al) Order(s)	Brig Operation Order No. 31 The Officer Commanding App 126		
Miscellaneous	Showing Arrangements For Attachment Of 1st And 4th South African Infantry To Battalions In The Line App 112	11/05/1916	11/05/1916
Operation(al) Order(s)	1st South African Infantry Brigade. Operation Order No. 24 App 106	04/05/1916	04/05/1916
Miscellaneous	Third South African Infantry The Officer Commanding App 108	08/05/1916	08/05/1916
Operation(al) Order(s)	1st South African Infantry Brigade. Operation Order No. 30 App 123	24/05/1916	24/05/1916
War Diary	Strazeele Area	01/06/1916	02/06/1916
War Diary	S.M. Area	02/06/1916	03/06/1916
War Diary	Quernes	03/06/1916	04/06/1916
War Diary	Rest Area	04/06/1916	15/06/1916
War Diary	Breilly	16/06/1916	18/06/1916
Operation(al) Order(s)	Headquarters, 1st S.A. Infantry Brigade. 1st June, 1916 Operation Orders No. 33. App 128	01/06/1916	01/06/1916
War Diary	Bois Celestins	26/06/1916	01/07/1916
War Diary		18/06/1916	19/06/1916
War Diary	Etinehem	19/06/1916	22/06/1916
War Diary	B.C.	23/06/1916	25/06/1916
Miscellaneous	Messages And Signals.		
Miscellaneous		14/07/1916	14/07/1916
Miscellaneous			
Operation(al) Order(s)	S.A.I. Bde Operation Order No. 48		
Miscellaneous	A Form Messages And Signals		
Miscellaneous	To O.C. 3rd S.A.I. App 154	14/07/1916	14/07/1916
Miscellaneous	To O.C. 3rd S.A.I. App 153		
Operation(al) Order(s)	1st South African Infantry Brigade. Operation Order No. 36	13/06/1916	13/06/1916
Miscellaneous	Headquarters, 1st S.A. Infantry Brigade.	12/06/1916	12/06/1916
Miscellaneous Map	Special Idea. Reference Map 5A 1/100,000		
Miscellaneous	General Idea. Reference Map 5.A. 1/100,000		
Miscellaneous	Headquarters, 1st S.A. Infantry Brigade. 10th June, 1916 Brigade Training Scheme For 11th Inst.	10/06/1916	10/06/1916
Operation(al) Order(s)	1st South African Infantry Brigade Operation Orders No. 36	10/06/1916	10/06/1916

Miscellaneous	Headquarters. 1st S.A. Infantry Brigade.	10/06/1916	10/06/1916
Operation(al) Order(s)	Operation Order 36 App 132	10/06/1918	10/06/1918
Miscellaneous	Map-Hazebrouck, No. 5.A. 1/100,000		
Miscellaneous	3rd S.A. Inf. Transvaal Rgt. Intelligence Report From 6. a.m. 13/5/16 to 6 a.m. 14/5/16	13/05/1916	13/05/1916
Miscellaneous	Messages And Signals App. 112	11/05/1916	11/05/1916
Operation(al) Order(s)	Move Orders by Lieut. Col. E.F. Thackeray, C.M.G., Commanding, Third South African Infantry.	13/06/1916	13/06/1916
Diagram etc	H.M.T. "Saxonia"		
Miscellaneous			
Miscellaneous	Headquarters, 1st S.A. Infantry Brigade.	28/06/1916	28/06/1916
Operation(al) Order(s)	1st South African Infantry Brigade. Operation Order No. 39 App 142	30/06/1916	30/06/1916
Miscellaneous	App 142	30/06/1916	30/06/1916
Miscellaneous	SC. B26 O/C 3 Regt SAI	01/06/1916	01/06/1916
Miscellaneous	Officer Commanding Company.	12/06/1916	12/06/1916
Operation(al) Order(s)	Move Orders 3rd S.A. Infantry. App 129	23/06/1916	23/06/1916
Operation(al) Order(s)	1st South African Infantry Brigade. Operation Order No. 38 App 129	28/06/1916	28/06/1916
Miscellaneous	1st Regt. S.A.I. 2nd Regt. S.A.I. 3rd Regt. S.A.I. 4th Regt. S.A.I.	27/05/1916	27/05/1916
Miscellaneous	C Form (Duplicate). Messages And Signals.		
Miscellaneous	Headquarters, 1st S.A. Infantry Brigade.	01/06/1916	01/06/1916
Miscellaneous	Billetting Instructions For Move From Strazeele To Rest Area.		
Miscellaneous	O/c A Coy.		
Map	1st Army Special Manceuvre Area.		
Operation(al) Order(s)	Headquarters, 1st S.A. Infantry Brigade. 3rd June, 1916 Operation Orders No. 35	03/06/1916	03/06/1916
Operation(al) Order(s)	Headquarters, 1st S.A. Infantry Brigade. 3rd June, 1916 Operation Orders No. 34 App 130	03/06/1916	03/06/1916
Miscellaneous			
Operation(al) Order(s)	Headquarters, 1st S.A. Infantry Brigade. Extracts From Standing Orders For The Brigade Whilst on the March, (issued in Egypt)		
Miscellaneous	XIII Corps. App 137	21/06/1916	21/06/1916
Miscellaneous	Issued at 2.45 PM B 102	28/06/1916	28/06/1916
Miscellaneous	B 4/83 App 135	22/06/1916	22/06/1916
Miscellaneous	1st South African Infantry Brigade. Parties Visiting Trench Area.	18/06/1916	18/06/1916
Miscellaneous	Headquarters 1st S.A. Infantry Brigade.	18/06/1916	18/06/1916
War Diary	Grovetown	01/07/1916	02/07/1916
War Diary	Copse Valley	03/07/1916	04/07/1916
War Diary	Stanley Av & Vicinity	05/07/1916	09/07/1916
War Diary	Silesia & Support Trenches	10/07/1916	13/07/1916
War Diary	Talus Boise	14/07/1916	15/07/1916
War Diary	Delville Wood	15/07/1916	31/07/1916
Miscellaneous			
Miscellaneous	Issued at 7.55 pm B 106	02/07/1916	02/07/1916
Operation(al) Order(s)	1st South African Infantry Brigade. Operation Orders No. 41	02/07/1916	02/07/1916
Miscellaneous	Headquarters, 1st S.A. Infantry Brigade. 1st July 1916	01/07/1916	01/07/1916
Operation(al) Order(s)	1st South African Infantry Brigade. Operation Order No. 41	02/07/1916	02/07/1916
Miscellaneous	To O.C. 3rd S.A.I.	22/07/1916	22/07/1916
Miscellaneous	B.M. 47/12/10	01/07/1916	01/07/1916

Miscellaneous	Intelligence		
Miscellaneous			
Miscellaneous	Extract from Brigade Operation Orders No 40 9.15 am	01/07/1916	01/07/1916
Miscellaneous		01/07/1916	01/07/1916
Miscellaneous	S.A.I. Brigade H.Q. 3rd Regiment	10/07/1916	10/07/1916
Miscellaneous	Headquarters, 1st S.A. Infantry Brigade.	26/07/1916	26/07/1916
Miscellaneous	Headquarters, 1st S.A. Infantry Brigade. App 157	25/07/1918	25/07/1918
Miscellaneous	Instructions No. 3 for move of 9th (Scottish) Division.	23/07/1916	23/07/1916
Miscellaneous	Headquarters, 1st S.A. Infantry Brigade. App 155	24/07/1916	24/07/1916
Miscellaneous	A Form Messages And Signals.		
Miscellaneous	B. M 11	18/07/1916	18/07/1916
Miscellaneous	3rd S.A.I. 4/5 7.16. A Diary XXX Div.		
Miscellaneous	War Diary.	06/07/1916	06/07/1916
Miscellaneous	O/C 3rd & 4th Regiment SAI	05/07/1916	05/07/1916
Miscellaneous	Head Street - No. Communication Trenches used as Such are to be occupied		
Operation(al) Order(s)	1st South African Infantry Brigade. Operation Order No. 43	08/07/1916	08/07/1916
Miscellaneous		06/07/1916	06/07/1916
Miscellaneous	Infantry to-night will be at four Willows, East of Machine Gun Wood.		
Miscellaneous	Headquarters, 1st S.A. Infantry Brigade Operation Order No. 43 App 149	06/07/1916	06/07/1916
Miscellaneous	Working Party Issued at 3/20	06/07/1916	06/07/1916
Miscellaneous	A Form Messages And Signals		
Miscellaneous	A Form Messages And Signals	05/07/1916	05/07/1916
Miscellaneous	C Form (Original). Messages And Signals		
Miscellaneous	Headquarters 1st S.A. Infantry Brigade App 148	06/07/1916	06/07/1916
Miscellaneous	Issue 3/40 Pm. B/109	04/07/1916	04/07/1916
Miscellaneous	Issued at 3/5 PM B/108	04/07/1916	04/07/1916
Miscellaneous	Headquarters 1st S.A. Infantry Brigade	04/07/1916	04/07/1916
Miscellaneous	Issued at 2/55 pm B/107	04/07/1916	04/07/1916
Miscellaneous			
Operation(al) Order(s)	1st south African Infantry Brigade. Operation Orders No. 42. App 147	04/07/1916	04/07/1916
Miscellaneous	O.C. 3rd S.A.I. App 146	03/07/1916	03/07/1916
Miscellaneous	Working Party	03/07/1916	03/07/1916
Miscellaneous	Officer Commanding 3rd S.A. Infantry.	13/07/1916	13/07/1916
Miscellaneous	A Form Messages And Signals		
Miscellaneous			
Miscellaneous	O/c "A" Coy, App 152	13/07/1916	13/07/1916
Miscellaneous	Working Party	12/07/1916	12/07/1916
Miscellaneous	C Form (Duplicate). Messages And Signals.	12/07/1916	12/07/1916
Miscellaneous	A Form Messages And Signals. App 157		
Miscellaneous	C Form (Duplicate). Messages And Signals		
Miscellaneous	Headquarters 1st S.A. Infantry Brigade.	09/07/1916	09/07/1916
Operation(al) Order(s)	African Infantry Brigade Operation Order No. 46	10/07/1916	10/07/1916
Miscellaneous			
Miscellaneous	C Form (Duplicate). Messages And Signals.		
Miscellaneous	O/C 3rd 1/4 SAI	08/07/1916	08/07/1916
Operation(al) Order(s)	1st South African Infantry Brigade. Operation Order No. 44	08/07/1916	08/07/1916
Miscellaneous		09/07/1916	09/07/1916
Miscellaneous	To O/C D Coy. Walter.		
Miscellaneous	Working Party App 150	08/07/1916	08/07/1916
Miscellaneous	C Form (Duplicate). Messages And Signals.		

Miscellaneous			
Operation(al) Order(s)	Operation Orders No 40 App 144	01/07/1916	01/07/1916
Miscellaneous	O.C. 1st S.A.I. App.143		
Heading	3rd South African Regiment August 1916		
War Diary	Fresnicourt	01/08/1916	15/08/1916
War Diary	Guoy Servins	15/08/1916	23/08/1916
War Diary	Front Line Trench	23/08/1916	30/08/1916
War Diary	Trenches	30/08/1916	31/08/1916
Miscellaneous		26/08/1916	26/08/1916
Miscellaneous		29/08/1916	29/08/1916
Miscellaneous		28/08/1916	28/08/1916
Operation(al) Order(s)	O.O. No. 50	21/08/1916	21/08/1916
Operation(al) Order(s)	1st South African Infantry Brigade Operation Order No. 40 App 158	15/08/1916	15/08/1916
Operation(al) Order(s)	1st South African Infantry Brigade Operation Order 51 App 166	28/08/1916	28/08/1916
Operation(al) Order(s)	1st South African Infantry Brigade Operation Order No. 50 App 162	21/08/1916	21/08/1916
Miscellaneous	App. 166	26/08/1916	26/08/1916
Miscellaneous	Move Orders By Lt. Colonel E.F. Thackeray. CMG. Commanding 3rd South African Infantry.	15/08/1916	15/08/1916
Miscellaneous	Move Orders by Major B Young From Commanding 3rd South African Infantry App 164	22/08/1916	22/08/1916
Miscellaneous	North Of International Ave.	28/08/1916	28/08/1916
Miscellaneous	Daily Intelligence Report	26/08/1916	26/08/1916
Miscellaneous	Enemy Artillery Corps.		
Miscellaneous	Daily Intelligence Summary	24/08/1916	24/08/1916
Miscellaneous	Intelligence Report	25/08/1916	25/08/1916
Miscellaneous			
Operation(al) Order(s)	To. Recipients Of 1st S.A.I. Bde Operation Order No. 40	13/08/1916	13/08/1916
Miscellaneous	App 160		
Miscellaneous	To Rowlock.	29/08/1916	29/08/1916
Miscellaneous	Patrol Report.	28/08/1916	28/08/1916
Miscellaneous	3rd Regiments	29/08/1916	29/08/1916
Miscellaneous	Patrol Report	29/08/1916	29/08/1916
Miscellaneous	H.Q., S.A. Bde. 20th August 1916 App 163	20/08/1916	20/08/1916
Miscellaneous			
War Diary	Cabaret Rouge Trenches.	01/09/1916	03/09/1916
War Diary	Villier Au Bois	04/09/1916	17/09/1916
War Diary	Carency II. Trenches	18/09/1916	19/09/1916
War Diary	Carency No 2	20/09/1916	21/09/1916
War Diary	Villier Au Bois	21/09/1916	22/09/1916
War Diary	Estree Cauchie Chellers	23/09/1916	23/09/1916
War Diary	Chellers	24/09/1916	24/09/1916
War Diary	Magnicourt sur Canche	25/09/1916	28/09/1916
War Diary	Grand Rullecourt	29/09/1916	30/09/1916
Miscellaneous	9th. Div. No. X. 5/1826 Training. App 186	21/09/1916	21/09/1916
War Diary	Solum	03/04/1916	04/04/1916
War Diary	Alexandria	04/04/1916	15/04/1916
War Diary	H.M.T. Megantic	20/04/1916	20/04/1916
War Diary	Marseilles	20/04/1916	20/04/1916
War Diary	Steenwerck	23/04/1916	25/04/1916
War Diary	Solum	03/04/1916	04/04/1916
War Diary	Alexandria	04/04/1916	15/04/1916
War Diary	H.M.T. Megantic	20/04/1916	20/04/1916

War Diary	Marseilles	20/04/1916	20/04/1916
War Diary	Steenwerck	23/04/1916	25/04/1916

Page 14.

Instructions regarding War Diaries and Intelligence Summaries are contained in F. S. Regs., Part II. and the Staff Manual respectively. Title pages will be prepared in manuscript.

WAR DIARY

or

~~INTELLIGENCE SUMMARY.~~

(Erase heading not required.)

Army Form C. 2118.

3RD S. A. INF. (TRANSVAAL RGT)

Hour, Date, Place	Summary of Events and Information	Remarks and references to Appendices
3pm. 26-4-16. STEENWERCK	7 Officers and 40 other ranks proceeded to the trenches for instruction.	
2pm 27-4-16 -do-	6 Officers and 40 other ranks proceeded to trenches for instruction.	
5pm. 28 4 16 -do-	Orders received for 16 Platoons to proceed to Trenches for instruction. Div order No X 4/1374/4 d/28 April 1916	App 104

A W McDonald Captn
Capt. & Adjutant,
3rd S.A. Infantry (Transvaal Regt.)

O/adt

2

App. 99 3

HEADQUARTERS,

1st S. A. INFANTRY BRIGADE.

Sidi Bishr Camp, Alexandria,

6th April, 1916.

To the Officer Commanding,

3rd Regiment.

Orders have been received for the Brigade and Field Ambulance to embark for France.

No vehicles, animals or harness are to be taken, except

(1) Officers' chargers actually in possession.

(2) Saddlery for same.

AMMUNITION. 120 rounds per man, and 3500 rounds per machine gun will be taken.

STORES AND EQUIPMENT. Machine guns and all stores and equipment constituting the loads of all vehicles, but not vehicles equipment will be taken.

All personnel belonging to the Brigade and Field Ambulance should accompany them, i.e., with the exception of Hospital Patients there should not be any personnel left behind. Any men detached or on command should be recalled for embarkation immediately.

CLOTHING. All Units proceeding to France up to May are to embark in bulk with

1 Woollen Vest. 1 Woollen Drawers. 1 Satchel.
2 P. Helmets. 1 Pocket Patch per man

all of which are not to be issued on a voyage. Please arrange to indent for these. Service dress will be worn, and any kharki drill clothing and helmets are to be withdrawn prior to embarkation, and returned to Ordnance.

With reference to the return to the various departments of the transport animals, extra ammunition, and helmets now in possession of your Unit, you will be notified as soon as authority for same is received.

A. L. Pepper

Captain.

Staff Captain.

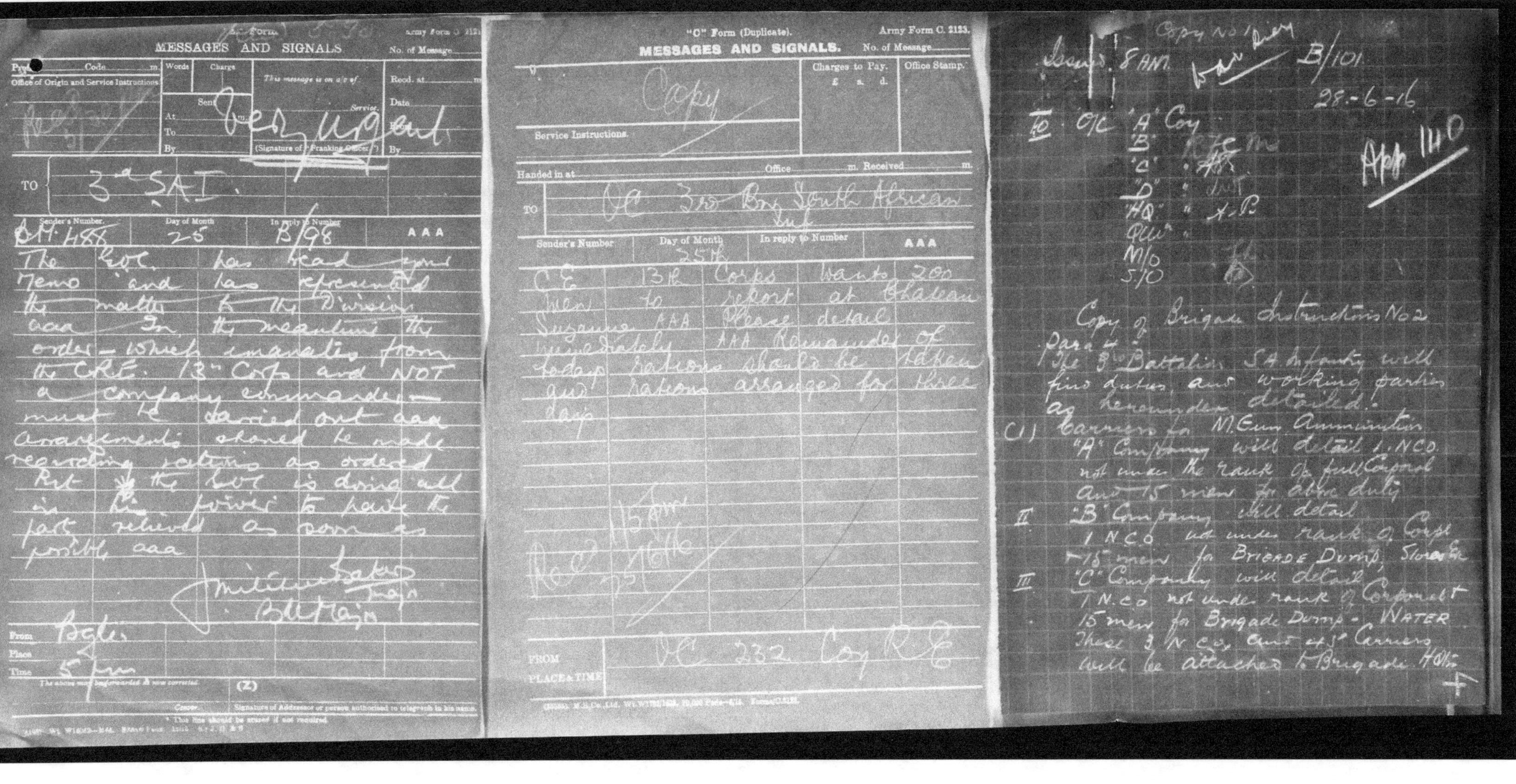

"C" Form. Army Form C. 2121.
MESSAGES AND SIGNALS. No. of Message

Very Urgent

TO 3rd S.A.I.

Sender's Number	Day of Month	In reply to Number	AAA
BM 488	25	B/98	

The G.O.C. has read your Memo and has represented the matter to the Division aaa In the meantime the order – which emanates from the C.R.E. 13th Corps and NOT a Company Commander – must be carried out aaa Arrangements should be made regarding rations as ordered But the G.O.C. is doing all in his power to have the party relieved as soon as possible aaa

J Mitchell-Baker Major
BM Major

From Bgde.
Time 5 pm

"O" Form (Duplicate). Army Form C. 2123.
MESSAGES AND SIGNALS. No. of Message

Copy

TO O.C. 3rd Bn South African Inf

Sender's Number	Day of Month	In reply to Number	AAA
	25th		

C.E. 13th Corps wants 200 men to report at Chateau Susanne AAA Please detail immediately AAA Remainder of todays rations should be taken and rations arranged for three days

Recd 15 pm 25/6/16

FROM O.C. 232 Coy R.E.

Copy No 1 War Diary

Issued 8 AM. B/101
28-6-16

To O/C "A" Coy
"B"
"C"
"D"
"HQ"
QM
M/O
S/O

App 140

Copy of Brigade Instructions No 2
Para 4.
The 3rd Battalion S.A. Infantry will find duties and working parties as hereunder detailed.

(1) Carriers for M.Gun Ammunition
"A" Company will detail 1 N.C.O. not under the rank of full Corporal and 15 men for above duty

II "B" Company will detail 1 N.C.O. not under rank of Corpl 15 men for BRIGADE DUMP, Stores &c

III "C" Company will detail 1 N.C.O not under rank of Corporal 15 men for Brigade Dump – WATER
These 3 N.C.O.s and 45 Carriers will be attached to Brigade HQrs

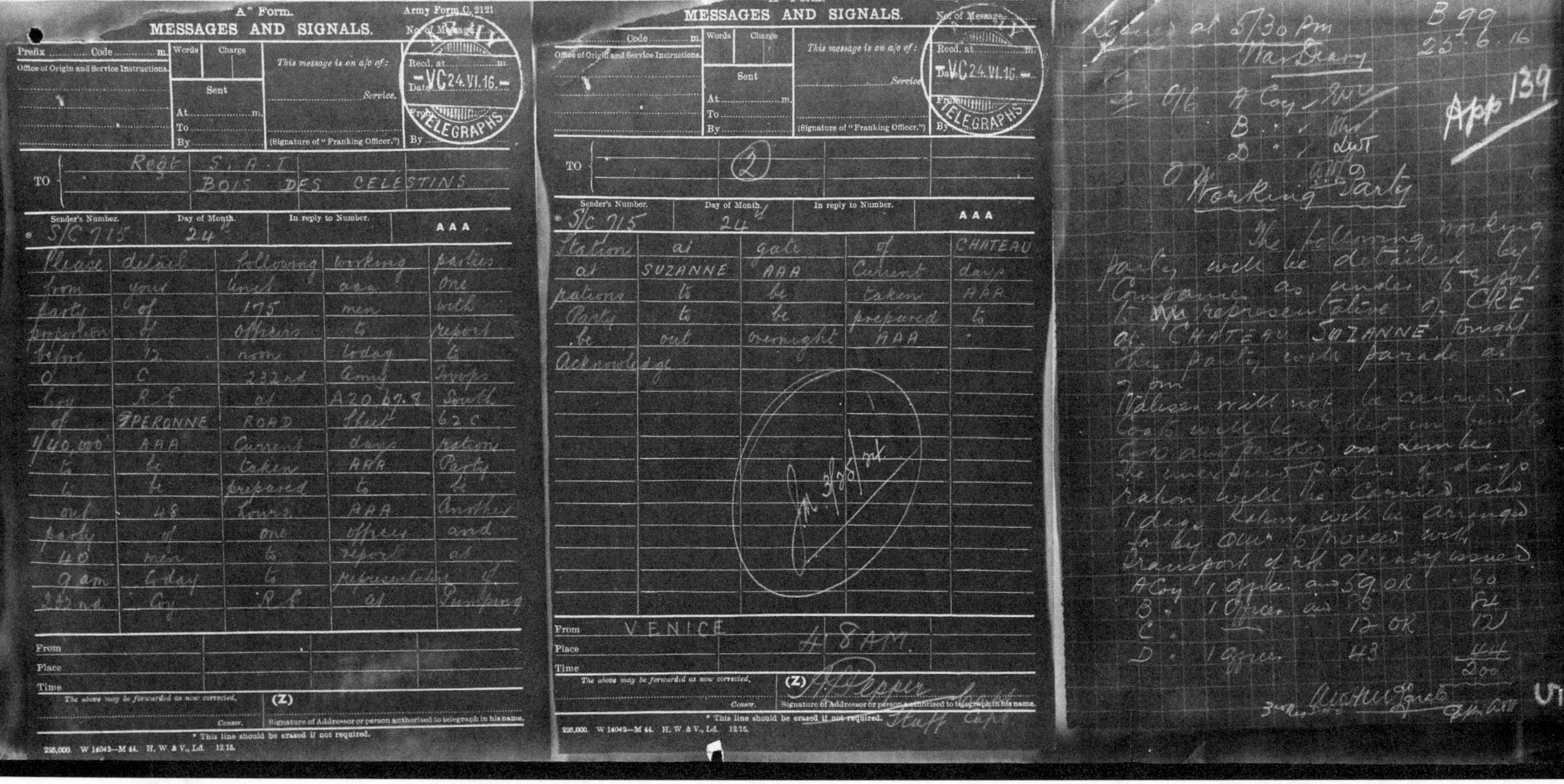

"A" Form. Army Form C. 2121
MESSAGES AND SIGNALS.

Recd. at -VC 24.VI.16.- TELEGRAPHS

TO Regt S.A.I. BOIS DES CELESTINS

Sender's Number: S/C 715 | Day of Month: 24th | In reply to Number: | AAA

Please detail following working parties from your unit aaa One party of 175 men with proportion of officers to report before 12 noon today to O C 232nd Army Troops Coy R E at A20 b7.8 South of PERONNE ROAD Sheet 62 C 1/40,000 AAA Current days rations to be taken AAA Party to be prepared to be out 48 hours AAA Another party of one officer and 40 men to report at 9 am today to representative of 232nd Coy R E at Pumping

From
Place
Time

225,000. W 14043—M 44. H. W. & V., Ld. 12.15.

MESSAGES AND SIGNALS.

Recd. at -VC 24.VI.16.- TELEGRAPHS

TO (2)

Sender's Number: S/C 715 | Day of Month: 24th | In reply to Number: | AAA

Station at gate of CHATEAU at SUZANNE AAA Current days rations to be taken AAA Party to be prepared to be out overnight AAA Acknowledge

From VENICE
Time 4 8 AM.

(Z) [illegible] Pepper Capt
Staff Capt.

225,000. W 14043—M 44. H. W. & V., Ld. 12.15.

Recd at 5/30 pm B 99
War Diary 25.6.16
App 139

O/C A Coy
B
D

Working Party

The following working party will be detailed by Companies as under to report to representative of CRE at CHATEAU SUZANNE tonight. The party will parade at 7 pm.
Valises will not be carried. Coats will be [illegible] and packed on limber. The unexpired portion of days ration will be carried and 1 days ration will be arranged for by QM to proceed with transport of rations already issued.

A Coy 1 Officer and 59 OR 60
B " 1 Officer and [illegible] 84
C " 12 OR 12
D " 1 Officer 43 44
200

[illegible] Capt
3rd Regt SAI

5

6

14

O.C. A, B, C & D
Coys, M.G. Offr. & T.O.

O.C. Coy.

Orders have been received for the Brigade to embark for France.

Transport – No vehicles animals or harness are to be taken except (1) Officer's chargers actually in possession
(2) Saddlery for same

S.A.A. – 120 rounds per man & 3500 per machine gun.

Stores & Equipment – Machine guns and all stores & equipment constituting the loads of all vehicles but not vehicle equipment will be taken.

Clothing – All units proceeding to France up to being due to embark – bulk with –

1 woollen vest	1 woollen drawers	1 satchel
2 P. helmets	1 pocket patch	per man

all of which are to be issued on voyage. Indents to be submitted at once. Service dress will be worn, any drill clothing & helmets withdrawn & returned to Ordnance.

Notification will be issued re return of Transport, animals, extra S.A.A. & helmets.

[illegible]
Capt.
Adjt. 3 S.A.I.

Sidi Bishr
6.4.16

App 100 7

HEADQUARTERS,

1st S. A. INFANTRY BRIGADE.

Sidi Bishr Camp, Alexandria.

7th April, 1916.

To the Officer Commanding,

3rd Regiment

Re Move.

In continuation of my minute of yesterday's date, authority has now been received for the return of surplus ammunition, etc.,

The vehicles and harness can be handed in to No. 1 Section, Gabbari, any day during working hours; the ammunition to Ammunition Store; and the animals to the Remount Department.

Please arrange accordingly.

A L Pepper

Captain.

Staff Captain.

app 101

8

HEADQUARTERS.

1st S. A. INFANTRY BRIGADE.

Recd 2-30 pm 11.4.16

Sidi Bishr Camp, Alexandria.

11th April, 1916.

To the Officer Commanding,

3rd S. A. INFANTRY.

With reference to the move of the Brigade, please note the following :-

All stores and baggage, except blankets and kits required for use to-day and to-morrow, will be embarked this afternoon.

Four trollies per u it will be at the lines at 2 p.m. to-day to convey baggage to the docks, and as these trollies will be required at 5 p.m. to-day expedition is to be used in loading and off-loading.

A baggage party of 1 officer and 22 other ranks will accompany the trollies to the docks and take charge of the baggage, etc., until the arrival of the unit. This party will take rations for to-night and to-morrow.

The horses, and men detailed to look after them, will not proceed until the 13th. The T. O., will be in charge of these.

The tents will be left standing, and all Camp Equipment is to be placed by units in the hut nearest their own cookhouse.

The Quartermaster, or other officer, will be present at the handing over of Camp to the Camp Quartermaster, and a written report will be sent to Brigade Headquarters that the lines of the unit were left clean, and Equipment handed over correctly.

A. D. Pepper

Captain.

Staff Captain.

Recd 11-30 P.

B.M. 1[illegible]/5. 9

EMBARKATION ORDERS.

App 102

SECRET.

1. SHIPS. The Brigade and the 1st S. A. Field Ambulance will embark for overseas on the following ships :-

MEGANTIC,	At Quay 4[illegible].
ORIANA,	" 26.
SCOTIAN,	" 45.
TINTORETTO,	" 44.

A schedule of the numbers to embark on each ship is attached, marked "A".

2. TRANSPORT TO DOCKS.

(a) Personnel.

The Brigade, less those detailed as Baggage Guard; in charge of horses, etc., will be conveyed by tram to the nearest point to the Docks.

Dress:- Marching order. Service dress will be worn.

All personnel belonging to the Brigade will accompany them; i.e., with the exception of hospital patients and an Orderly Room Clerk left attached to 3rd Echelon, Base, no personnel will be left behind.

A timetable of entramming is attached, marked "B".

(b) Baggage, Stores and Equipment.

Transport will be provided for the conveyance of all baggage, stores and equipment.

Tents will not be taken.

Field and base kits only will be taken, and the weight given in the Field Service Pocket Book must be adhered to.

Machine guns and all stores and equipment constituting the loads of vehicles, but not vehicles' equipment will be taken.

3. RATIONS. Rations for the day of embarkation will be carried. Tea will be the first meal issued on board.

4. AMMUNITION. 120 rounds per man and 3,500 rounds per machine gun will be taken.

5. VEHICLES, ANIMALS & HARNESS. No vehicles or harness

/will

10

SCHEDULE "B".

ENTRAMMING TIMETABLE.

13th April,

Unit.	Nos. All ranks.	Hour at which to parade at Sidi Bishr Tram ~~Station~~ Siding
2nd S. A. I.	250	7.30 a.m.
do	250	7.45 a.m.
do	250	8. a.m.
3rd S. A. I.	250	8.15 a.m.
do	250	8.30 a.m.
do	250	9.30 a.m.
4th S. A. I.	250	9.45 a.m.
do	250	10. a.m.
do	250	10.15 a.m.
1st S. A. I.	250	10.30 a.m.
2nd S. A. I.	Balance of regiment embarking on 'Megantic'	11.30 a.m.
3rd S. A. I.	do 173 do	11.45 a.m.
4th S. A. I.	Balance of regiment embarking on 'Oriana'	12 noon.
1st S. A. I.	250	12.15 p.m.
do	Balance of regiment embarking on 'Oriana'; and portion of Field Ambulance embarking on 'Oriana'; A.S.C. Details and Brigade Headquarters embarking on 'Megantic'	12.30 p.m.

13th April.

Unit.	Nos. All ranks.	Hour
1st S. A. I.	250	9. a.m.
do	Balance embarking on 'Scotian', and details to the aggregate of 250	9.15 a.m.
	Portion of 1st Field Ambulance embarking on 'Scotian', and balance of details of Brigade embarking on 'Scotian'	9.30 a.m.

ALLOTMENT of accomodation

UNIT	To embark on 12th apl — H.T. MEGANTIC Offs	O. ranks	H.T. ORIANA Offs	ranks	To embark on 13th apl — H.T. SCOTIAN Offs	O. ranks	H.T. TINTORETTO Offs	O. Rks	Horses
Maximum Accomodation	101	1897	204	1667	87	1300	15	206	500
Southafrican Brigade									
Headquarters	5	20			1	25		7	10
1st Batt			20	594	15	398	1	8	11
2nd — " —	34	998					1	13	11
3rd — " —	28	895			2	50	1	13	11
4th — " —			35	1049			1	13	11
204 Coy A.S.C.	2	14							
S.A.M.C.			5	134	5	95		11	10
Detail officers proceeding to Depot England			7						
3rd Echelon Base Record Staff			1	9					
133 A.E. Coy R.E.					3	90			
134 — do —					3	89			
136 — do —					1	133		5	5
167 — do —					2	137			
Heavy artillery							1	3	3
29th Div. Base Details							1	68	137
	69	1927	68	1786	32	1007	6	141	209

12

SECRET App. 103 Copy No. 1 64

Embarkation Order

by Lt-Col. C.F. Thackeray, Cdg. 3rd. S.A.I.

SIDI BISHR

12.4.16

Ships 1. The Battalion will embark for overseas in the following ships:-

MEGANTIC Quay 42 12.4.16	Bn Hqrs.	6 officers	136 other ranks
	A Coy.	7 ..	189 ..
	B ..	5 ..	191 ..
	C ..	6 ..	200 ..
	D ..	4 ..	179 ..
ORIANA Quay 26 12.4.16	5 officers proceeding to BORDON.		
SCOTIAN Quay 45 13.4.16	2/Lts. RITCHIE & BARTON and 52 other ranks.		
TINTORETTO Quay 44 13.4.16	2/Lt. DICK, 13 other ranks and 11 horses.		

Transport to Docks 2. The Battalion, less baggage guard of 1 NCO and 12 men of A Coy. and officers' batmen and less details embarking on SCOTIAN & TINTORETTO will be conveyed by tram from SIDI BISHR station to the nearest point to the docks.

Dress.- Heavy marching order. Service dress. Rifles to be labelled.

The time-table of trams is as follows and companies and parties will be at the SIDI BISHR tram station ~~at~~ 5 minutes before the times stated -

13

Copy No. 1 65

8.15 am. { R.Q.M.S. & 4 Company Q.M.S.
B Coy.
50 all ranks "C" Coy.

8.30 am. { Remainder of C Coy.
100 all ranks D Coy.

9.30 am. { Remainder of D Coy.
Bn. Hqrs.
45 all ranks "A" Coy.

11.45 am. Remainder of A Coy.

Baggage 3. Transport will be in the lines at 8.45 am for conveyance of baggage stores and equipment.

Tents will not be taken.

Field and base kits only will be taken and the weight given in the Field Service Pocket Book will be adhered to.

Machine guns and all stores and equipment constituting the loads of vehicles will be taken.

Rations 4. Rations for the day of embarkation will be carried. Tea will be the first meal issued on board.

S.A.A. 5. 120 rounds per man and 3,500 per machine gun will be taken.

Details 6. 2/Lts. RITCHIE and BARTON and 52 other ranks (which will include 1 N.C.O. per company) embarking on the SCOTIAN and the Transport Officer & 13 other ranks (11 grooms, 1 batman & 1 L/Cpl) all embarking on the TINTORETTO will report to Major HEAL, Lt. S.A.L. on departure of the Battalion from SIDI BISHR.

HEADQUARTERS,

1st S. A. INFANTRY BRIGADE.

Officer Commanding,
3rd S. A. Infantry.

B.M.47/33/5. 17th June, 1918.

The unit under your command will proceed by train from AILLY at 14.15 to-morrow for [illegible].

It will march from [illegible] to [illegible] CAMP for work under the G.O.C., 30th Division. That Division will arrange for an officer to meet you at [illegible], with full instructions as to camping site and work.

The baggage wagons have been ordered to report to you at 6 a.m. tomorrow.

You will send a guide to the cross roads at K.21.b.[illegible]. (Sheet 62d N.E.) to meet supply wagons at 13.30 to-morrow.

On arrival at your new camp please forward at once to this office the usual report regarding the number of men who fell out on the march, and the hour at which your unit was settled in camp.

Major.
Brigade Major.

HEADQUARTERS,

1st S. A. INFANTRY BRIGADE.

Officer Commanding,
1st S. A. Infantry.
2nd do do
3rd do do
4th do do
9th Division.
107th Coy, A.S.C.,
28th Bde. M.G. Coy.
S.A. Bde. L.T.M. Battery.
1st S.A. Field Ambulance.

B.M.12/11/B. 18th June, 1916.

With reference to paragraph 8 of Operation Order No.38 issued to-day, all transport and animals must be at the entraining point three hours before time of departure of train, together with the necessary entraining parties.

Major,
Brigade Major.

16

66

1 (3) Copy No. 1

The Transport Officer will obtain from the Adjutant and hand to Major HEAL a state showing the strength of the details reporting.

Officers proceeding to the Reserve Battalion, BORDON, will proceed on the ORIANA and will ascertain from the Adjutant, 1st S.A.I. the means of transport of themselves and their kit to the docks. These officers will not take batmen with them.

Camp. 7. The tents will be left standing, flies looped. All camp equipment is to be placed in the hut nearest the cookhouse. Lines must be left clean.

[signature]
Captain.
Adjutant 3 S.A.I.

Issued at

Copy No. 1 War Diary
2 Adjutant, Qr-mr. & M.O.
3 O.C. A Coy.
4 B
5 C
6 D
M.G. Offr.
7 T.O.
8

44/3

5th app 10 IV 17

26th Infantry Brigade.
27th Infantry Brigade.
28th Infantry Brigade.
1st South African Infantry Brigade.
9th Divisional Train
"Q"

No. X. 4/1274/4 28th April '16

Reference 9th Division No X. 4/1274/ para 10 of 23rd April.

1. The attachment of Platoons of the 2nd & 3rd South African Infty Battalions to companies of battalions in the line will commence on Monday next May 1st.
The attachment will be carried out as follows:-

2. First Party.

(a) To 27th Infantry Brigade, 10 Platoons.

~~Each Platoon will join the battalions~~

These Platoons will be billeted with the battalions of the 26th Infantry Brigade in their rest billets on the night 1st/2nd May & will go into the trenches on the morning of May 2nd attached to battalions of the 27th Infantry Brigade.

Two platoons to be accommodated for the night by the battalion at Dapot will rendezvous at road junction B.3.d.8.6. at 6-30 pm on May 1st.

The other platoons will rendezvous at the 26th Infantry Brigade Headquarters, T.29.d.8.5., the leading platoon arriving at the rendezvous at 6.30 pm, the other platoons following at intervals of five minutes.

27th Infantry Brigade will arrange in direct communication with 26th Infantry Brigade to provide guides to conduct these platoons to the trenches on the morning of May 2nd.

These platoons will come out of the trenches with the 27th Infantry Brigade when it is relieved on the 3rd of May.

(B) To 28th Infantry Brigade. 6 Platoons.

These platoons will be billeted with the reserve battalions of the 28th Infantry Brigade on the night 1st/2nd May & will go into the trenches on the morning of May 2nd.

The leading Platoon will rendezvous at cross roads B.23.A.9.4. at 6 pm on May 1st the other platoons following at intervals of five minutes.

G.O.C. 28th Inf Brigade will arrange for these platoons to come out of the trenches at a suitable hour on May 3rd.

(C) Transport from the Divisional train for conveyance of mans packs & rations will report at the headquarters of the 2nd & 3rd South African Inf regiments at 3 pm on May 1st.

3. Second Parties

(a) To 26th Inf Bde. 10 Platoons.

Each platoon will join the battalion of which it is attached on the evening of May 2nd & will go into the trenches with it on May 3rd.

2 Platoons for the battalion at Lapot will rendezvous at road junction B.3.C.8.6. at 6.30 pm on May 2nd.

The other platoons will rendezvous at the 26th Inf. Bde. Headquarters, T.29.D.8.5., the leading platoon arriving at this rendezvous at 6.30 pm, the other platoons following at intervals of five minutes.

G.O.C. 26th Inf. Brigade will arrange for these platoons to come out of the trenches at a suitable hour on May 4th.

(B) To 28th Inf Bde. 6 Platoons.

These platoons will be billeted with the reserve battalions of the 28th Inf. Bde. on the nights of May 3rd/4th & will go into the trenches on the morning of May 4th.

The leading platoons will rendezvous at cross roads B23.a.9.4. at 6 pm on May 3rd, the other platoons following at intervals of five minutes.

G.O.C. 28th Inf. Bde. will arrange for these platoons to come out of the trenches at a suitable hour on May 5th.

(C) Transport from Divisional Train for the conveyance of mans packs & rations will report at the headquarter of the 2nd & 3rd S.A. regiments as follows:-

At 3 pm on May 2nd (for parties attached to 26th Inf. Bde), & at 3 pm on May 3rd (for parties attached to 28th Inf Bde)

4. Brigades will inform Divisional headquarters at what hours transport is required for bringing back mens packs rations from the trenches.

5. Brigades will arrange to have guides to meet parties at rendezvous.

6. 1st South African Brigade should communicate direct with 26th, 27th & 28th Infantry Brigades as to any details concerning the attachment which may arise.

Signed. A. Stewart.

Lt Col.
General Staff.
9th (Scottish) Division.

Page 15

Instructions regarding War Diaries and Intelligence Summaries are contained in F. S. Regs., Part II. and the Staff Manual respectively. Title pages will be prepared in manuscript.

WAR DIARY
or
~~INTELLIGENCE SUMMARY.~~
(Erase heading not required.)

Army Form C. 2118.

3RD S. A. INF. (TRANSVAAL REGT.)

Hour, Date, Place	Summary of Events and Information	Remarks and references to Appendices
6 am 2/5/16 STEENWERCK	2nd Lieut E. WILSON found dead - gunshot wound. Buried 7 pm STEENWERCK CEMETERY.	
3.45 pm do do	10 Platoons detailed to report trenches for ~~orders~~ instruction. Strength 10 Officers 402 O.R. Right and ~~Left~~ Sector Trench line LE BIZET. Entered trenches 8.15 pm.	App 105
11.45 am 3/5/16 do	10 Platoons returned from trenches for Corps Commanders Inspection	App 105
3.45 pm do	6 do detailed to report trenches for Instruction. Strength 6 Officers 264 O.R. Right Sector attached 9th Scottish Rifles. Entered trenches 8.15 pm - 2 days.	App 105
2.15 pm do do	Inspection by Corps Commander - 19 Officers 479 OR. on parade. One man wounded in trenches.	
3 pm 4/5/16 do	Received operation order No 24. SAI Brigade re move of Battalion from STEENWERCK to LE BIZET. Issued Battalion operation order	App 106
9.30 am 5/5/16 do	Issued Battalion Move Order 30/9 furtherance BHQ 24 - X4/13/10	App 107
6 pm do do	6 Platoons returned from trench line and billeted ARMENTIERRES.	
2.45 pm 6/5/16 do	Battalion less 6 Platoons left STEENWERCK to occupy billets in LE BIZET	
6 pm do LE BIZET	Arrived LE BIZET. Reserve to front line. 6 Platoons rejoined Battalion	
3.30 pm 7/5/16 do	Brigade Operation Order No 25 received, to take over trench line - Left Sector.	App 108
6.0 pm do do	Battalion move order issued	App 108
do do	2 men wounded as a result of enemy's shelling.	
10 am 8/5/16 do	Battalion move order issued to take over Left Sector of trenches.	App 108 - Time Table attached.
7.40 pm do do	Battalion commenced to move off by Platoons	App 108 - Time Table attached.
10.30 pm do TRENCHES	Trench line taken over and relief completed of 10th H.L.I.	
6 am 9/5/16 do	In TRENCH LINE LEFT SECTOR 95 to 102.	App 109. Intelligence Report
6 am 10/5/16 do	do do do do	App 110 do do

20

Instructions regarding War Diaries and Intelligence Summaries are contained in F. S. Regs., Part II. and the Staff Manual respectively. Title pages will be prepared in manuscript.

PAGE 16

WAR DIARY
or
~~INTELLIGENCE SUMMARY~~.
(Erase heading not required.)

Army Form C. 2118.

Hour, Date, Place			Summary of Events and Information	Remarks and references to Appendices
8 pm	10/5/16	TRENCHES	One Officer 125 OR left Trenches proceeding to billets in ARMENTIERRES under instructions to reduce strength in trenches due to overcrowding	
	do	do	8 Casualties (all wounded) 1 died later.	
6 am	11/5/16	do	In trench line - Left Sector 95-102	App 111. Intelligence Report.
8 pm	do	do	Relief of 200 NCOs and men, consisting of 1 Platoon per Coy - relieved by 4th SAI, and proceeded to ARMENTIERRES to occupy Billets	App 112
10-30 pm	do	do	Relief effected	
6 am	12/5/16	do	In front line - Left Sector 95/102 One man wounded	App 112a Intelligence Report
6 am	13/5/16	do	In front line - Left Sector 95/102	App 113 Intelligence Report
7 pm	do	do	Operation order BHQ 26 received for relief on 14th inst	App 114
8 pm	do	do	Relief of 200 NCOs & men consisting of 1 Platoon per Coy - relieved by 4th SAI and proceeded to ARMENTIERRES to occupy Billets	
10-30 pm	do	do	Relief completed.	
6 am	14/5/16	do	In front line - Left Sector 95/102	App 115 Intelligence Report
8 pm	do	do	Relief of balance of Officers, NCOs & men by 4th S.A.I.	App 116.
11-30 pm	do	do	Relief completed. Occupied billeting area at LE BIZET. Details joined up from ARMENTIERRES	
6 am	15/5/16	LE BIZET	In billets. Shelled frequently during the day.	
6 am	16/5/16	do	do do do do do	
8-30 do	do	do	do Shelled by HE Shells 5.9. 2 men killed 3 wounded. Capt. S Liebson slightly wounded.	

21

PAGE 17

Instructions regarding War Diaries and Intelligence Summaries are contained in F. S. Regs., Part II. and the Staff Manual respectively. Title pages will be prepared in manuscript.

WAR DIARY
or
~~INTELLIGENCE SUMMARY~~.
(*Erase heading not required.*)

Army Form C. 2118.

3RD S. A. INF. (TRANSVAAL RGT)

21A

Hour, Date, Place			Summary of Events and Information	Remarks and references to Appendices
7-40pm	16/5/16	LEBIZET	2 Officers and 100 O.R. detailed for working party F.L. Trenches, under R.E.	App 117.
2 am	17/5/16	do	Working party of 2 Officers and 100 O.R. returned.	
5-30 am	17/5/16	do	Shelling resumed by enemy with H.E. Shells 5·9. One man severely wounded and died during day. Two civilians severely wounded.	
7.45 pm	17/5/16	do	1 Officer 50 O.R detailed as wiring party with R.E at GLASGOW REDOUBT	App 117
2 am	18/5/16	do	Working party 1 Officer 50 OR returned.	
1 pm	do	do	Received BHQ Order 28 for relief in trenches of left Sector	App 118
6 pm	do	do	Battalion Operation Order - furtherance BHQ Order 28, issued	
7.50 pm	do	do	2 NCOs 20 Men detailed as RE Fatigue. F.L. Trenches	
2 am	19/5/16	do	Working party 2 NCOs 20 men returned	
	do		Vicinity of Billets shelled during day.	
7.45 pm	19/5/16	do	2 Officers 100 OR working party under RE in F.L. Trenches	
do	do	do	1 do 50 " wiring party under RE at Glasgow Redoubt.	
2 am	20/5/16	do	3 Officers 150 O.R. working parties returned.	
	do	do	Vicinity of Billets shelled during day.	
8 pm	do	do	Commenced relief of 4th S.A.I. in terms of BHQ order 28. 17 Officers 680 O.R. Balance of Battalion proceeded to ARMENTIERRES.	
11 pm	do	TRENCHES	Relief of 4th S.A.I. in trenches completed. One man seriously wounded.	

(73989) W4141—463. 400,000. 9/14. H.&J.Ltd. Forms/C. 2118/10.

Page 18

Instructions regarding War Diaries and Intelligence Summaries are contained in F. S. Regs., Part II. and the Staff Manual respectively. Title pages will be prepared in manuscript.

WAR DIARY
or
~~INTELLIGENCE SUMMARY~~.
(Erase heading not required.)

Army Form C. 2118.

3RD S. A. INF. (TRANSVAAL RGT.)

Hour, Date, Place			Summary of Events and Information	Remarks and references to Appendices
6 am	21/5/16	TRENCHES	In front line trenches — 95-102	App 119 Intelligence Report
6 am	22/5/16	do	In front line trenches 95-102	App 120 do
6 am	23/5/16	do	In front line trenches 95-102.	App 121 do
	do	do	One man wounded.	
6 am	24/5/16	do	In front line trenches. 95-102 3 men wounded	App 122 do
9 pm	do	do	Received Operation Order No 30	App 123.
6 am	25/5/16	do	In front line trenches. 95-102.	App 124 do
			One man wounded	
8 am	do	do	Issued Battalion Move Order	App 123
6 am	26/5/16	do	In front line trenches 95-102	App 125 do
8 pm	do	do	Relief commenced by 4th SA Scottish	
11 pm	do	do	Relief completed & same billets occupied at LE BIZET. Details joined up from ARMENTIERRES	
6 am	27/5/16	LE BIZET	In Billets.	
3 pm	do	do	Received BHQ Move Order No. 31	App 126
5 pm	do	do	Issued Battalion Move Order for relief by 10th Batt. West Kent Regt.	App 126
6 am	28/5/16	do	In Billets	
12 Noon	do	do	Advance party of relief took over billets	
6 pm	do	do	Battalion moved off by Platoons at intervals of 5 minutes.	
11 pm	do	NOOTEBOOM	Arrived and billeted at NOOTEBOOM.	

22

(73989) W4141—463. 400,000. 9/14. H.&J.Ltd. Forms/C. 2118/10.

Page 19

Instructions regarding War Diaries and Intelligence Summaries are contained in F. S. Regs., Part II. and the Staff Manual respectively. Title pages will be prepared in manuscript.

WAR DIARY

or

~~INTELLIGENCE~~ SUMMARY.

(Erase heading not required.)

Army Form C. 2118.

3RD S. A. INF. (TRANSVAAL RGT.)

Hour, Date, Place	Summary of Events and Information	Remarks and references to Appendices
6 am 29/5/16 NOOTEBOOM	In Billets	
9 am do do	Issued Battalion Move Order	App 127
4-30pm do do	Battalion moved from NOOTEBOOM via OUTERSTEEN and MERRIS.	
7-45pm do STRAZELLE	Battalion arrived and billeted.	
6 am 30/5/16 do	In Billets	
6 am 31/5/16 do	In Billets	

A. H. McDonald
Capt. & Adjutant,
3rd, S. A. Infantry (Transvaal Regt.)

23

Secret

7.5.16

Preliminary Move

App 108

To O/C A [illegible]
B [illegible]
C [illegible]
D [illegible]
HQ [illegible]
SO [illegible]
MO [illegible]
Other [illegible]

Issued 6 pm 7.5.16

O/Commanding Companies will report at Btn Head Quarters at 9 am 8/5th and will proceed with Commanding Officer to Trenches in connection with tomorrow's move, the Signalling Officer, Machine Gun Officer, and Bombing Officer (Trench Stores) will also accompany this party.
The 4 Company Sergeants Major will accompany their O/C Companies and will not return to Billets; but will take over trenches and trench stores. The Signalling Sergeant with 5 (five) Regt Signallers will also proceed with this party.
The Machine Gun Officer will detail 1 man to accompany him, also 1 man per Company will be detailed from Maxim Sections to report to this Officer. 1 man per Company also 1 man from HQ will be detailed to report to Bombing Officer to assist to take over all bombs etc.
Great Coats and Waterproof Sheets will be carried by above party, also Emergency Kit.
All spare Kit, blankets etc to be packed and labelled and handed into Company Qm Store by 8.45 am. The parties proceeding under their respective Commanders and will rendezvous at Despierre Farm.
Rendezvous first at Btn Head Quarters, and will move off as follows:

C/O and Company Commanders 9 am
9.3 am Signalling Officer & Party
9.6 " Bombing " & Party
9.9 " Machine Gun Officer & Party
9.12 " 4 Company Sergts Major

3 mins
[signature]
Capt
a/Adjt 3rd Regt SA Infty

Note
I Waterbottles to be filled.
II Emergency ration (Company Comdrs are responsible that every man is in possession of same.
III Company Commanders will return for lunch.

24

from the Quartermasters' store and issue steel helmets handed in by them before 12 Noon.

7. SURPLUS KIT. Company Commanders will arrange for all surplus kit to be collected and packed in sacks clearly labelled and will be handed into Regimental Quartermaster's store by 12 Noon.
It is unlikely that this kit (if any) can be forwarded to the new destination and men should caary all essential requirements.
It must clearly understood that no transport is available other than that already laid down in para. 5.

8. DAVANCE PARTY. Companies will detail a reliable N.C.O. to report to 2nd Lieut. A.R. Barton at "B" Company headquarters, PIPPERMONT at 2-30 p.m. to proceed to LILLERS station to allocate train accomodation.

9. MARCHING OUT STATES. Companies will render Marching Out states by 9-0 a.m. - the reverse to shew names of Officers marching out and details of all ranks NOT marching out.

10. REAR GUARD. "C" Company will detail one platoon under an Officer to act as Rear Guard.

[signature] Lieut.,
Acting Adjutant,
3rd Regt., S.A. Infantry.

Copy No. 1, War Diary.
2. Brigade Headquarters.
3. "A" Company.
4. "B" Company.
5. "C" Company.
6. "D" Company.
7. Headquarter Details.
8. Transport Officer.
9. Quartermaster.

Issued at 10-0 p.m. by orderly.

120

SECRET

[illegible]

[illegible] a.m. [illegible]

[illegible]

[illegible]

[illegible] 1 [illegible]

[illegible]

[illegible] FRELINGHEIN

[illegible]

[illegible] hand [illegible] HALTE and one on FRELINGHEIN BRIDGE.

Between 6 p.m. and 7 p.m. [illegible] 18 pdr. fired about 30 shots near BLANCHISSERIE.

Enemy's Activity

Attitude Artillery active during day. Trench area quiet during day, [illegible] active in the [illegible].

2

Artillery Between 8 + 11 a.m. he fired 89 10 Cent. at HAYSTACK

Between 9 + 10 he fired about 20 77 MM into LE BIZET.

Between 12.45 and 3.15 p.m. he fired about 100 12 Cent. in vicinity of LE TOQUET STATION and at 3.45 p.m. a further 43 were fired at the same objective.

Movements in rear

A small party were seen at 7 a.m. throwing sand out of Trench at C.4.d.2.4.

A few men were seen at 11 a.m. walking at C.4.b.4.5.

New earth is observed around RED HOUSE (C.4.d.1.2) and it is suspected that this place is being used for some purpose by the enemy at night time.

3.

Identifications What appeared to be an officer wearing peaked cap with broad crimson band, was seen at 4.30. p.m. at C.4.d.2.4.

At 5 p.m. three men were seen at FRELINGHEIN BARRICADE two wore dark uniforms and caps & the third had on a white jersey.

[signature], Lt. Col.
Commanding 2nd S. A. Infantry
(Transvaal Regt.)

26

Mine Operations. Our miners destroyed an enemy plate and a periscope.

Wiring was carried out as usual in front of saps C & D the crater

Enemy's Activity

Attitude. Aggressive.

Artillery. At 7.30 a.m. he fired some H.E. and Shrapnel about 10 rounds into LE BIZET.
8.40 a.m. he fired 5 rounds of Shrapnel into GLASGOW REDOUBT and SUFFOLK AVENUE.
At 1.40 p.m. 6. 77 MM into our support trenches 96–97.
Between 4 and 5 p.m. he fired 10. 12 CM 16. 10 CM and 25. 77 MM into our support Trenches, HARNIAN AVENUE and PATERNOSTER ROW.

Bombing. In retaliation the enemy fired between 4.15 p.m. onto our front & support Trenches 91–98. 60 Rifle Grenades, 90 T.M. and 30 [illegible] causing damage to [illegible] Avenue parapets and dug outs.

Movements in rear. Men were seen for a few moments at intervals during the day at C10 b 1.4 and at C11 b 1.2.

Enemy's Defences

Front & Support Lines. Work was being carried on at the following places during the day, [illegible] action was taken to disperse them as they could not be seen from our front line. Approximately at C4 d 2.5 to C4 d 9.7 & C4 d.15 timber was being carried along and hammering was heard.

During the evening our [illegible] harassed a working party on their parapet

Issued 8 AM

SECRET

The Officer Commanding,

Company.

MOVE

Copy of Operation Order No 30, 24th May 1916

1. **RELIEF.** The 1st and 4th Regiments, S.A.I. at strength approximately 600 all ranks (each Battalion) will relieve the 2nd and 3rd Regiments, S.A.I. on Friday night, the 26th inst.

2. THE LEWIS GUN Teams and TRENCH MORtAR personnel will be relieved during the day on Saturday, under arrangements being made between Battalion Commanders.

3. **BILLETS.** The Battalion will take over billets at LE BIZET, vacated by the 4th Battalion, S.A.Scottish.
O.C.Companies will arrange that C.Q.M.Sgts take over their billets tomorrow, the 26th inst by 6 p.m. also take over all ammunition, bombs etc, from the 4th Battalion, viz:- 12 cases of ammunition and 250 bombs (each company).
Lieut Hirtzel, will report from ARMENTIERRES to O.C. 4th S.A.I. to take over Battalion billeting area at Le BIZET by 4 p.m.

4. **MOVEMENT.** The relief will be acrried out by Platoons. Platoons must move at intervals of al least five minutes. Leading Platoon to move off at 8 p.m.

5. MOVE of the REMAINDER OF BATTALION. The remainder of the 1st and 4th Battalion, S.A.I. will move from the billets at LE BIZET to the billets at present occupied by the remainder of the 2nd and 3rd S.A.I at ARMENTIERRES the same evening, and those portions of the 2nd and 3rd Regiments at present billeted at ARMENTIERRES will move to LE BIZET. These moves must not commence until 8 p.m.

6. TRENCH STORES. Great care must be exercised in compiling Trench Store lists on Yellow Form, which must be signed by both Officers handing and taking over.

7. STEEL HELMETS. Company Commanders must ensure that on leaving Trenches they are in possession of the numbers issued to them by the Quartermaster. Surplus steel helmets will be handed over to 4th Battalion and receipt obtained.
Companies are reminded to take out all stores on Regimental charge which may have been taken into the trenches by their orders.

8. PETIT RABECQUE FARM POST. The O.C."C" Coy will detail (1) one Platoon under an Officer to relieve platoon of the 4th S.A.I now in occupation of this post.
The Officer detailed with an N.C.O and guard of at least 3 men, must take this post over by 8 p.m. and give receipt on Yellow Form for all ammunition, Stores etc.,

A. H. McDonald
Captain and Acting Adjutant,
3rd S.A.Infantry.

4

MOVEMENTS IN REAR.

At [illegible] pm [illegible] of the enemy were seen crossing the bridge at FRELINGHEIN PONT ROUGE.

ENEMY'S DEFENCES.

FRONT & S. LINES. At 2.30 pm a party of the enemy were seen working at C.4.C.10.8. and at 12 noon the enemy were heard working underground near the crater at about C.4.a.7.2½.

Between 2 and 3.30 am enemy at 14/13th a working party was dispersed by our [illegible] Rifle fire opposite T.97.

IDENTIFICATIONS.

At 4.15 pm one of the enemy was seen in a communication trench wearing a [illegible] blue cap and [illegible] with gold band.

5

MISCELLANEOUS.

[illegible] to go
A gun was seen firing from a house at C.11.d.9½.2½.

[illegible signature]

.................................Lt. Col.
Commanding 3rd. S. A. Infantry.
(Transvaal Regt.)

SECRET 112a

12/5/16

INTELLIGENCE REPORT

From 6 am 11/5/16 to 6 am 12/5/16.

① OUR OPERATIONS

Artillery At 12.30 pm a number of 18 Pounder shells were fired on Enemy Support Lines in vicinity C4D2.8

During our bombing activity we fired several salvos of Shrapnel over enemy front & support line

② Bombing Between 5 pm and 6.15 pm we fired forty Trench Mortar Bombs and 35 Rifle Grenades at enemy lines Opposite T102 and T96-98

HAYSTACK. At C3B72 and at 4.30 pm eight 77 mm at LETOQUET STATION and four shells into PATERNOSTER ROW damaging our equipment.

BOMBING He fired 14 Rifle Grenades into GLASGOW REDOUBT and between 12 Noon and 1-30 pm, he sent about thirty Trench Mortar Shells in and over BACHELOR'S WALK and 98S, with slight damage to parapets, causing four casualties

Enemy's snipers active

③ OUR ACTIVITY

Between 12 Noon & 1 pm we fired 62 Trench Mortar Bombs and 16 Rifle Grenades into enemys line opposite T96-99. Good results were observed. The enemy retaliated.

4 SNIPING

Our Snipers claimed two certain hits and a box periscope was smashed. [illegible] claimed from vicinity of Trees

5 Enemy Movements in rear

During the day the enemy were seen working at C4B1.2.

6 Enemy Defences

Front and Support line at 11 pm enemy working party on his wire was driven in by our Lewis Gun Fire. Opposite T98

E F Thackeray. Lt. Col.
Commanding 3rd. S. A. Infantry (Transvaal Regt)

113

Secret 3RD S. A. INF. (TRANSVAAL REGT.) 13/5/16

INTELLIGENCE REPORT.

From 6 am 12/5/16 to 6 am 13/5/16

I Our operations

Artillery. Between 9.30–10 am 11 18 pounder shells were fired in direction of Frelinghien and again between 6 and 6.30 pm a further 12 were fired in the same direction

Between 11 and 11.30 a m our 12 in Howitzer gun fired 25 rounds at Deulemont chimney.

2

Between 2.20 pm and 2.45 pm we fired eleven 18 pounder shells in direction of Blanchmerie wood and also between 4 and 4.30 pm a further 9 shots were fired.

2) Bombing.

3

3) Sniping Our snipers claim to have hit four box periscopes

4) Enemy Activity

Attitude. Quiet.

5) Artillery Between 9.30 and 9.45 am the enemy fired 4. 77 m/m at Trench 103. and between 8 am and 9.30 am he fired 50 77 m/m in the direction of Motor Car Corner.

31

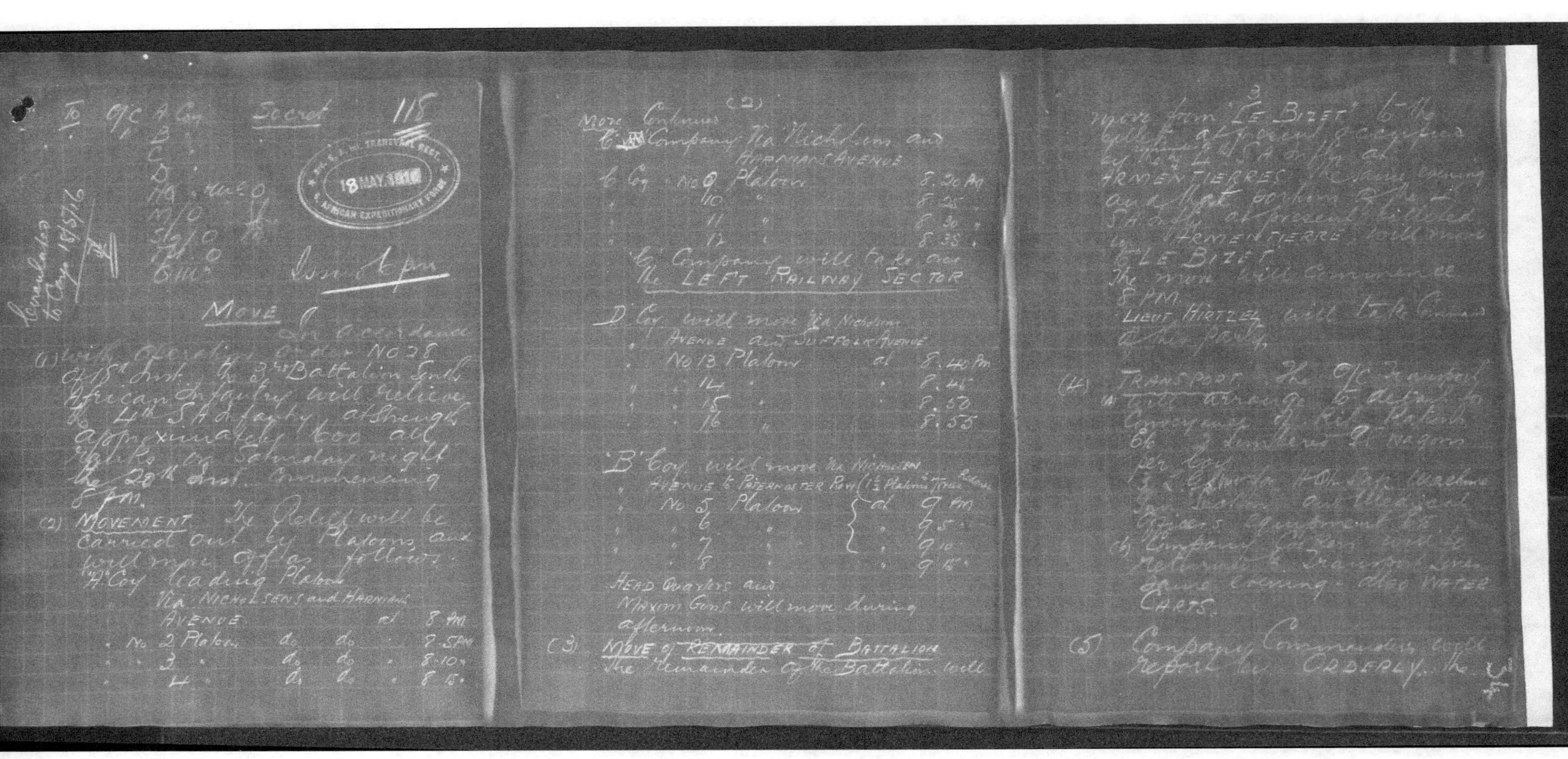

To O/C A Coy
" B "
" C "
" D "
HQ. Mess O
M/O
Sig/O
TPt O
QM

Secret 118

Issued 4 pm

Recirculated to Coys 18/5/16

MOVE

(1) In accordance with Operation Order NO 28 of 15th Inst. the 3rd Battalion South African Infantry will relieve the 4th S.A. Infantry, although approximately 600 all ranks on Saturday night the 20th Inst. Commencing 8 PM.

(2) **MOVEMENT** The Relief will be carried out by Platoons and will move off as follows.
"A" Coy leading Platoon
Via NICHOLSONS and HARMANS AVENUE at 8 AM
No 2 Platoon do do 8.5 PM
" 3 " do do " 8.10 "
" 4 " do do " 8.15 "

(2)

Move Continued
"C" Company Via Nicholsons and HARMANS AVENUE
C Coy No 9 Platoon 8.20 AM
" 10 " 8.25 "
" 11 " 8.30 "
" 12 " 8.35 "
"C" Company will take over the LEFT RAILWAY SECTOR

D Coy will move Via Nicholsons AVENUE and SUFFOLK AVENUE
No 13 Platoon at 8.40 Pm
" 14 " " 8.45
" 15 " " 8.50
" 16 " " 8.55

"B" Coy will move Via NICHOLSON AVENUE to PATERNOSTER ROW (1½ Platoons Trench Reserve)
No 5 Platoon at 9 PM
" 6 " " 9.5 "
" 7 " " 9.10 "
" 8 " " 9.15 "

HEAD Quarters and MAXIM Guns will move during afternoon.

(3) **MOVE of REMAINDER of BATTALION** The Remainder of the Battalion will

3

move from "LE BIZET" to the billets at present occupied by the 4th S.A. Infty at ARMENTIERRES the same evening and that portion of the 4th S.A. Infty at present billeted in ARMENTIERRES will move to LE BIZET.
The move will commence 8 PM.
LIEUT HIRTZEL will take Command of this party.

(4) **TRANSPORT** The O/C Transport (a) will arrange to detail for Company the Kit Rations etc. 2 Limbers 2 wagons per Coy.
[illegible] Machine Gun Section and Quartermaster's equipment etc.
(b) Company Cookers will be Returned to Transport Lines same evening – also WATER CARTS.

(5) Company Commanders will Report by ORDERLY the

3/4

3

Machine Guns & Rifle Fire

Fairly active during evening.

Movements in rear

Enemy were busy repairing support and communication trenches opposite MONMOUTH HOUSE from daybreak until 9.30 a.m. [illegible] bags being used to hold earth.

Working parties seen at
C4 a 1½ 6
C4 c 8 9½
C4 B 5.7.

Apparently repairing damages caused by our bombing on the previous evening.

4

ENEMY DEFENCES.

SAPS The O.C. D Company reported that noises suggesting sapping were heard at C.T. 102. Two officers of Tunnelling Company were notified and proceeded to the spot where the noise was heard and which appeared to come from a point near Sap D. however nothing was heard by these officers and attention is being paid to the spot and in the event of a recurrence the officers referred to will make the necessary tests.

IDENTIFICATIONS.

An officer in grey uniform peaked cap, [illegible] [illegible] blue or black band and a very bright cap badge was seen at U.25 d 1½.4.

5

ENEMYS AIRCRAFT.

At about 9.30 pm while relief was taking place the sound of an aeroplane engine [illegible] was heard proceeding in the direction of the [illegible] [illegible] lights were [illegible] [illegible] the aeroplane and [illegible] after a searchlight was seen in the direction of MESSINES.

One Company Commander is of opinion that it was a Zeppelin and was [illegible] to [illegible] [illegible] by [illegible] SEVEN TREES REDOUBT.

[illegible] [illegible] [illegible] [illegible] [illegible] [illegible] [illegible] 4th S.A.

Enemy aeroplane again heard at 2 a.m. [illegible] [illegible] [illegible] direction at 3.40 a.m. [illegible] [illegible] [illegible] [illegible] [illegible] T.10 [illegible] SE [illegible]

[illegible] [signature]

Commanding [illegible]

([illegible])

33

SECRET. 3rd S.A.I. 119

6am 20th May to 6am 21st May 1916

INTELLIGENCE REPORT

OUR OPERATIONS

ARTILLERY

At 9.30 a.m. our Artillery fired on enemy houses at FRELINGHEIN, and at 6.30 p.m. usual shots were fired on enemy support and front line. No effective results were observed.

PATROLLING

A patrol of two men penetrated towards Red House going through No man's Land, met no opposition but could not get near Red House on account of enemy machine Gun fire and watchfulness of enemy dog.

2

Minor Operations

SNIPING

One enemy sniper was seen falling out of a tree as result of our snipers shooting opposite T.102.

ENEMY'S ACTIVITY.

Attitude Normal.

Artillery. Between 6.30 & 8.30 a.m. enemy fired about 100 rounds at Station, H.E. Schrapnel 25 and 75. 77 M.M. at 10.30 a.m. about twenty five 77 M.M. were fired at the church in LE BIZET.

Between 7 & 7.30 p.m. about thirty 77. M.M. were fired near DESPIERRE FARM, HARNIAN AVENUE and SEVEN TREES' REDOUBT.

4

... Completion of the move as soon as possible after taking over.

(6) Company Commanders will arrange to report in Trenches for the purpose of taking over [struck through] Stores etc. accompanied by C. Sergeant Major. During the afternoon and [illegible] remain.

(7) Party RABECQUE FARM POST.

Arrangements are being made with O/C 4th "SAI" for the relief of Platoon stationed here, to be effected before 8 pm.

(8) Stores. All Ammunition & bombs in Company Stores will be handed over to 4th S.A. Scottish, and receipts taken on the yellow form by Company. The same order applies to RABECQUE FARM.

A H M [illegible] Capt.

Capt. & Adjutant.

3rd S.A. Infantry (Transvaal) Regt.

32

SECRET.

Copy No. 3..

35

126

1st SOUTH AFRICAN INFANTRY BRIGADE.

OPERATION ORDER No. 31.

1. RELIEF. The 1st S. A. Infantry Brigade will be relieved by the 123rd Infantry Brigade. The relief will be carried out as per attached table.

2. MORTARS, etc., The Light Trench Mortar Battery personnel and all Stokes' Guns will accompany the Brigade. All Light Guns, other than Stokes', to be handed over to the 41st Division, i.e., in Right Sector, four 3.7" Guns.

3. M.G. Coy. The 28th Infantry Brigade M.G. Coy. will not move with the Brigade, and will be temporarily attached to the 41st Division. It will remain in its present position in the Right Sector.

4. DOCUMENTS. All documents relating to the Area will be handed over on relief.

5. MOVEMENT. Units moving from their billetting areas will march by Platoons at 200 yards interval, and will take the usual precautions against observation by hostile aircraft.

6. MARCH ORDERS. The times and other arrangements for the march from LE BIZET to STRAZEELE will be left to the discretion of the Battalion Commanding Officers.

7. TRANSPORT. First Line Transport will march 500 yards in rear of each Battalion.

8. M. G. SECTION. Will march in rear of the Battalion.

9. COMMAND. The Command of the Right Sector will be handed over by the G.O.C., S. A. Infantry Brigade, to the G.O.C., 123rd Infantry Brigade, at 5 p.m. on 31st inst.,

10. REPORTS. The completion of relief by each unit will be at once reported to Brigade Headquarters by wire. Progress of moves will be reported daily to Brigade Headquarters.

11. RECEIPTS. All receipts for trench and other stores handed over to relieving units will be handed in to Brigade Headquarters on 31st inst.,

12. ROADS. Roads in the II Corps Area West of Bailleul are allotted as follows:-

41st Division,	CAESTRE - METEREN - BAILLEUL.
	STRAZEELE - MOOENACKER - BAILLEUL.
9th Division,	BAILLEUL - OUTTERSTEENE - STRAZEELE.

Please acknowledge.

R L Pepper
Captain.
a/ Brigade Major.

Copy No. 1 to	1st S. A. I.,	
2	2nd do	
3	3rd do	
4	4th do	
5	9th Division.	
6	26th Inf. Brigade.	
7	27th do do	
8	123rd do do	
Copy No. 9 to	Bde M.G. Company.	
10.	O.C. L.T.M. Battery.	
11	107th Coy. A.S.C.,	
12	Right Group, Artilly.	
13	O.C. Bde. Signal Sec.,	
14	233rd Fld. Coy. R.E.,	
15	3rd N.Z. Inf. Brigade.	
16	Office Copy.	
17	OC. SA Fd Ambce	

Issued by Orderly at....7.30 am........

3PM

1st S. A. INFANTRY BRIGADE HEADQUARTERS,

27th May, 1918.

SECRET 121 3rd S.A.I.

Intelligence Report Section

From 6 a.m. 22/5/16 to 6 a.m. 23/5/16

Our Operations

Between 9 and 11.30 pm our 18 pdrs fired several shell into enemy front support line at C.11 B.5.9 FRELINGHEIN, USINE and HALTE and also BURNGHISSERIE at 6.45 pm our 18 pdrs fired one salvo into area C.4.d.3.5.

Patrolling

An N.C.O.s patrol went out opposite Gap E at 10 pm to take observations of Red House they returned at 12.30 a.m. and reported that there was no sniper's post there and no machine guns were in use.

Minor Operations

An N.C.O. & three men carried out wiring operations in front of Gap C parapet.

2

Minor Operations

Sniping

On evening of 21st instant one of the enemy snipers was shot by our sniping opposite Northern end of Gap D.

Four enemy sniper plates were hit to day at intervals snipers not used for shooting from after being hit for the rest of the day.

3

Enemy's Activity

Attitude Quiet during the day. Machine gun rifle fire fairly brisk during evening.

Artillery Between 8.45 a.m. and 9.15 a.m. the enemy fired 35 10 Cent. shells at LE TOQUET STATION, HEADQUARTERS FARM and WIDOWS HOUSE.

At intervals during the rest of the day shell fire seemed to be directed to PLOEGSTEERT WOOD

Movements in rear

At 6 a.m. a party of three were seen at C.11 B.5.6 walking towards USINE

At 3.45 pm several men were seen attired in dark outfits at C.10 b.8.4 very near a house in enemy line.

At the side of the house 3 [illegible] wings can be seen apparently coming from the French walls

36

CONFIDENTIAL.

Copy No. 3.

1st SOUTH AFRICAN INFANTRY BRIGADE.

OPERATION ORDER No.28.

1. **RELIEF.** The 2nd and 3rd Regiments, S. A. Infantry, at strength approximately 600 all ranks each Battalion, will relieve the 1st and 4th Regiments, S. A. Infantry, on Saturday night, 20th inst.,

2. **LEWIS GUN TEAMS & T. M. PERSONNEL.** The Lewis Gun teams and Trench Mortar personnel will be relieved during the day on Saturday under arrangements to be made between Battalion Commanders.

3. **BILLETS.** Units will make their own arrangements for taking and handing over billets.

4. **MOVEMENT.** The relief will be carried out by platoons. Platoons must move at intervals of at least 5 minutes. Leading platoon to move off at 8 p.m.

5. **MOVES OF REMAINDERS OF BATTALIONS.** The remainder of the 2nd and 3rd S. A. Infantry will move from LE Bizet to the billets at present occupied by the remainder of the 1st and 4th S. A. Infantry at Armentieres the same evening, and those portions of the 1st and 4th S. A. Infantry at present billetted in Armentieres will move to Le Bizet. These moves are not to commence until 8 p.m.

6. **COMPLETION OF RELIEF AND MOVES.** Completion of relief and moves to be reported to Brigade Headquarters.

Please acknowledge.

Major.

Brigade Major.

Copy No.1	to 1st S. A. Infantry.	Copy No.9	to O.C. L.T.M. Batty.
2	2nd do	10	107th Coy. A.S.C.,
+ 3	3rd do	11	Right Group, Arty.
4	4th do	12	Bde Signal Section.
5	9th Division.	13	223rd Field Co. R.E.,
6	26th Inf. Brigade.	14	2nd N.Z. Inf. Bde.
7	27th do	15.	Office Copy
8	O.C. Bde M.G.Coy.	16	do

Issued by Orderly at 11.30 am

Headquarters,
1st S. A. I. Brigade.
18th May, 1918.

SECRET 109/110

3RD S. A. INF. (T... REGT.) 9/5/16

Intelligence Report

From 6 am 9/5/16 to 6 am 10/5/16

(1) Our Operations

At 2-15 pm and 4 pm our Artillery fired about 12 - 18 pounders in the direction of FRELINGHEIM

(2) Enemy Activity

The Enemy's attitude was quiet he was sniping occasionally during the day causing no damage.

(3) Enemy's Artillery

Between 8 am + 9 am

(2)

The enemy fired about twenty 77 MM in the vicinity of Plummers Farm x.

(4) Movements in Rear.

At 9-30 am a small working party was observed throwing sand out of the trench at C.4.A 9½ 3.

(5) Enemy's Defences

A small enemy wiring party was dispersed by our Lewis Gun Fire opposite T98.

(6) Identifications

Working parties of the enemy have been seen wearing dark blue coats, light grey caps with metal badges.

E. [illegible]

SECRET 111/109

3RD S. A. INF. (T... REGT.) 11/5/16.

Intelligence Report

From 6 am 10/5/16 to 6 am 11/5/16

(1) Our Operations

At 10-30 am our Artillery fired 4 Salvos on enemy front and support line in direction C.11.D 3½.5½ Between 4.30 pm & 5 pm we fired 12 6" at buildings in Frelinghem.

There was further artillery activity between 11-30 pm and 12.30 am.

(2) Enemy Activity

Attitude - normal.

Artillery. At 11-30 am he fired 12 - 10 cm at Hay Stack

38

Army Form C. 2123.

MESSAGES AND SIGNALS.

No. of Message ....

Service Instructions.	Charges to Pay. £ s. d.	Office Stamp. D13 13-5-16

Handed in at .... Office .... m. Received .... m.

TO

Sender's Number	Day of Month	In reply to Number	AAA

[illegible] D 13 and D 18 [illegible] ARMENTIERES [illegible]

FROM

PLACE & TIME

W 15660 M/151. 75,000 Pads. McC. & Co., Ltd., London. 1/16. Forms/C.2123.

MESSAGES AND SIGNALS.

No. of Message ....

Service Instructions.	Charges to Pay. £ s. d.	Office Stamp. D13 13-5-16

Handed in at .... Office .... m. Received .... m.

TO D.B.

Sender's Number	Day of Month	In reply to Number	AAA

[illegible]

FROM

PLACE & TIME

W 15660 M/151. 75,000 Pads. McC. & Co., Ltd., London. 1/16. Forms/C.2123.

39

5

Identifications of

Two men were seen in dark blue uniforms with blue feathers caps one of these men was also wearing a dark apron

J. J. Hackney

Commanding [illegible]

([illegible] Regt.)

SECRET

Intelligence

From 6 a.m. 25/5/16 to 6 a.m. 26/5/16.

Our Operations

Artillery Our artillery fired between 10.45 a.m. and 3.30 p.m. about 180 rounds of 18 pdr. Shrapnel and HE into ~~[illegible]~~ FRELINGHEIN and BLANCHISSERIE WOOD.

Between 2.45 and 5 p.m. we fired 30 rounds of 5.7 [illegible] enemy front support trenches, Machine Gun Head quarters, [illegible] direct hits [illegible] in the latter place.

Minor Operations

Our sniping destroyed four enemy periscopes and several plates which seemed to impress enemy sniping [illegible]

42

127

To O/C "A" Coy
B "
C "
D "
HQ. "
S/O "
T/O "
Qmr. "
M/O

Issued 9 am

MOVE

I Move — The Battalion will parade at 4.30 pm to day 29th at Company billets and will rendezvous at Tunnel Road 4K9 and Nooteboom 4K12 leaving off at 4.45 PM and will proceed to STRAZEELE via OUTTERSTEENE and MERRIS. Transport will move off from Billets and will rendezvous at Btn Hd Qrs Billets 4.30 pm. [illegible] B.C.D.A Companies

II Transport Baggage — 1 G.S. Wagon attached for A and B Coy with Hd Qrs [illegible] Kits
1 G.S. Wagon for C & D Coy

43

with Pioneer & Ammunition Tools.
No 1 Wagon will report Hd Qtrs 4 pm
No 3 Wagon to O/C "C" Coy at same hour.
Any spare surplus Company Kits to be picked up and loaded on G.S. Limbered Wagons.

(3) Sanitary Companies are requested to ensure that their billets are left thoroughly clean and Latrines filled in

Arthur H Arnold
Capt
A/Adjt 3rd Reg 'SAI

2

Enemy's Artillery

Observation Posts

An observation post is suspected at point C.11.d.4½.6 the windows of the building are barricaded with sandbags there appears to be a loop hole in door on left of building and one in the roof, movement was today seen in the house and it was from this point that a man was seen proceeding along a trench in the direction of BLANCHISSERIE WOOD

Communications

Light Signals

At 8 p.m. two rockets were sent up behind OSIME WOOD

6

Identifications.

A man was seen at 11 a.m. wearing a khaki peaked cap with gold braid band, [illegible] also [illegible] seen at point C.4.d.2.5½ adjusting a [illegible] plate.

Enemy's Aircraft

An aeroplane came over our lines at 6-20 p.m. and dropped a message when ~~[illegible]~~, [illegible] Plugstreet Wood

Observation Balloons

A magnetic bearing which read 10[illegible]° was taken from Battalion Headquarters of enemy balloons, two were seen during afternoon one was down when bearing taken.

[signature]

................Lt. Col.

Commanding 3rd. S. A. Infantry.

(Transvaal Regt.)

Secret App 108

Copy No. 4

1st S. A. INFANTRY BRIGADE OPERATION ORDER No.25. 45

Reference Trench Map 1/10,000.

1. The following reliefs will be carried out on the evening of May 8th :-

   2nd S. A. Infantry relieve 11th H. L. I., in T.90-95 inclusive.

   3rd S. A. Infantry relieve 10th H. L. I., in T.96-101 inclusive.

2. The 2nd S. A. Infantry will move into the trenches via Station Avenue (Motorcar Corner), and the 3rd S. A. Infantry via Nicholson's Avenue (Gasometer Corner).

3. Relieving units and those to be relieved will arrange direct with each other regarding taking and handing over of stores and billets.

4. The relief will be carried out by platoons. Platoons must move at intervals of at least 300 yards. The leading platoons of the 2nd and 3rd S. A. I., will not leave LE BIZET before 7.30 p.m.

5. Defence schemes will be handed over.

6. Completion of relief to be reported to Brigade Headquarters.

   Kindly acknowledge.

J Mitchell Baker

Major.

May 7th, 1916. Brigade Major.

Copies No.			
1 to	10th H. L. I.,	7 to	27th Inf. Brigade.
2	11th H. L. I.,	8	O/C M.G. Coy.
3	2nd S. A. I.,	9	O/C L. T. M.,
× 4	3rd S. A. I.,	10	O/C 107th Coy A.S.C.,
5	9th Division.	11	O/C 2nd Arty. Group.
6	26th Inf. Brigade.	12, 13	Office

7th

Issued by Orderly at 3.15 pm.

Received 3/30 P.M. 7/5/16

46

106

THIRD SOUTH AFRICAN INFANTRY.

May 4th 1916

The Officer Commanding,

Copy of operations order No 24.

In accordance with 9th Division X4/1310 of the 2nd inst, the following move will take place:-

(1) The Third Battalion South African Infantry will proceed on Saturday 6th inst, to billets at Le Bizet.

(2) Billeting Party of 1 Officer, 5 N.C.O's and 5 men (one N.C.O and one man each from A.B.C.D and H.Q Coy) will report to headquarters 9th Scottish Rifles, at Le Bizet, at 10 a.m. This party will take over all camp equipment, grenade carriers and reserve S.A.Ammunition, at the billets.

(3) Remainder of Battalion will leave present billets by Platoons, with intervals between Platoons of at least 200 yards, in time to enable the Battalion to be at LeBizet by 6 p.m. Order and time of move will be issued later. When halts are made, care must be taken that the interval is maintained.

(4) Regimental Transport will be used to move stores, kits etc, from present to new billets.

(5) The following guns, transport stores etc, and ammunition will be handed over to each battalion:-

Lewis Guns	4 Per Battalion	
2 Horse Limbers for same	2	do
Gun and Regimental S.A.A for same		
Steel Helmets		
Telescopic sighted rifles		
"Very" Pistols		
Periscopes		

The above named stores will be taken over at 10 a.m. on the 6th inst, from the 6th Royal Scots Fusiliers at La Papot (Sheet 36 B3 C.9.2) and transport them to Regimental Quartermaster's Stores in the billeting area, to be occupied at LeBizet. A motor trolley will be at the former place.

A fatigue party of 1 Officer and 20 men will be detailed for taking over these stores.

Receipts to be signed by the Officer handing over and receiving in each case - duplicate receipt to be retained by the Officer handing over

(6) Transport of the Third Regiment will be billetted at Sheet 36 B 4.6.10.0.

(7) The Billets at present occupied by the Third Regiment will be taken over by the 6th Royal Scots Fusiliers and are to be left in a perfectly clean state.

(8) Brigade Headquarters moves on same date to present Headquarters 28th Infantry Brigade at Pont de Neppe,

A.W.H. McDonald

Captain and Actg Adjutant,
3rd S.A.Infantry.

47

(2) of Copy No 1

Head Quarters for RATIONS from the 30th Inst.
All Carriers will parade alongside working parties at 3pm today 28th for checking by a Staff Officer in the open ground at K 33 d. 8. 6 Sheet 62d N.E.
They will parade at Battalion Orderly Room at 2.45 pm.

(4) **Brigade Police** para 5 A7

O/C Hd Qt Detail Coy will detail 3 O Ranks as Brigade Police to take with them M.P. Armlets and will parade with Carriers at 2.45 pm today – They will be rationed with Bgd H Qts from the 30th Inst.

5 Trained Bombers for detonating Bomb – para 7
O/C D Coy will detail 2 Trained Bombers who will parade at 2.45 pm today with Carrier party – They will be attached to B H Qts for Rations from the 30th Inst

6 Advance Detachment – 2 Lieutenant with 5 N.C.O. already detailed

3

will report to Lieut BROADWOOD Brig H Q Staff at 1pm today 28th Inst at point K 33. d. 8. 2 to proceed to GROVETOWN ahead of the Regiment.
All Carriers will wear distinguishing badge which will be issued by Brigade

A. O. H. McDonald
Capt
Adj
3rd Regt S. A Infty

War Diary

[illegible] 13th Bn [illegible]

App 138

To O.C. "A" Coy

[illegible]

The undermentioned working party to parade at once with current days rations to be prepared to [illegible] over night and to report at 9 am today 24/6/16 to representative of 233 Coy R E at PUMPING STATION at GATE of CHATEAU at SUZANNE. Of Map 62C NWB 1/10000 G8 D4.1.

[illegible]

[illegible]

[illegible] Capt & Adjt

3rd Reg[illegible] [illegible]

War Diary Issued 6 am

24/6/16

To O.C. "B" Coy

" D "

WORKING PARTIES

[illegible]

Troops Coy

R.E. at [illegible] 20. 678 [illegible]

[illegible]

[illegible]

arrange to [illegible] of [illegible] party at 9.30 am.

[illegible]

Capt 3rd Reg [illegible]

will be taken, and the only animals to be taken will be officers' chargers actually in possession. Saddlery for same w ill be taken.

The Transport Officer bel onging to the 4th S. A. Infantry will supervise the work of the N.C.O., and men in charge of the Field Ambulance horses, and the Transport Officer of the 1st S. A. Infantry will supervise the work of the N.C.O., and men in charge of Headquarters horses.

6. DETAILS. Details not embarking with their units on either the "Megantic" or "Oriana" will report to Major Heal, 1st S. A. Infantry, on departure of their units from Sidi Bishr.

The senior officer or N.C.O., in charge of unit details will hand to Major Heal a State, signed by the Adjutant of the unit, showing the strength of the details reporting.

2 8 52
1 8 13
3 65
11 horses

Officers proceeding to the Reserve Battalion at Bordon will proceed on the "Oriana". These officers will not take servants with them.

J. Mitchell Baker
Major.
Brigade Major.

11. 4. 16
11 pm.

50

Urgent Bde Hdqrs.

S A Bde

3rd Regt S A I

Transport will move by road

to ETINEHEM, as there

is no accommodation on train.

Please instruct your

Transport Officer to

report to Town Major

at ETINEHEM on

arrival.

They should be sent off

as soon as possible.

18/6/16 [illegible] Lieut-
6.30 AM for Bde Major

Daily Intelligence Report
Unit Rowlock
From 4 30pm to 4:30 pm 27 & 28 /8 1916
Part I

I Artillery during the evening the enemy's artillery put over a few heavy shells in ZOUAVE VAL during the hours of 1 & 2 pm they put over a number of H.E. shells on front line trenches and ZOUAVE VALLEY.

II Trench Mortars The enemy's trench mortars have been more active during the past 24 hours the positions of EASATZ and GUBRON AVE being the principal places of the enemies bombardment.

III Working parties A working party was heard in front of INTERNATIONAL AVE at about 2-30 am.

IV General the enemy have been more active during the last 24 hours, and his activity with H.E. shells - schrapnel & trench mortars was fairly active.

PART II

I Artillery Our artillery have been firing large quantities of 18 pdrs on enemy wire in front line trenches. Effect not yet observed.

II Trench mortars. Our trench mortars & M.T.M.B.R.A have been very active during the past 24 hours in strafing the enemy in retaliation. It was observed at point S.5.c. 3.5½ that a bomb store or magazine was blown up.

III Lewis Guns Our Lewis guns fired on enemy working party at 4-30 am with success. The enemy working immediately dispersing. We believe that two or three hits took place.

IV Patrol A patrol went out at 9-30 pm to examine enemy wire returning at 11-00 pm.

V General Our & also the enemy action has been not active during the last 24 hours.

Major
Comdg. [illegible]

Rowlock
Daily Intelligence Report
From 4-30pm 28.8.16 To 4-30 pm 29.8.16
PART I

I Artillery During the last 24 hours the enemy artillery has been fairly active. Using H.E. & schrapnel

II Trench Mortars. Fairly active.

III Lights At about 10-20 pm one green light went up followed by slight artillery fire.

IV General The enemy has been on the alert during the past 24 hours & shows himself fairly active.

Part II

I Artillery Our artillery burst 2 shells on graze on N slope leading to ZOUAVE VALLEY.

II Trench motors. Our M.T.M.B.R.A. and S.A.L.T.M.B were very active in retaliation to enemies fire.

III Patrols Several patrols went out to inspect & report upon the condition of enemies wire. All patrols agree that same is still impassable.

IV General The action of our trench mortars & action generally has been more active during past 24 hours

Major

51

from each Regiment will be detailed for taking over above stores.

(e) Receipts to be signed by the officer han ding over and receiving in e ach case -- duplicate receipt to be retained by the officer handing over.

(6) Transport of 2nd S. A. Infantry will be bi lletted at Sheet 36.B.8.a.2.10. and that of the 3rd S. A. Infantry a t Sheet 36.B.4.b.10.0.

(7) The billets at present occupied by the above units of the South African Brigades will be taken over by the 8th Go rdon Highlanders and 6th Royal Scots Fusiliers res pectively, and are to be left in a pe rfectly clean sta te.

(8) Maps of new billetting areas, with details of bille ts, are attached here to. These are to be returned to Brigade Headquarters on t he 7th inst., together with schedules showing how the Battalions have been distributed in the billetting areas.

(9) Brigade Headquarters will move on same date to present Headquarters of the 28th Infantry Brigade at PONT DE NIEPPE.

(10) Reports to be sent to Brigade Headquarters as soon as units have occupied their new billets .

Acknowledge.

[signature]
Major.

Brigade Major.

Copy No.1 to 2nd S. A. In fantry.
2 " 3rd do
3 " 9th Division.
4 " 26th Infantry Brigade.
5 " 27th do do
6 " 28th do do
7 Office.
8 do

(Copies 3–6: For information)

Issued by ord erly at ____________

SECRET

53

Headquarters
1st Inf Bde SAOEF
4/5/16.

[illegible] 30/5/16

O.C.
3rd Regt

In connection with the move of Battn on Saturday next please note

(1) The 29 men of 2nd Regt now looking after transport of 4th Regt will be relieved at 3 pm tomorrow by similar number from 1st Regt. Officers Commanding Units have been advised - please inform T.O. 4th Regt

(2) The transport 4th Regt will be at your disposal on Saturday to assist in moving your stores - please inform T.O. accordingly.

(3) The Transport personnel 4th Regt & men attached from 1st Regt are to occupy transport lines in billeting area 4th Regt from tomorrow. Please ensure the Transport Officer knows all particulars about his Regts billeting area, so that on arrival of his Unit he can point out billets of Battn Hd Qrs, companies &c.

(4) In addition to motor lorry mentioned in move order one will be at your Battn H-Qrs at 8 am Saturday to move baggage &c.

5 Marching In and Out States to be

rendered

2

rendered in duplicate please.

Acknowledge by telephone message please.

P. L. Pepper [?]
Captain
Staff Captain.

when the enemy bombed us.
I kept 6 men with me all carrying bombs. We retaliated throwing 15 bombs. The enemy's bombs were falling short at first. Our bombs were bursting in the air. It seems that the Germans were trying to cut us off because bombs came from our right & these bombs fell amongst us. We retired back to our own trench.
We all returned safely at 11.15 pm.

20. 8. 16.

2nd Lieut

FROM: O/C. ERSATZ CRATER. App.
TO, HARTUNG ST. PATROL.
TO. O.C. 3RD S.A.I.

I with four men, one an interpreter left point A in the crater & proceeded in an EASTERLY direction towards the enemy wire. I came up to wire at point B. and lay quiet for 15 minutes. The wire at this point had been twisted & churned up by our artillery fire but I found no opening to get to the trench. I then proceeded in a NORTHERLY direction for some 25 yards or 30 and was fired on by a machine gun. Finding that each time I attempted to move the machine gun would open fire I started to crawl in a westerly direction to escape detection. I attempted to make for the wire at point C but was again fired on by the machine gun. I eventually

---

reached the wire at D. I lay there some time & heard sounds of knocking & hammering & I thought it was hammering stakes in the wire but could not detect anyone. The wire is low at this point & has been cut by our shell fire. I attempted to crawl through & look over parapet but was sniped at several times. Coming back I examined our advanced wire & found that several gaps had been cut in it. I eventually reached HARTUNG SAP at 11-35 pm.

54

Lieut
3rd S.A.I.

Daily Intelligence Report
ROWLOCK 30.8.16 55

Part I.

I Artillery Intermittent during past 24 hours.
II Trench Mortars Fairly active.
III Lights. Red light was sent up about 10 pm followed by rifle grenade fire.
IV General The general disposition of the enemy was alert.

Part II

I Artillery Our artillery fire was very quiet
II Trench Mortars Retaliated to enemy's trench mortar & artillery fire.
III Patrols Three patrols went out at at 9.15 pm one 10-30 pm & one 12 mn. The first patrol got within 15 yards of enemy lines & where unable to proceed further owing to alertness of the enemy who bombed them from front line and Right flank. 2nd Patrol examined enemies wire & when fired on by enemy machine gun 3rd Patrol inspected enemies wire which was [illegible] impassable.
IV General the enemy have been very quiet during the past 24 hours.

Major
Temp Commanding

Daily Intelligence Report

ROWLOCK 31.8.16.
From 4.30 pm 30.8.16 TO 4-30 pm 31.8.16

PART I

I Artillery Exceeding quiet during night shelling at about 9 am. shells falling in LOVAVE VALLEY – our shells evidently searching for our artillery firing from point SW ridge.

PART II

I No retaliation.

Major
Temp Commanding

1st SOUTH AFRICAN INFANTRY BRIGADE

Annexure to Operation Order No.50

Relieving Unit	Unit being relieved	Hour at which guides will meet leading platoon at point "G"	Hour at which leading platoon to pass point W.18.a. central
S.A.Bde.M.G.Company	26th Bde.M.G.Company	8.am	6.am
S.A.Bde.T.M.Battery	26th Bde.T.M.Battery	8.15.am	6.15.am
4th S.A.Infantry	6th Black Watch	9.am	7.am
3rd S.A.Infantry	5th Cameron Highlanders	noon	10.am
1st S.A.Infantry	7th Seaforth Highlanders	3.pm	1.pm

The 2nd S.A.Infantry, less working party in the MAESTRE LINE will move to CAMBLAIN L'ABBE under regimental arrangements, but will not pass point W.5.c.central before 1.pm, and must be in billets by 6.pm.

58

S E C R E T.

Date.	Unit.	From.	To.	Approximate Distance.	S.P. and Time.	Remarks.
May 28.	3rd Regiment. a 2nd do a	LE BIZET. LE BIZET.	NOOTE BOOM. BAILLEUL.	9 miles. 7½ miles.	Relief to commence at 6 p.m.	Each Battalion will move under orders of its Regtl. Commander
29.	1st Regiment. b	FRONT LINE.	LE BIZET.			
	3rd Regiment. 2nd do	NOOTE BOOM. BAILLEUL.	STRAZEELE Area. (Via Outtersteene)	5 miles. 4 miles.	To be clear of Bailleul & Noote Boom by 6 p.m.	Not to enter new billets till 7 p.m.
	S.A. Fd. Amb.	LA CRECHE Area.	STRAZEELE Area.	6 miles.		
30th	4th Regiment. c	FRONT LINE.	LE BIZET.			
31.	1st Regiment. d 4th do d	LE BIZET. LE BIZET.	BAILLEUL. NOOTE BOOM.	7½ miles 9 miles.	Relief to commence at 6 p.m.	Each Batt. will move under orders of its Regtl. Commander.
June 1.	1st Regiment. 4th do	BAILLEUL. NOOTE BOOM.	STRAZEELE Area. STRAZEELE Area.	6 miles. 5 miles.	Not to march before 6 p.m.	do do
2.	S.A. Brigade. S.A. Fd. Amb.	STRAZEELE Area.	STEENBECQUE-MORBECQUE Area.	9 miles via HAZEBROUCK.	Not to enter STEENBECQUE-MORBECQUE Area before 7 p.m.	S.A. Fd. Amb. to move under orders of G.O.C. S.A. Brigade.
3.	S.A. Brigade. S.A. Fd. Amb.	STEENBECQUE-MORBECQUE Area.	WITTERNESSE.	8½ miles via AIRE.	To be clear of STEENBECQUE-MORBECQUE Area by 6 p.m.	Not to enter WITTERNESSE till 6.30 p.m.
4.	S.A. Brigade. S.A. Fd. Amb.	WITTERNESSE.	ERNY-St JULIEN Area.	6 miles.	To be clear of WITTERNESSE by 6 p.m.	

a Will be relieved by the 10th Batt. Royal West Kent Regt., and 20th Batt. Durham L.I., respectively.
b Will be relieved by the 20th Batt. Durham L.I.,
c Will be relieved by the 10th Batt. Royal West Kent Regt.,
d Will be relieved by the 23rd Batt. Middlesex Regt., and 11th Batt. Queen's Regiment respectively.

59

HEADQUARTERS,

1st S. A. INFANTRY BRIGADE.

To:- 3rd Regiment

B.M. 47/10 26th May, 1916.

[illegible]

Herewith instructions in connection with the move of the Brigade to 1st Army Training Area.

1. BILLETTING PARTIES. These will precede their units by 24 hours, and will be composed of 1 Officer and 4 N.C.O's, who should be mounted on cycles. Interpreters will accompany Billetting Parties when possible.

2. REPORTING. Units billetting in Boullion, Herbecque, Steenbecque and Cuillieul, will instruct their Billetting Parties to report as under :-

BOULLION, To Area Officer, Lieut. Christian, near Church, Boullion.

STEENBECQUE, HERBECQUE, } To Area Officer, Lieut. McLeod, near Mairie, Herbecque.

[illegible], Town Major, [illegible].

3. GUIDES. Billetting Parties will arrange to meet their units, and guide them by the most direct route to their billets.

4. FIELDS which have already been used as Transport and Wagon Lines should be occupied, and care taken not to damage crops, grass, fields and trees.

5. BILLETTING CERTIFICATES. Must be rendered for all billets occupied.

6. Units occupying billets at STEENBECQUE are on no account to interfere with the 1st Army Sniping School.

7. TRANSPORT. For the move from [illegible] to [illegible] one Motor Lorry will be allotted to each Regiment. From [illegible] to Training Area one Motor Lorry between two Regiments.

8. DRIVERS. Units will arrange for rations and billetting of the drivers of above vehicles.

9. [illegible]. O.C. Divisional Train will arrange for Baggage Wagons of Units to join their units on day prior to move. These Wagons will remain with and accompany their units.

Captain.

a/ Brigade Major.

app 105 61

RELIEFS

TIME ——— TABLE

May 8th 1916

Time	Coy	Platoons	Route		Destination
7-40 P.M	B Coy	1 Platoon	Via	To	Trench 98
7-43 "		1 do	HARNIAM		" 99
7-46 "		1 do	AVENUE		To Bachelors' Walk
7-49 "		1 do			Trench 97 S

Time	Coy	Platoons	Route		Destination
7-~~40~~ 30 p.m	A Coy	1 Platoon	Via	To	Trench 96
7-~~43~~ 33 "		1 Do	LONG AVENUE		" 97
7-~~46~~ 36 "		1 do			" 96 S
7-~~49~~ 39 "		1 do			" 96 S

Time	Coy	Platoons	Route		Destination
7-52 p.m	D Coy	1 Platoon	Via	To	Trench Glasgow Rt
7-55 "		1 do	HARNIAN'S AVENUE		" " Lt
7-58 "		1 do	&		FORT PAUL & RESERVE TRENCH ~~FARM~~
8-1 "		1 do	SUFFOLK AVENUE		RESERVE FARM

Time	Coy	Platoons	Route		Destination
8-4 p.m	C Coy	1½ Platoon	Via	To	7 Trees Redoubt
8-9 "		1½ do	HARNIAN'S		PATERNOSTERROW
8-11 "		1 do	AVENUE		do do

A. McDonald

Capt. & Adjutant

3rd. S. A. Infantry (Transvaal Regt.)

Brig Operation Order No 31

S E C R E T

27 MAY 1916

62

The Officer Commanding, A Coy, B " C " D " HQ "

MOVE

I. **RELIEF.** The 10th Battalion Royal West Kent Regiment will relieve the 3rd S.A.Infantry, commencing at 6 p.m. 28th inst

2. **MOVE.** The Battalion will move from LE BIZET at 6 p.m. in the following order, maintaining intervals between Platoons of 5 minutes. (1) Headquarter Details (2) "A" Coy (3) "B" Coy, (4) "C" Coy, (5) "D" Coy, (6) Lewis Gun Section, (7) Transport.

3. **TRANSPORT.** The Transport will maintain a distance of at least 500 yards from the Battalion.

4. **REAR GUARD.** "D" Company will furnish a rear guard of 1 Officer with Platoon for the collection of probable straglers. Company Commanders will enforce strict march discipline. The Officer detailed for rear guard to report to Adjutant for instructions at 5 p.m. re ammunition guard.

5. **BAGGAGE.** The following vehicles are available for Regimental Baggage and will be detailed by Transport Officer to report at Battalion Headquarters at 6 p.m.

Headquarters, Officers Kits, Orderly Room "A" Coy Officers Kits, & Coy Orderly Room "B" " do & do do Shoemaker's Tools, Oils etc	One G.S.Wagon.
"C" Coy Officers Kits & Coy Orderly Room "D" " do & do do Armourer's Tools, Carpenter's Tools, Oils etc	No 2 G.S.Wagon

All kits to be piled at Company Headquarters where it will be picked up by Transport

SIGNALLING EQUIPMENT.	No 1 Tool Wagon. In rear portion G.S.Limbered Wagon. In fore portion	
TOOLS, PICKS, SHOVELS.	No 2 Tool Wagon. Fore portion.	G.S.L.Wagon
PANNIERS SIGNALLING.	No 2 do Hind portion.	do

Companies will return all Tools to Q.M.Store by 4 p.m. 28th inst. The Quartermaster will arrange distribution on wagons, G.S. Limbered, as above.

TRAVELLING KITCHENS. All Camp Kettles and unexpired portion of day's ration will be carried on these kitchens also other Company Cooking Utensils.

6. **DRESS** The Battalion will parade in Heavy Marching Order with Steel Helmet strapped to valise.

7. **RECEIPTS.** The Yellow form must be handed in to Orderly Room as soon as possible after handing over to O/C Company taking over ammunition, bombs etc. This form must be signed by both Company Commanders and a certificate added with regard to the cleanliness of the lines.

8. **BAGGAGE GUARD.** Companies will detail 2 men per Company as Baggage Guard.

A.W.H. McDonald

Captain and Actg Adjutant,
3rd S.A.Infantry.

App 112

S C H E D U L E.

SHOWING ARRANGEMENTS FOR ATTACHMENT OF 1st AND 4th SOUTH AFRICAN INFANTRY TO BATTALIONS IN THE LINE.

	Parties to be attached.	Unit & Coy. to which to be attached.	Date of entering trenches.	Date of leaving trenches.	Remarks.
	RIGHT SUB-SECTOR.				
	1st S.A.I.				
(a)	50 other ranks A Coy.	2nd S.A.I. A Coy.	11th May.	13th May.	(a) This party relieves a similarly constituted party of 2nd S.A.I.- 200 other ranks - who proceed to the billets vacated by 1st S.A.I. party.
	50 do do B Coy.	do B Coy.	do	do	
	50 do do C Coy.	do C Coy.	do	do	
	50 do do D Coy.	do D Coy.	do	do	
(b)	Similarly constituted parties.	As above.	13th May.	15th May.	(b) This party relieves (a).
(c)	do do do	do	15th May.	17th May.	(c) do do (b)
(d)	do do do	do	17th May.	19th May.	(d) do do (c)
	LEFT SUB-SECTOR.	3rd Regt SAI			(e) As at (a), substituting 3rd S.A.I. for 2nd S.A.I. and 4th S.A.I. for 1st S.A.I.
	4th S. A. I.				(f) This party relieves (e)
(e)	50 other ranks A Coy.	3rd S.A.I. A Coy.	11th May.	13th May.	(g) do do (f)
	50 do do B Coy.	do B Coy.	do	do	(h) do do (g)
	50 do do C Coy.	do C Coy.	do	do	
	50 do do D Coy.	do D Coy.	do	do	
(f)	Similarly constituted parties.	As above.	13th May.	15th May.	
(g)	do do	do	15th May.	17th May.	
(h)	do do	do	17th May.	19th May.	

All officers will be attached for a tour of duty in the trenches in accordance with arrangements to be made between the O.C. 1st and 2nd and O.C. 3rd and 4th S.A.I.

[illegible signature]
Bde Major

11.5.16

63

app

3 pm 4/5/16

106

64

SECRET.

Copy No. 2

1st SOUTH AFRICAN INFANTRY BRIGADE.

OPERATION ORDER No. 24.

In accordance with 9th Division "X4/1310" of the 2nd inst., the following moves will take place :-

(1) 2nd and 3rd Battalions S. A. Infantry will proceed on Saturday, 6th inst., to billets at LE BIZET.

(2) Billetting parties of the 2nd and 3 rd S.A.I., will arrive at LE BIZET, at Headquarters of the 6th K.O.S.B., and 9th Scottish Rifles respectively, at 10 a.m. These parties will take over Camp Equipment, Grenade Carriers and reserve S.A.A. at the billets.

(3) Remainder of each Battalion will leave present billets by platoons, with intervals between platoons of at least 200 yards, in time to enable the whole Battalion to be at LE BIZET by 6 p.m. When halts are made care must be taken that the interval mentioned is maintained.

(4) Regimental transport will be used for moving stores, kits, etc., from present to new billets.

(5) (a) The following guns, transport, stores and ammunition will be handed over to each Battalion :-

Lewis Guns, 4 per Battalion.
Two 2-horse Limbers for same (per Batt).
Gun and Regimental S.A.A. for same.
Steel helmets.
Telescopic Sighted Rifles.
"Very" Pistols.
Periscopes.

(b) The 2nd Regiment will take over above stores at 10 a.m. on 6th inst., from the 8th Gordon Highlanders, at Soyer Farm (Sheet 36.B.6.d. centre), and transfer them to Regimental Q.M. Stores in the billetting area to be occupied by them at LE BIZET. For this purpose a motor trolly will be at the former place.

(c) The 3rd Regiment will take over the above stores at 10 a.m. on 6th inst., from the 6th Royal Scots Fusiliers at PAPOT (Sheet 36.B.3. c.9.2.), and transfer them to Regimental Q.M. Stores in the billetting area to be occupied by them at LE BIZET. A motor trolly will be at the former place.

(d) A fatigue party of one officer and 20 men

1h 4th 5th

65

(13) COMMUNICATION will be established by "A" and "D" Companies, with the Regiments on their flanks, and PATROLS between all gaps constantly sent out under an N.C.O. Such patrols will invariably initial patrol slips on meeting each other. A post of 1 sentry and its relief will be posted in centre of each gap.

(14) TRENCH STANDING ORDERS. Every Officer and N.C.O should be in possession of a copy issued in Egypt which will be adopted pro tem.

(15) WARNING. It is impressed on all ranks, that in some places the parapet is not high enough to be absolute cover especially for tall men, and has been known to be penetrated by a bullet, causing casualties in consequence. These should be pointed out to all sentries who will allow NO ONE to loiter near such spots.

Great care must also be exercised in the handling of periscope and telescopic rifles and that all bombs in trenches are kept free from rust and ready for use, but men warned against interfering with the pin.

(16) ALARM In case of alarm, all ranks will immediately "STAND TO" at their station. Men should be made to learn quickest route.

(a) Notice Sentries will only fire if a definite or suspicious movement is seen. No indiscriminate firing is to take place.

(b) All N.C.O's and men to be warned against giving any notification to the enemy by their conduct, that a relief is taking place, or enable them to find out the Regiments effected by the relief.

(c) "STAND DOWN" will not be given unless Company Commanders are satisfied that weather and light is clear enough to see any Suspicious movement on the part of the enemy.

(d) "STAND TO" for all ranks, 3-30 a.m. each morning.

(e) All spare ammunition, old clothing etc, to be collected and placed in DUMP to be collected by Salvage Company.

(f) The Line held by the Brigade is a series of defended positions, which MUST be held till the last man, and is the proud boast of some Brigades that they have never lost a Trench.

[signature]

Captain and Acting Adjutant,
3rd South African Infantry.

Note Magazines will be charged before leaving billetting area.

Transport has been arranged and will call at Company's lines about 7 p.m.

SECRET. War Diary app 108

THIRD SOUTH AFRICAN INFANTRY

Issued 10 am

May 8th 1916

66

The Officer Commanding,

MOVE

In accordance with operation order No 25, reference Trench Map 1/10,000, the following move will take place:-

3rd Regiment, S.A.I relieve 10th H.L.I in T96 - 102 inclusive. The 3rd Regiment, S.A.Infantry will move into Trenches via Nicholson's Avenue (Gasometer Corner). The relief will be carried on by Platoons. Platoons must move at intervals of at least 300 yards

Reliefs will move off and report as per time table attached, at various positions. 1 Guide per platoon will be detailed to report to Companies at 6-30 p.m. Companies to send Orderly Corporal to take over these guides, at Battalion Headquarters

(2) Signalling Officer and Battalion Bombing Officer will take over at 5 p.mand will report at Headquarters of Battalion being relieved.

(3) Company Commanders are reminded of their responsibility in handing over billets and all equipment, stores etc and that Trench Store Sheet is completed in duplicate.

(4) The 2nd in Command with Medical Officer will inspect all billets at 6 p.m.

(5) DRESS Great Coats will be worn. Gas Helmet satchel over all equipment.

(6) No smoking will be allowed when proceeding to Trenches or in Fire Trenches.

(7) On arrival in Trenches, bayonets will be fixed and magazines previously charged 5 rounds, with safety catch turned over. All ammunition used in Trenches to be obtained from Trench Dump; only in cases of emergency will ammunition in men's pouches be used.

(8) Officers, N.C.O's and men will "Stand To" till the relief has been completed and all sentries posted and Company Commanders reported such to Battalion Headquarters. "Stand Down" will then be given when men may file to Dugouts and rifles placed in Box Racks in "Bays" near Dugouts. Rifle Covers will NOT be worn.

PACKS may be removed but belt with ammunition will at all times be worn - less waterbottle and haversack, which can be stored in Dugout.

(9) TRENCH HELMETS will be worn by all sentries. Officers will invariably wear Trench Helmets in any part of the line.

(10) SILENCE is to be maintained and it must be remembered that Talking, Shouting and also striking matches, is an indication to the enemy that reliefs are taking place.

(11) SENTRIES will challenge in low voice, and to all Officers will give the number of their post
Company
3rd S.A.I
Correct or otherwise.

(12) COOKING must be carried out at Company or Platoon Cook Houses. Individual cooking will not be permitted.

CONFIDENTIAL.

Copy No...3.....

App 123 67

1st SOUTH AFRICAN INFANTRY BRIGADE.

OPERATION ORDER NO. 30.

1. RELIEF. The 1st and 4th Regiments, S. A. I., at strength approximately 300 all ranks, each Battalion, will relieve the 2nd and 3rd Regiments, S. A. I., on Friday night, 26th inst.,

2. L. G. & T. M. PERSONNEL. The Lewis Gun teams and Trench Mortar personnel will be relieved during the day on Saturday, under arrangements to be made between Battalion Commanders.

3. BILLETS. Units will make their own arrangements for taking and handing over billets.

4. MOVEMENT. The relief will be carried out by Platoons. Platoons must move at intervals of at least five minutes. Leading Platoons to move off at 8 p.m.

5. MOVES OF REMAINDERS OF BATTALIONS. The remainder of the 1st and 4th S. A. I., will move from LE BIZET to the billets at present occupied by the remainders of the 2nd and 3rd S. A. I., at ARMENTIERES the same evening, and those portions of the 2nd and 3rd Regiments, S. A. I., at present billetted at ARMENTIERES, will move to LE BIZET. These moves must not commence until 8 p.m.

6. REPORTING RELIEF COMPLETE. Completion of relief and moves to be reported to Brigade Headquarters.

Please acknowledge.

[signature] Pepper
Captain.
a/ Brigade Major.

Copy No.	to	Copy No.	to
1	1st S. A. I.,	9	O.C. L.T.M. Battery.
2	2nd do	10.	107th Coy. A. S. C.,
3	3rd do	11	Right Group, Artillery.
4	4th do	12	Brigade Signal Section.
5	9th Division.	13	233rd Field Coy. R.E.,
6	26th Inf. Brigade.	14	2nd N.Z. Inf. Brigade.
7	27th do	15	Office Copy.
8	O.C. Bde M.G.Coy.	16	do

Issued by Orderly at...5 pm.........

received 9 pm

Headquarters,
1st S. A. I. Brigade.
24th May, 1916.

Page 20.

Instructions regarding War Diaries and Intelligence Summaries are contained in F. S. Regs., Part II. and the Staff Manual respectively. Title pages will be prepared in manuscript.

WAR DIARY
or
~~INTELLIGENCE SUMMARY.~~
(Erase heading not required.)

Army Form C. 2118.

3RD S. A. INF. (TRANSVAAL RGT.)

Vol

Hour, Date, Place	Summary of Events and Information	Remarks and references to Appendices
6 am 1/6/15 STRAZEELE AREA	In Billets.	
12. 30pm do do	Billeting party of 1 Officer NCOs left for STEENBECQUE MORBECQUE to secure accomodation	
9pm do do	Received Brigade Operation Order No 33	App 128
8 am 2/6/15 do	Issued Battalion Move Order from STRAZEELE AREA to STEENBECQUE - MORBECQUE AREA	App 129
1 pm do	Battalion moved off via HAZEBROUCK	
6 pm do S. M. Area	Arrived and billeted in STEENBECQUE - MORBECQUE AREA	
9 am 3/6/15 do	Received Brigade Operation Order No 34 to WITERNESSE AREA	App 130
10 am do do	Issued Battalion Move Order to QUERNES	
3. 30pm do	Battalion moved off via outskirts of AIRE	
8 pm do QUERNES	Arrived and billeted QUERNES.	
3 30pm 4/6/16	Received Brigade Operation Order No 35 Battalion left QUERNES for Rest Area	
6 pm do REST AREA	Arrived and billeted as follows:- Battalion HQrs, (Lewis Gunners, Signallers & Band) and "C" Coy at BONCOURT, "A" Coy "B" Coy & Transport at PIPPERMONT, "D" Coy at LE PLEOUY	App 131
5/6/16 6/6/16 7/6/16 do	Training under Company Arrangements	
8th, 9th & 10th do	do do Battalion ~~Brigade~~ Scheme.	
11/6/16	do do Brigade do.	App 132

68

(73989) W4141—463. 400,000. 9/14. H.&J.Ltd. Forms/C. 2118/10.

PAGE 21

Instructions regarding War Diaries and Intelligence Summaries are contained in F. S. Regs., Part II. and the Staff Manual respectively. Title pages will be prepared in manuscript.

WAR DIARY
or
~~INTELLIGENCE SUMMARY.~~
(Erase heading not required.)

Army Form C. 2118.

3RD S. A. INF. (TRANSVAAL RGT)

Hour, Date, Place	Summary of Events and Information	Remarks and references to Appendices
12/6/16 REST AREA	Training under Company arrangements.	
13/6/16 do		
2.40 pm do do	Received Brigade Operation Order No 36 re Training	
10 pm do do	Issued Battalion Move Order	
4 pm 14/6/16	Battalion moved off & marched through FLECHIN	
7 pm do	Arrived at LILLERS STATION	
9.51 do do	Completed entraining & left for LONGUEAU Station	App 133
7 am 15/6/16	Arrived at LONGUEAU Station and detrained	
11 am do	Marched from LONGUEAU station to BREILLY	
4 pm do	Arrived at billets at BREILLY	
16/6/16 BREILLY	Training under Company arrangements	
17/6/16 do		
do do	C/O, 2nd in Command, Capts Tomlinson, MacLachlan & Lt Paxton visited trenches	
11 pm do do	Received Brigade Operation Order - BM 47/26/5	App 134
10 am 18/6/16 do	C/O issued verbal instructions to C.Cs re Move	
1 pm do	Battalion moved off, marching to AILLY SUR SOMME Station	do.
2.50 do do	Completed entraining & left by train for HEILLY Station. Transport proceeding by road.	

69

(73989) W4141—463. 400,000. 9/14. H.&J.Ltd. Forms/C. 2118/10.

SECRET.

APP 128

rec'd 9 pm

Copy No. 3

70

HEADQUARTERS,

1st S. A. INFANTRY BRIGADE.

1st June, 1916.

OPERATION ORDERS No. 33.

1. MARCH. The Brigade will march to-morrow afternoon, 2nd inst., to the STEENBECQUE-MORBECQUE Area.

2. STARTING POINT. Point "X" on attached plan. To starting point

3. ROUTES TO BE FOLLOWED. As shown on attached plan.

4. ORDER OF MARCH & TIMETABLE.

(a) Brigade Headquarters. To be formed up at starting point at 3.15 p.m.

(b) 4th S.A.I. To be formed up at starting point at 3.15 p.m. to follow Brigade Headquarters at 50 yards distance.

(c) 2nd S.A.I. To be at point 0 on plan at 3 p.m. ready to move in rear of 4th S.A.I.,

(d) 1st S. A. I., To be at starting point at 3.18 p.m. Battalion to be clear of STRAZEELE by 2.30 p.m.

(e) 3rd S.A.I., To be at STRAZEELE by 2.30 p.m. and follow in rear of 1st S.A.I.,

(f) 1st S.A. Field Ambulance. To be at STRAZEELE by 2.30 p.m. and to follow in rear of 3rd S.A.I.,

5. DISTANCES. Usual distances, excepting that distance between transport and Battalion following will be increased to 50 yards.

6. TRANSPORT. First Line. To march in rear of Battalions as usual.

Baggage Wagons. To report to an officer of Divisional Train opposite the Church, STRAZEELE, at 4 p.m.

7. GUIDES TO BILLETS. Officers Commanding units will be notified later regarding the places at which their units will be met by guides to lead them to their billets.

8. MARCH STANDING ORDERS. Attention is directed to Nos. 6, 7 and 9 of Brigade March Standing Orders, issued in Egypt. The order regarding no smoking on line of march by night is temporarily suspended. (See copy attached)

9. ORDERS FOR FOLLOWING DAY'S MARCH. An officer from each unit will report at Brigade Headquarters, (House where Area Officer's Office is), MORBECQUE, at 9 a.m. on the 3rd inst., for orders for march on the 4th idem to WITTERNESSE Area.

J Mitchell Baker

Major.
Brigade Major.

Issued by Orderly at............

Copy No.1 to 1st S.A.I.,
2 2nd do
3 3rd do
4 4th do
5. 9th Division.
6 107th ... A.S.C.

Copy No.7 to O.i/c Bde Sig. Sec
8 1st S.A. Fd. Amb.
9 G.O.C. the Bde.
10 Brigade Major.
11 Staff Captain.
12 Office Copy

PAGE 23

Instructions regarding War Diaries and Intelligence Summaries are contained in F. S. Regs., Part II. and the Staff Manual respectively. Title pages will be prepared in manuscript.

WAR DIARY
or
~~INTELLIGENCE SUMMARY~~.

(*Erase heading not required.*)

Army Form C. 2118.

3RD S. A. INF. (TRANSVAAL RGT.)

Hour, Date, Place			Summary of Events and Information	Remarks and references to Appendices
11 am	26/6/16	BOIS CELESTINS	Draft of 53 NCOs & men arrived from Base	
1 pm	do	do	"C" Coy working party returned	
4·30 pm	do	do	Draft of 42 NCOs & men arrived from Base.	
	27/6/16	do	Training under Company arrangements	
8 am	28/6/16	do	Detailed various working parties in terms of Brigade Instruction No 2 para 4	App 140
1-45 pm	do	do	Received Brigade Operation Order No 38	App 141
2·45 pm	do	do	Issued Battalion Move Order (B102)	
7 pm	do	do	Received Brigade Minute cancelling Operation Order No 30	
7·45 pm	do	do	Working party 3 Off 197 OR returned	
	29/6/16	do	Training under Company arrangements & inspection by G.O.C	
9-30 am	30/6/16	do	Received Brigade Operation Order No 39	App 142
9·45 am	30/6/16	do	Issued Battalion Move Order (B104)	
			Training under Company arrangements	
10-30 pm	do	do	Battalion Moved off en route to GROVETOWN	
1-15 am	do and 1/7/16		Arrived GROVETOWN and bivouacked.	

A W H McDonald Capt
Adjutant
3rd S. A. Infantry (Transvaal Regt.)

PAGE 22

Instructions regarding War Diaries and Intelligence Summaries are contained in F. S. Regs., Part II and the Staff Manual respectively. Title pages will be prepared in manuscript.

WAR DIARY
or
~~INTELLIGENCE SUMMARY~~.
(Erase heading not required.)

Army Form C. 2118.

3RD S. A. INF.
(TRANSVAAL RGT

Hour, Date, Place	Summary of Events and Information	Remarks and references to Appendices
5 pm 18/6/16	Arrived HEILLY and detrained. Battalion marched to camp at ETINEHEM	App 134
11 pm do	Arrived at ETINEHEM.	
2·30pm 19/6/16 ETINEHEM	Supplied working party of 1 Officer 50 men for cable digging	
7·30 am 20/6/16 do	do do do 4 do 300 do do do	
1·30 pm do do	do do do 2 do 160 do do do	
21/6/16 do	Issued move order R4/83.	App 135
do	Draft of 1 Officer, 28 Men arrived from Base.	
8·30 am 22/6/16 do	Supplied working party of 8 Officers 300 men for R.F.A 9th Div.	App 136
2·30 pm do	Remainder of Battalion vacated camp and marched to BOIS CELESTINS	App 137
6 pm do	Arrived BOIS CELESTINS and occupied tents	
4 pm 23/6/16 B.C.	Working Party of B Coy returned. 2 Casualties both bullet wounds	
6 am 24/6/16 do	Working Party 1 Off 40 men left Camp to report to 232nd A.T. Coy RE.	App 138
9·30 do do	do do 3 Off 175 do do do do	
7·30 pm 25/6/16 do	do do 3 Off 197 men do for trenches	App 139

(73989) W4141—463. 400,000. 9/14. H.&J.Ltd. Forms/C. 2118/10.

72

15.

MESSAGES AND SIGNALS.

Prefix .... Code .... m. | Words | Charge

Office of Origin and Service Instructions.

Aw
8.35

Sent
At .... m.
To ....
By ....

This message is on a/c of: .... Service.

(Signature of "Franking Officer.")

Recd. .... m.
Date ....
From ....
By ....

TO { (1) WALTER
(2) EDWARD
(3) JOHN

* Sender's Number.	Day of Month.	In reply to Number.	AAA
B.M. 236	17.7.16		

The 76th Infy Bde will attack LONGUEVAL ~~town~~ at 3.45 a.m. and they will advance from West to East as far as the STRAND where the company holding that line must be in position aaa All ranks must be warned so that they understand what is on

J Mitchell Baker Major
Bde Major

From VENICE
Place
Time 1 am.

The above may be forwarded as now corrected. (Z)

Censor. Signature of Addressor or person authorised to telegraph in his name

* This line should be erased if not required.

925,000 W 14042—M 44 H W & V Ld 12/15

(pads of 50 dupls.) "C" Form (Duplicate). Army Form C. 2123.

MESSAGES AND SIGNALS. No. of Message ....

Charges to Pay. £ s. d. | Office Stamp.

Service Instructions.

Handed in at .... Office .... m. Received .... m.

TO Edward and Walter

Sender's Number	Day of Month	In reply to Number	AAA
BM 230	17.7.16		

The enemy is to be completely driven out of LONGUEVAL this morning by Infantry of 53 Bde attacking from West and our Heavy Artillery is to be registered on their objectives by our FOOs who will be given suitable targets at the North end giving time for our Infantry [illegible] if necessary to positions south of present trenches aaa Any [illegible] to be [illegible] to this [illegible] by Infantry [illegible] time pressure after Hour of attack will be notified later

FROM Venice
PLACE & TIME [illegible]

W 15660 M/151. 75,000 Pads. McC. & Co., Ltd., London. 1/16. Forms/C.2123.

73

Bombing posts will be made at such points as C.Os consider necessary

(4) Machine & Lewis Guns

A Machine gun and a Lewis Gun will be placed in each strong point on the perimeter. Garrisons of strong points to be two sections

(5) Flares

Flares will be lit when ~~that portion of the~~ the objective ~~to go and~~ between and to the east of S 12 C 6,7 and S 18 b 5 1 is reached

(6) Bde HQ

Bde. HQ. will be at S 27 d 3,7

(7) Ration rendezvous

Ration rendezvous will be at ~~8.30~~ 10 pm. tonight at S 28 a. 0.3½ where guides & carrying parties should meet transport. If possible to get transport nearer it will be done

(8) Dump

Bde dump will be at S 22 d 1,4

J Mitchell Baker
Major
Bde Major

In the field
14.7.16
3pm

Copy No 1 to O.C. 2nd S.W.B.
2 to O.C. 3rd
3 " "
personally to C.Os.

~~Brigade Headquarters the C.O. concerned will state the hour at which he will be ready~~ JMS

~~If no such message is received at Brigade Headquarters~~ JMS the artillery barrage which will be on BUCHANAN STREET – STRAND will lift to CAMPBELL STREET REGENT STREET at 7.30 (JMS) o'clock ; ~~and~~ to KING STREET – BOND STREET at ~~7.30~~ 8 and to a line clear of the wood at 8.30 pm.

(3) Defensive ~~Flanks~~ perimeter

The ~~C~~Os. C. 3rd and 2nd S.A.I. will each form a defensive perimeter as they move forward by making strong points and garrisoning them and making machine gun emplacements in suitable points at

S 11 d. 7,6 }
S 12 c 1,6 } by 3rd S.A.I.
S 12 c 5,7 }
S 12 c 9,5 }
S 12 d 3,4 }
S 18 b 6,9 } by 2nd S.A.I.
S 18 d 9,5 }
S 18 b 6,1 }

Supporting points will be made by 64th F Coy. RE at

S 18 b 5,7
S 18 a 5,4

a section Field Coy RE will accompany each of the attacking battalions

Secret

Reference Map
MONTAUBAN Sheet

Copy No I 76

S.A.I. Bde Operation Order No 48

(1) Our Troops

Our Troops are in possession of LONGUEVAL and the enemy's second line as far as BAZENTIN le GRAND

(2) Attack

The Brigade ~~will attack~~ less one Battalion will attack DELVILLE Wood from the west

The 3rd S.A.I. will attack the sector North of PRINCES STREET

The 2nd S.A.I. will attack the sector South of PRINCES STREET

The 4th S.A.I. will be in reserve in the trenches South of MONTAUBAN

The attack on each sector will be launched in column of half companies :- The right of the 3rd S.A.I. resting on PRINCES STREET and the left of the 2nd S.A.I. keeping close touch with that "street".

x. The base from which the attack will be launched will be roughly from S 11 d 3 2 to S 18 a 2 0

The attack x will be launched at 7 p.m. today

J.W.B.

~~If for any good reason one or other of the 2nd or 3rd SAI is NOT ready to move forward at 5 o'clock the O.C. of the Battalion NOT ready must advise the O.C. of the other battalion and also Brigade headquarters. In notifying~~

J.W.B.

77

"A" Form. Army Form C.2121.

MESSAGES AND SIGNALS.

No. of Message

Prefix ... Code ... m.	Words	Charge	This message is on a/c of:	Recd. at ...
Office of Origin and Service Instructions.	Sent		... Service.	Date
	At ... m.			From
	To			By
	By		(Signature of "Franking Officer.")	

TO VENICE

Sender's Number.	Day of Month	In reply to Number	AAA
*G 527	15		

Before	forming	up	for	the
attack	on	DELVILLE	WOOD	at
5	AM	be	sure	to
obtain	reliable	information	regarding	situation
in	LONGUEVAL	It	may	be
unsafe	to	form	up	west
of	village	unless	village	is
in	our	hands	aaa	If
enemy	is	still	in	North
of	village	and	we	in
occupation	of	SE	of	same
it	would	probably	be	better
to	enter	wood	at	SW
corner	aaa	acknowledge		

From 9th Division

Place

Time

The above may be forwarded as now corrected. (Z)

Censor. Signature of Addressor or person authorised to telegraph in his name.

* This line should be erased if not required.

(4198) Wt. W14042—M44. 300000 Pads. 12/15. Sir J. C. & S.

To
O.C.
3rd SAI

BM 45

A copy of 9th Div.
Telegram G 457 issued
1.15 am today is attached
for your information.

On arrival at LONGUEVAL
Col TANNER will ascertain
the position and then confer
with you. If the position
is such as to necessitate
attack from the S.W.
it will be made on a
one Bn front the 3rd
SAI leading supported
by the 2nd.

If the enemy
is NOT in possession
of LONGUEVAL the
attack on DELVILLE
WOOD will be launched
as originally ordered.

The attack will
be launched at

On receipt of this order you
can move on to LONGUEVAL

[illegible] Baker Major
Bde Major

14.7.16
2.23 am

154/78

79

3/

cover and await orders.
Two Machine Guns
have been detailed to
join your Bn.

J Mitchell Baker
Major
BdeMajor

14.7.16
11.37 am

B.M. 35

To O.C. 3rd S.A.I.

App 153

Following is an extract from telegram received from 9th Division

"Combined attack will be made on WATERLOT FARM and DELVILLE WOOD aaa 26th Bde reinforced by a Bn. of S.A. Bde. will attack WATERLOT FARM and DELVILLE WOOD South of PRINCES ST."

You will at once send an officer of your Bn which is placed at the disposal of 26th Bde, to HQ. of that Bde at S 27 d 3,6 for instructions.

The Bn. under your command is to move off without delay in the direction of MONTAUBAN. It will be met en route by the Officer you are sending on to the 26th Bde with the instructions of the G.O.C. that Bde.

If you have no orders from 26th Bde by the time your Bn arrives on the line running north of S 3 and 4 you will halt the Bn. under

SECRET.

Map Reference:-
Hazebrouck, No.5.A.
1/100,000.

App 133

Copy No. 3

81

In the Field,

13th June, 1916.

1st SOUTH AFRICAN INFANTRY BRIGADE.

OPERATION ORDER No. 36

1. MOVE BY RAIL. The Brigade will move by rail from BERGUETTE and LILLERS as shown on the attached table.

2. MARCH TO POINTS OF ENTRAINMENT. All units will march to points of entrainment under orders issued by their own Commanding Officers. Units must be at the place of entrainment two hours before the time stated on the attached table. Each Commanding Officer will forward a copy of March Orders issued by him to Brigade Headquarters as soon as possible, but at the latest so as to reach Brigade Headquarters six hours before unit moves.

3. TRANSPORT. First Line/and unit train Transport will accompany units. No additional Transport will be provided.

4. MARCHING OUT STATES. Marching Out States will be sent to Brigade Headquarters as soon as possible, but in any case so as to reach that office before the unit to which they relate marches.

[signature]
Major.
Brigade Major.

Copy No.1 to 1st S. A. I.,
2 2nd do
3 3rd do
4 4th do
5 9th Division.
6 107th Coy. A.S.C.
7 1st S.A. Field Amb.

Copy No.8 to O.C. 28th Bde M.G. Coy.
9 O.C. L.T.M. Battery.
10 Brigade Signal Section.
11
12
13
14

Issued by Orderly at 1. 30 pm

9/4 [illegible] 1.40 pm

13 JUN 1916

S E C R E T.

HEADQUARTERS,

1st S. A. INFANTRY BRIGADE.

Officer Commanding,
1st S. A. Infantry.
2nd do do
3rd do do
4th do do
O.C., 64th Field Coy. R.E.,
28th Brigade M.G. Company.
Brigade L.T.M. Officer.
O.C., 1st S.A. Field Ambulance.
Brigade Signal Section.

B.M.46/7/9. 12th June,/16.

Owing to a change of orders my minute of to-day under the above number is cancelled.

Orders and instructions for Operations on the 14th inst., are also cancelled.

Please instruct accordingly the officers under your command who were to act as Umpires on that day.

Major.
Brigade Major.

88

83

SPECIAL IDEA.

Reference Map 5A 1/100,000.

The 9th Division is a portion of the Reserve Army, and the South African Infantry Brigade is ordered to make an approach march on the night 10th/11th from Blessy to the north-east of ERNY ST JULIEN - to be there before dawn on the 11th. This approach march has been carried out.

An hour before daybreak on the 11th patrols report ERNY ST JULIEN and the wood surrounding the village to be clear of the enemy.

The Brigadier received orders that in the event of ERNY ST JULIEN being reported clear of the enemy he was to move forward through the village and deploy on a frontage of 900 yards along the open ground immediately to the south-west; the attack being timed to commence at daybreak on a previously arranged signal.

The portion of the enemy's trenches to be attacked by the Brigade extends for 900 yards from the most westerly point of BOMY WOOD to the high ground just above PETIGNY.

For the purpose of the present training 10 am. will be equivalent to daybreak, and will be the hour at which the signal to move forward to the attack will be given.

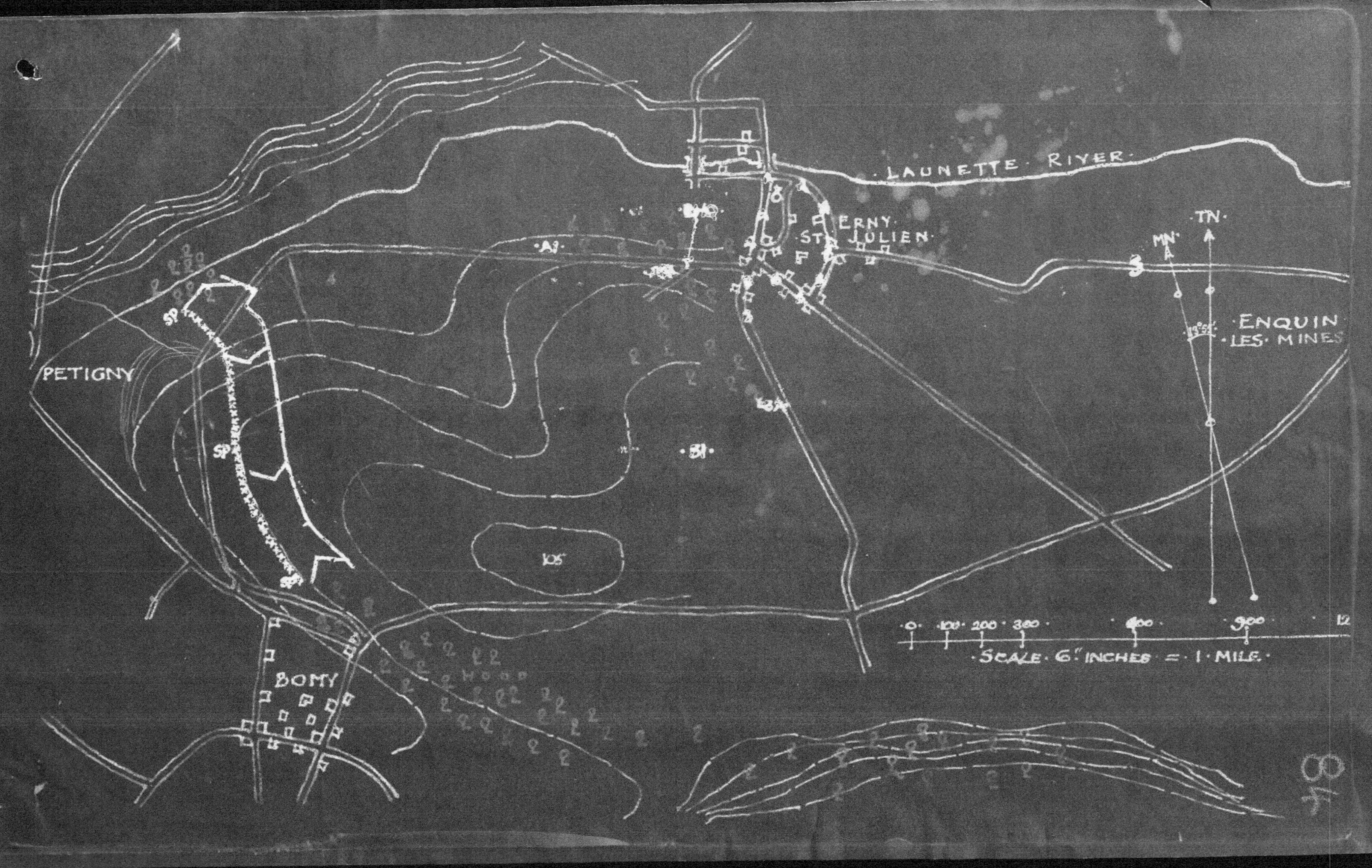

LAUNETTE RIVER
ERNY
ST JULIEN
TN
MN
ENQUIN
LES MINES
PETIGNY
SP
SP
SP
105
BOMY
WOOD
0 100 200 300 600 900 12
SCALE 6" INCHES = 1 MILE
84

85

GENERAL IDEA.

Reference, Map 5.A. 1/100,000.

The general line of enemy's entrenchments faces North East. Our forces have made a thrust, and on the evening of the 10th June taken some five (5) miles of the enemy's trenches, roughly between ESTREE BLANCHE and DELETTE.

In view of the nature of the country to the South West of that line the enemy has fallen back on a previously prepared position running along the high ground between ESTREE BLANCHE and CUHEM; the Northern edge of BOMY WOOD; through PETIGNY and along the high ground towards COYECQUE, and there linking up with their original line of trenches running North West from DELETTE.

The Commander-in-Chief, in anticipation of this success, has held an Army in reserve with orders to follow up immediately any success gained and endeavour to dislodge the enemy from the position described above.

On the evening of the 10th our Forces are in possession of the ridge running from SERNY to ENQUIN-les-MINES; through the high ground marked 140 - to the North West of ERNY St. JULIEN - and on to our original line opposite the enemy trenches at DELETTE.

86

HEADQUARTERS,

1st S. A. INFANTRY BRIGADE,

10th June, 1916.

BRIGADE TRAINING SCHEME for 11th inst.,

As explained verbally by the Brig. Genl. commanding the Brigade on the ground this morning to Officers Commanding units the training to-morrow will embrace two distinct phases, the first being an advance from the Base A.1 - B.1 on the sketch plan issued with the Operation Order, under distant Artillery fire to commence with, and later on long range rifle fire and effective Artillery fire.

In making this advance the Brigade will be considered as moving to the support of our own troops in occupation of the "objective" laid down in the Operation Order.

The second phase will commence when the first wave has reached within 200 yards of the enemy's first trench. The Brigade will be halted, and the "objective" will then be considered as being in the possession of the enemy, who is holding the line of trenches as shown on the plan.

The second phase will thus consist of an attack on the enemy's trenches, launched from our own line of trenches within 200 yards of the enemy's first line.

When the first wave of the Brigade has halted the succeeding waves will close up to a distance of 5 yards between waves.

The enemy's first line of trenches will be marked by white flags; the communication trenches by white and blue flags; and the "objective" of the Brigade by another line of flags.

Flags in the line of advance of the Brigade during the first phase of the training will indicate a barrage of Artillery fire.

In the second phase of the training the two leading platoons of the supporting Battalions will clear the communication trenches, and the remainder of these Battalions will occupy and consolidate the enemy's first line of trenches, constructing 'strong points' at the heads of communication trenches.

All material and tools as laid down must be carried, and arrangements should be made for replacing carriers who may become casualties.

Arrangements must also be made for bringing on the Lewis Guns in the event of the crews becoming casualties.

Machine Guns attached to Battalions should accompany the second line of carriers.

From the left of the "objective" to the sunken road in the Right Sector the enemy's second line of trenches will be lightly held when captured, and the enemy's first line of trenches will form our strong line of resistance - the object being to make use of ground and to avoid exposing an unnecessary number of men to direct Artillery fire. From the sunken road on the right of the "objective" the second line of enemy's trenches will form our strong line of resistance.

At the conclusion of the training the "Cease fire" will be sounded. The Officer Commanding, 1st S. A. Infantry, will detail a bugler for this purpose. The bugler will report to the Brigade Major as soon as the supporting Battalions enter the enemy's first line of trenches.

All "casualties" will rejoin their units on the "Cease fire" sounding.

87

the plan by "S.P." - roughly speaking, the right, centre and left of our objective. All these strong points will be made on the westerly side of the slope, i.e., the reverse side from our line of attack.

11. CLEARING OF ENEMY'S FIRST LINE TRENCHES. Two platoons of each of the 1st and 3rd S.A. Infantry will be detailed to clear up the enemy's first line of trenches and communication trenches on the forward slopeof our objective - shewn on plan.

12. MACHINE GUNS & TRENCH MORTARS. The Officers Commanding 28th Brigade M.G.Coy., and Brigade L.T.M.,Officer, will report to the Brigade Major at 8.45.am., at the Starting point.

13. COMMUNICATIONS. The Officer i/c Brigade Signal Section will advise Battalion Commanders of his arrangements for communications between Headquarters of Battalions and Brigade Headquarters, and will ascertain from them what their communication arrangements are before the Brigade moves.

14. MEDICAL ARRANGEMENTS. The Officer Commanding 1st S.A.Field Ambulance will advise the Brigade Major and all Commanding Officers of the Medical arrangements made by him before the Brigade moves.

15. BRIGADE HEADQUARTERS. Marked "B.H.Q." on plan. All reports and messages for the Brigadier General Commanding the Brigade to be sent to that spot.

J Mitchell Baker

Major,
Brigade Major.

	Copy No.	
Issued personally at 11.30 pm	1	to 1st S.A.Infantry
	2	2nd -do-
	×3	3rd -do-
	4	4th -do-
	5	Brigade Signal Section
	6	Brigade L.T.M.Officer,
	7	Brigade M.G.Coy.,
Issued by Orderly at...............	8	9th Division
	9	O.C., Right Group Artillery
	10	O.C.,107th Coy., A.S.C.,
	11	O.C., 1st S.A.Field Ambulance
	12	Office copy
	13	G.O.C., the Brigade
	14	Brigade Major
	15	Staff Captain.

rec'd 7am 13/4/16

S E C R E T

Copy No..3...... 88

1st SOUTH AFRICAN INFANTRY BRIGADE

OPERATIONS ORDERS No.36

Map Reference :-
Sheet 5.A
1/100,000
(Enlarged plan of Sector of operations attached)

ERNY ST. JULIEN,

10th June 1916

1. ENEMY'S MOVEMENTS. The enemy has fallen back on a previously prepared position, running along the high ground between ESTREE BLANCHE and CUHEM; the northern edge of BOMY WOOD; through PETIGNY and along the high ground towards COYECQUE, from there linking up with his original line of trenches, running north-west from DELETTE.

2. ARMY COMMANDER'S INTENTION. It is the intention of the Army Commander to drive the enemy from the position mentioned in para : 1.

3. POSITION OF BRIGADE IN ATTACK. The South African Brigade will be the Right Brigade of the 9th Division, with the 26th Brigade on its left, and the Left Battalion of the 24th Division on its right.

4. OBJECTIVE OF BRIGADE. The objective of the Brigade will be the enemy's second line of trenches from a point on the high ground just above PETIGNY to the most westerly corner of BOMY WOOD, approximately 900 yards. (Shewn on the enlarged map by xxxxxxxxx).

5. MOVE.

(a) Routes to be followed. The Brigade will move at 9.am: The 2nd and 3rd S.A.Infantry by the route marked "A" on plan; and the 4th and 1st S.A.Infantry by the route marked "B".

(b) Order of moving off. The 4th Regiment will lead, followed by the 2nd, 1st and 3rd Regiments.

(c) Starting point. Marked "S" on plan.

6. GUIDES. Six guides will report to the Brigade Major at the Starting point at 8.45.am. They will be placed at the various turns in the routes to direct their units to the points of deployment, in order to avoid any possibility of mistake in direction being made.

7. POINTS OF DEPLOYMENT. When units reach points "AX" and "BX" respectively they will deploy. The limits of the Brigade front at the base from which the attack will be launched are indicated on the plan by "A1" and "B1" - total length of base, 900 yards.

8. ATTACK FORMATION. The Brigade will form up for the attack with the ~~2nd and 4th~~ 4 and 2nd S.A.Infantry in front, and the ~~1st and 3rd~~ S.A.Infantry in support.

9. ATTACK. The attack will be launched at 10.am., Watches will be set at 8.45.am., each unit to send an officer to the Starting point for that purpose.

10. CONSOLIDATION AND STRONG POINTS. On the objective being gained the ground captured will be consolidated immediately, strong points being made at the spots indicated on

Rec'd 10pm

HEADQUARTERS,

1st S. A. INFANTRY BRIGADE.

Officer Commanding,
1st S. A. Infantry.
2nd do do
3rd do do
4th do do
9th Division.
28th Brigade M.G. Coy.
Brigade L.T.M. Battery.
Brigade Signal Section.
1st S. A. Field Ambulance.

B.M. 46/7/8 10th June, 1916.

With reference to the scheme of training for to-morrow, I attach further instructions which, inter alia, make certain changes in the scheme as originally decided upon.

As explained by the Brigadier-General Commanding the Brigade these changes have been made to meet the wishes of the Divisional Commander.

[signature]
Major.

Brigade Major.

89

Issued 6/10 pm. Operation order 36

App 132

9/6 A
B
C
D
HQ
M/O
L.G.O.
S/O
Qm
T/O

Battalion Orders by Lt. Col. Christian Comdg. Commanding

1. Training. The Battalion will parade for Brigade Training and will rendezvous at Battn Head Quarters ready to move off at 7.45 AM tomorrow 11th Inst and will march to Brigade Starting Point under the [illegible] letter R of RIVER on main road ERNY ST JULIEN and EQUIN LES MINES. (Shewn on sketch map handed to Company Commanders) to arrive by 8.45 AM.

(2)

II Dress. Review marching order with Haversack on back. Mess tin in haversack and Ground Sheet under flap of same.

III Stores. All R.E. Stores for trenching, wiring etc. will be taken, also dummy tools & sandbags.

IV Transport. The following transport will accompany the Battalion, and be ready to move off from Battn Head Quarters at 7.45 am. No vehicle will be permitted to be detached from the convoy.

1 G.S. Wagon for use of A B and D Coy.

2 G.S. Wagon for R.E. Stores & report Qm Stores for completion of load.

1 Tool wagon with tools for entrenching limber filled with Battalion Complement of Tools.

(3)

Transport Company Cooks will accompany the Regiment also water carts. [illegible] [illegible] for [illegible] to be [illegible].

(4) Mid day Meal } Company Commanders will arrange for the issue of the mid day meal on completion of the days training.

(5) Time. Lieut Paxton will report to Brigade Major at 8.45 am to take Brigade Time at Starting Point.

(6) Guides. Head of Coy will furnish 6 Guides to report to Brigade Major at Starting Point at 8.45 am. [illegible] [illegible] [illegible] at H.Q. Officer at 7.30 am.

7 (Signallers) L.G.O. and Sig. Officer will detail Signallers to Companies and [illegible] march with same.

[signature]

Capt. & Adjutant,
2nd S.A. Infantry (Transvaal Regt.)

90

MAP -- Hazebrouck, No.S.A. 1/100,000.

No. of Train.	Date.	Unit.	** Hour of Departure of Train.	Station of entrainment.
11.	14th June.	S. A. Field Ambulance. Sanitary Section.	19.40	BERGUETTE.
16.	15th June.	4th S. A. Infantry.	8.40	do
16.	16th June.	1st S. A. Infantry.	11.40	do
12.	14th June.	3rd S. A. Infantry.	21.51	LILLERS.
13.	15th June.	2nd S. A. Infantry.	1.51	do
14.	15th June.	107th Coy. A.S.C. Div. Trn.	4.51	do
15.	15th June.	Brigade Headquarters. Brigade Signal Section. 28th Bde. M.G. Coy. S.A. Bde. L.T.M. Battery.	7.51	do

** In the above, account has been taken of the change which will take place at 11 p.m. on the 14th inst., in connection with Daylight Saving.

115

SECRET 3RD S. A. INF. 14/5/16
(TRANSVAAL RGT.)

INTELLIGENCE REPORT

From 6. a.m. 13/5/16 to 6 a.m. 14/5/16

① Our Operations

Artillery Between 9 and 11.0 a.m.
our 18 pounders fired several
rounds in the direction of
BLANCHISSERIE WOOD.
At 11.30 a.m. our 18 pdrs fired three
rounds in the enemy support
trench at about C.4.c.10.8.
At 3.30 p.m. about six 18 pdrs were
fired at BLANCHISSERIE WOOD
At 4.30 p.m. and 5 p.m. our 18 pdrs
fired ten rounds at ENGLINGHEIM
BRIDGE.
Between 6.30 p.m. and 9.15 p.m.
our artillery fired several rounds
at BLANCHISSERIE WOOD and
enemy support & front line of
trenches, in retaliation.
About 200 18 pdrs and
100 12 in Howitzers were
fired by our guns

2

guns during the time.

Sniping Our snipers claim one
hit and broke three periscopes

II ENEMY ACTIVITY. (a) Attitude Normal.

(b) Artillery Between 10 a.m. and 11.15 a.m.
enemy fired six 77 M.M. in the
direction of PATERNOSTER ROW.
11.45 a.m. four 77 M.M. near RESERVE
FARM.
12.45 and 1.15 p.m. nine rounds of 77 M.M.
and H.E. Schrapnel near FORT PAUL
Between 6.30 p.m. and 9.10 p.m.
the enemy fired about 50 rounds
of 77 M.M. and H.E. Shrapnel near
PATERNOSTER ROW.

3

About twenty five 77 M.M.
were fired near GLASGOW
REDOUBT and fifty 15 C.M.
and thirty five 42 C.M. in
the vicinity of RESERVE
and DESPIERRE FARMS.

56

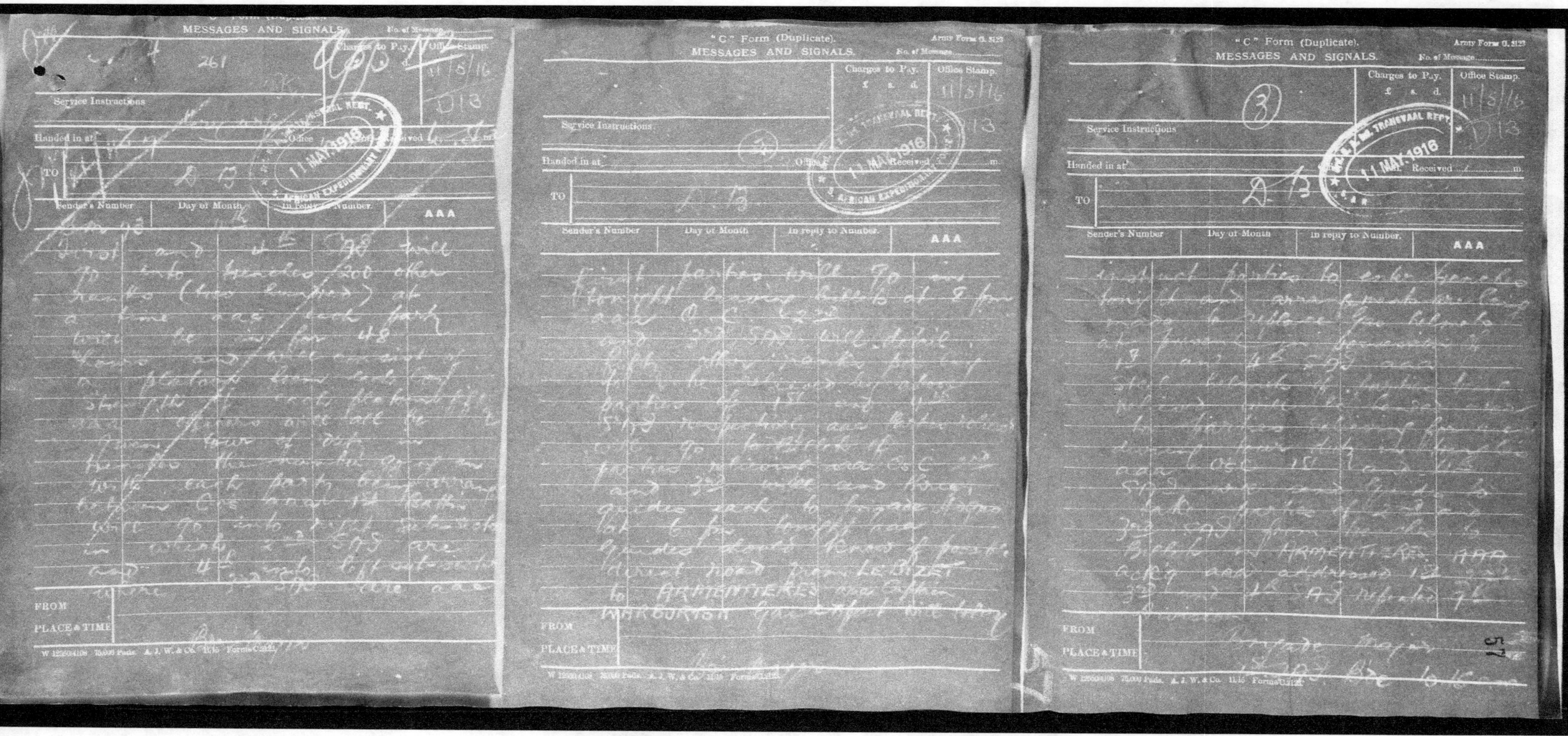

"C" Form (Duplicate).
MESSAGES AND SIGNALS.
Army Form C. 2123

261

Service Instructions

Handed in at

TO: B B

Sender's Number | Day of Month | In reply to Number | AAA

First and 4th [illegible] will go into trenches 200 other ranks (two hundred) at a time aaa each party will be in for 48 hours and will consist of a platoon from each Coy [illegible] officers [illegible] [illegible] tour of duty [illegible] each party [illegible] will go into [illegible] SAS are [illegible] left [illegible] aaa

FROM

PLACE & TIME

W 12500/4108 75,000 Pads. A. J. W. & Co. 11/15 Forms/C2123

"C" Form (Duplicate).
MESSAGES AND SIGNALS.
Army Form C. 2123

(2)

Charges to Pay. £ s. d. | Office Stamp. 11/5/16 D13

11 MAY 1916 — TRANSVAAL REGT. — AFRICAN EXPEDITIONARY

Service Instructions

Handed in at | Office | Received | m.

TO: B B

Sender's Number | Day of Month | In reply to Number | AAA

First parties will go in tonight leaving billets at 8 pm aaa O.C. 2nd and 3rd SAI will detail [illegible] [illegible] parties of 1st and 4th SAI [illegible] [illegible] parties [illegible] O.C. 2nd and 3rd [illegible] and [illegible] guides each to Brigade [illegible] 6 pm tonight [illegible] guides [illegible] road from LE BIZET to ARMENTIERES [illegible] WARBURTON [illegible]

FROM

PLACE & TIME

W 12500/4108 75,000 Pads. A. J. W. & Co. 11/15 Forms/C2123

"C" Form (Duplicate).
MESSAGES AND SIGNALS.
Army Form C. 2123

(3)

Charges to Pay. £ s. d. | Office Stamp. 11/5/16 D13

11 MAY 1916 — TRANSVAAL REGT.

Service Instructions

Handed in at | Received | m.

TO: B B

Sender's Number | Day of Month | In reply to Number | AAA

[illegible] parties to [illegible] trenches tonight and arrangements [illegible] [illegible] aaa [illegible] 1st and 4th SAI aaa [illegible] O.C. 1st and 4th SAI [illegible] take [illegible] 3rd SAI from [illegible] to [illegible] of ARMENTIERES aaa Ackg aaa addressed 1st [illegible] 3rd and 4th SAI repeated 76 [illegible]

FROM

PLACE & TIME

Brigade Major

W 12500/4108 75,000 Pads. A. J. W. & Co. 11/15 Forms/C2123

57

92

S E C R E T .

Move Orders by Lieut. Col. E. F. Thackeray, C.M.G. Commanding, Third South African Infantry.

....

13th June, 1916.

Reference Map :- Hazebrouck, 5A, Scale 1/100,000.

1. MOVE. In compliance with Brigade Operation Order No 36., dd. 13/6/16., the Battalion will march by road to Lillers and entrain for destination to-morrow, 14/6/16.

2. PARADE. The Battalion will rendezvous at starting point on PIPPERMONT - LE TIRMAND ROAD, the head of the column at a point on the road under the N in FLECHIN., and ready to move off at 4-0 p.m.
The Battalion will march via LIGNY LEZAIRE - AUCHY AU BOIS - LIERE - ECQUEDECQUES - a distance of 10 miles.
Order of March :- Signallers, Band, "A", "B", "D" "C" and Headquarter Company.

3. DRESS. Heavy marching order. Spare shirt to be carried. Ground sheet to be folded under flap of valise. Steel helmets will be carried by the man and strapped to the pack as heretobefore.

4. RATIONS. The unexpired portion of the day's ration in addition to the iron ration will be carried on the man. Unexpired portion of day's feed on the animal.

5. TRANSPORT. One G.S. wagon will report to O.C., "D" Coy., at 2-0 p.m. and from there will report ~~to~~ O.C., "A" and "B" Companies at once for conveyance of officers' kit and Company Orderly Room boxes. (One per Company.)
One G.S. wagon will report to the Quartermaster, Boncourt, at 2-0 p.m. for conveyance of officers' kits, Headquarters' and "C" Company, also artificers' tools and Orderly Room boxes.
The Maltese Cart to be loaded and ready to move off at 2-0 p.m.
First Line Transport will leave PIPPERMONT at 3-0 p.m. The Transport Officer will arrange for two front limbers of tool wagons to report to the Quartermaster at 1-30 p.m. for loading signalling equipment, etc.
Lieut. Paxton and the Lewis Guh Section will accompany the Trasnport leaving PIPPERMONT at 3-0 p.m.

6. STEEL HELMETS. Company Commanders will arrange to draw from

H.M.T. "SAXONIA"

ARRANGEMENT OF BOATS & RAFTS.

23 Rafts = 460

4 RAFTS = 120

Port side

Crew's	Boat accdn	Total accdn
12	53 + 42 =	95
	5 RAFTS =	115
12	54 + 43 =	97
12	51 + 42 =	93
12	52 + 42 =	94
12	52 + 54 =	106
	6 RAFTS =	138
12	52 + 50 + 40 =	142
	2 RAFTS =	46
12	51 + 40 =	91
	2 RAFTS =	46
24	51 + 44 + 42 + 42 + 42 + 23 =	244

108

Total accdn. (P) 1307
Less Crew 108
Available for Troops (P) 1199

Starboard side

Boat accdn		Crew
52 + 43 + 23 =	105	12
5 RAFTS =	115	
52 + 42 =	81	12
4 RAFTS =	92	
43 + 42 =	85	12
51 + 42 =	93	12
52 + 40 =	92	12
7 RAFTS =	161	
52 + 53 + 40 =	145	12
2 RAFTS =	46	
52 + 40 =	92	12
2 RAFTS =	46	
50 + 48 + 42 + 42 + 42 + 23 =	247	

Total Accdn (S) 1980
Less Crew 108
Available for Troops (S) 1872

Total [illegible] accdn for troops 3071.

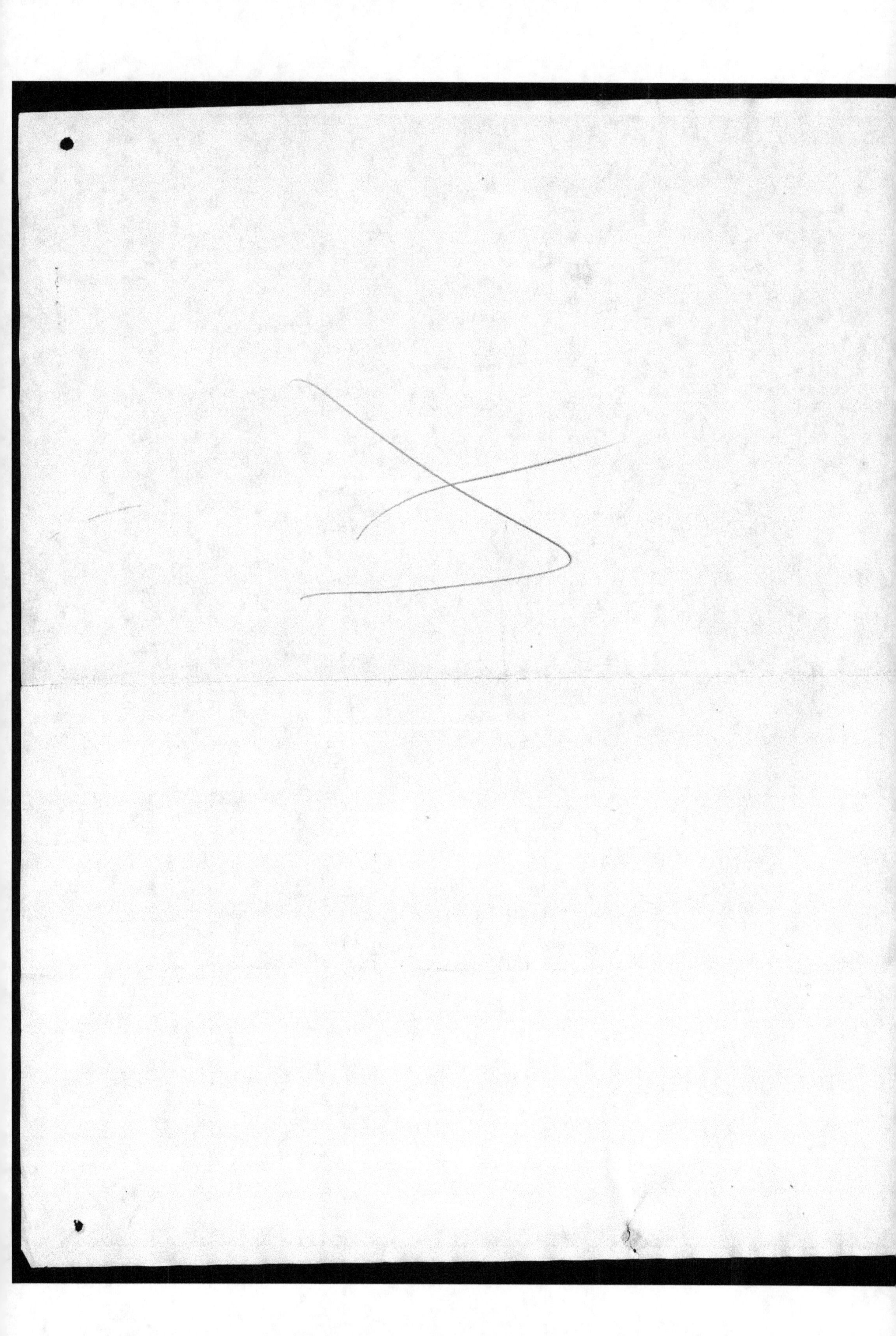

War Diary

S E C R E T.

HEADQUARTERS,

1st S. A. INFANTRY BRIGADE.

Officer Commanding,
1st S. A. Infantry.
2nd do do
3rd do do
4th do do
S.A. Bde. L.T.M. Battery.
28th Coy. M.G. Corps.
Bearer Section, S.A.F.A.
51st Brigade, R.F.A.
64th Field Coy. R.E.
107th Coy. A.S.C.
Brigade Signal Section.
Brigade Transport Officer.
9th Division.
28th Inf. Brigade.
27th do do

Acknowledged

B.M. 47/12/10. 28th June, 1916.

Operation Order No.38, issued to-day, is cancelled, and the Brigade will stand fast for further orders.

Please acknowledge

[signature]

Major.
Brigade Major.

94

95

SECRET.

Copy No. 3

App 142

Map reference-
62d N.E.

1st SOUTH AFRICAN INFANTRY BRIGADE.

OPERATION ORDER No. 39

In the Field.

30th June, 1916.

1. MOVE. The 1st S. A. Infantry Brigade, 64th Field Coy. R.E., 28th Bde. M.G. Coy., and Bearer Section, S.A.F. Ambulance will move to GROVETOWN to-night by "X" Route.

2. STARTING POINT. Starting Point will be at K.34.b.9.7.

3. ORDER OF MARCH & TIMES OF PASSING STARTING POINT. Units will march in the following order, passing the Starting Point at the times stated:-

Brigade Headquarters,	9.50 p.m.
1st S. A. Infantry,	10.00 p.m.
4th do do	10.10 p.m.
2nd do do	10.20 p.m.
3rd do do	10.30 p.m.
64th Field Coy. R.E.	10.40 p.m.
28th Brigade M.G. Coy.	10.50 p.m.
Trench Mortar Battery,	10.55 p.m.
Bearer Section,	11.00 p.m.
Transport, under Brigade T'port Officer, (to march in same order as units)	11.15 p.m.

4. ADVANCE PARTIES & GUIDES. Units, on reaching GROVETOWN, will be led to their camping sites by a member of their Advance Party which visited GROVETOWN on 28th inst., Advance Parties, as follows, will be detailed by Officers Commanding units to proceed to GROVETOWN at 7 p.m. this evening by other than "X" Route. These Advance Parties will proceed from GROVETOWN to TRIGGER WOOD, etc., to-night with the units of the 27th Inf. Brigade, whose camping sites in TRIGGER WOOD, etc., will be taken over by the units to which the respective Advance Parties belong:-

Infantry Battalions,	1 officer	5 Other Ranks.
64th Field Coy, R.E.	1 do	2 do do
28th Brigade M.G. Coy.	1 do	2 do do
Trench Mortar Battery.	1 do	2 do do
Bearer Section,	-	1 do do

These Advance Parties will rejoin their units in GROVETOWN VALLEY on the morning of the 1st July, not later than 9 a.m., marching by "X" Route so as not to miss their units should they be on the march by that hour.

5. MACHINE GUNS. The Officer Commanding, 28th Bde. M.G. Coy. will detail, to accompany each of the 1st, 2nd and 4th S. A. Infantry when they leave GROVETOWN, two Machine Guns with their teams, under an Officer. These Machine Guns will not, for the present, be attached to the units which they accompany, but they will march immediately in rear of them from GROVETOWN.

6. WORKING PARTIES & CARRIERS. The Working Parties and Carriers detailed in Brigade Instructions No.2, para 3, (dated 27th inst.,) will march with their units, but after the Brigade leaves GROVETOWN these parties will be at the disposal of the O.C. 64th Feild Coy. R.E., who will advise Battalion Commanders where and when he wishes them to report to him or his representative.

7. BRIGADE HEADQUARTERS. Brigade Headquarters in GROVETOWN VALLEY will be about L.8.c.2.9.

Please acknowledge.

[signature]

0047

96

(2)

Copy No.	to	Copy No.	to
1	1st S. A. Inf.	9	Bde L.T.M. Battery.
2	2nd do	10	28th Coy M.G. Corps.
3	3rd do	11	Bearer Section.
4	4th do	12	Brigade Signal Section.
5	9th Division.	13	Brigade Transport Off.
6	52nd Brigade, R.F.A.	14	26th Inf. Brigade.
7	64th Field Coy. R.E.	15	27th do do
8	107th Coy. A.S.C.	16	Office Copy.

Issued by Orderly at...7.15 am...........

Received 9/3? am

G. T. J.

APP 142

B/O11

Issued at 9.45. AM.

SECRET.

30-6-16

To O/C A Coy
B "
C "
D "
HQ "
T/O " A.S.
M/O "
QM "
S/O "
Lt Jenner

File

(1) In Compliance with operation order No 39 of this date The Battalion will move tonight to GROVETOWN by "X" route.
Map reference 62 d NE

II MOVE The Battalion will parade at 10.15 pm tonight and will march past starting point at 10.30 pm at K34 b 9.7
Transport under Brigade Transport Officer to march in same order as Units and to pass starting point at 11.15 PM.

(3) Advance Parties and Guides } Units on reaching GROVETOWN

2nd Sheet

GROVETOWN will be led to their Camping sites by a member of their advance party which visited GROVETOWN on the 28th inst.
2/Lieut JENNER with the N.C.O.s detailed as per A, B, C, D and H.Q Coy will proceed to GROVETOWN at 7 pm this evening by other than "X" route.
This advance party will proceed from GROVETOWN to TRIGGER WOOD Ek tonight with the Units of the 27th Inf Brigade whose Camping sites in TRIGGER WOOD Ek will be taken over.
This advance party will rejoin the Battalion at GROVETOWN on the morning 1st July not later than 9 am. marching by X route so as not to miss their Units should they be on the march by that hour.

4 WORKING PARTIES as detailed for Brigade Dump will march with the Battalion to Grovetown

5 TRANSPORT. All Transport to be packed and ready to

Sheet 3

to move by 10.15 PM

ORDER of MARCH HQrs
B Coy
C "
D "
A "

Ammunition & Baggage Guard } one Platoon under an Officer will be furnished by "A" Coy who will take over escort duties at Transport Lines at 10.15 PM. of all 1st Line Transport and Baggage wagons of the Battalion

ES CELESTIN

[illegible] Capt & Adjt
3rd Regt S.A. Infty

97

98

SC · B26

O/c 3 Regt SAI

Move from Strazeele to Morbecque, Steenbecque area

Please note that your Camp for the night of the 2/3 June will be approximately in the neighbourhood of the Etaminet Grand Hasard

Your Billeting guides will meet you at D.9.a.0.8 Map 36A at the cross roads with the tower in off hand side.

W. MB Mitchley Capt
A/Staff Captain

1.6.16

SC B30

3rd Regt SAI

From Strazeele on please note that the motor lorry that you have hitherto had for the move is to be halved with the 2nd Regt.

To day the 2nd Regt will be first to load up its half of the lorry & the lorry will then be passed on to you to load up your half.

For the future please arrange mutually with the 2nd Regt about the use of the lorry.

W. MB Mitchley Capt
A/Staff Captain

2/6/16

South African Infantry Brigade.

Copy

Officer Commanding

Company.

Pending definite move order which will be issued early tomorrow morning, the following order is passed to you for your information, having just been received from B.H.Q.

Order of march and Time Table 3rd S.A.I
To be at STRAZEELE by 2 ---- 30 p.m. 9/6/16.

Transport. 1st Line to march in rear of battalions as usual.

Baggage wagons. to report to an Officer Divisional Train STRAZEELE (opposite the Church) at 4 p.m.

Captain and Actg Adjutant,
3rd S.A. Infantry.

To War Diary

App 129

100

The Officer Commanding,

Move Orders 3rd S.A.Infantry.

The Battalion will rendezvous at 1-45 p.m. 2/6/16, at cross roads ½ mile south of "B" Company's Billets in FLETRE and STRAZEELE road and will march to STRAZEELE - MORBECQUE via HAZELBROOK.

ORDER OF MARCH. Headquarters, "C", "D", "A" and "B" Company. Officer Commanding "B" Company will detail one Platoon under an officer to act as rear guard and escort to ammunition convoy, which will march behind the Regiment.

Companies will fall in and move to place of rendezvous and to be ready to move off at the appointed time, with intervals of not more than 50 yards.

DRESS. Marching Order. *MARCH DISCIPLINE* ALL N.C.O's and men will march with their Companies and are not to be allowed to fall out without permission of an officer. Any case of straggling will be dealt with very severely by the Commanding Officer.

Water Bottles will be filled from water carts before moving from billets.

Officers Commanding Companies are reminded re orders for cleanliness of billets before vacating same. The Commanding Officer will inspect billets at 1 p.m. commencing with "A" Company.

On arrival at MORBECQUE, Companies will be met by their guides and conducted to their respective billets.

Water Carts will be filled before the march commences and will be sent to Companies immediately on arrival at new billets.

The Battalion will march to Brigade rendezvous STRAZEELE by 2-30 p.m. and follow in rear of 1st S.A.I.

DISTANCES The usual distances, excepting that distance between Transport and Battalion following will be increased to 50 yrds.

TRANSPORT First Line To march in rear of Battalion as usual.

Baggage Wagons To report to an officer of Divisional Train opposite Church, STRAZEELE at 4 p.m.

MARCH STANDING ORDERS Smoking on line of march is forbidden but men may smoke during halts and day time. The order regarding no smoking on line of march by night is temporarily suspended. Men may be permitted to smoke during halts.

A. W. H. McDonald
Capt and Acting Adjutant,
3rd S.A.Infantry.

S E C R E T.

War Diary

Copy No........3 .101

App 129 141

Rec'd 11.45 pm

1st SOUTH AFRICAN INFANTRY BRIGADE.

OPERATION ORDER No. 35.

Map Reference:-
62d N.E.

In the Field,

28th June, 1916.

1. MOVE. The 1st S. A. Infantry Brigade, 64th Field Coy. R.E., 28th Bde. M.G. Coy., and Bearer Section, S.A.F.Ambulance will move to GROVETOWN to-night by "X" Route.

2. MACHINE GUNS. The O.C. 28th Bde. M.G. Coy. will detail, to accompany each of the following units - 1st, 2nd and 4th S. A. Infantry - two Machine Guns with their teams, under an Officer. These Machine Guns will not, for the present, be attached to the units which they accompany, but they will march immediately in rear of these units.

3. STARTING POINT. Starting point will be at K.34.b.9.7.

4. ORDER OF MARCH & TIMES OF PASSING STARTING POINT. Units will march in the following order, passing the starting point at the times stated:-

1st S.A.I., (less Working Parties & Carriers detailed in Bde. Instructions No.2 para 3)	10.00 p.m.
4th S.A.I., do do do do	10.10 p.m.
2nd S.A.I., do do do do	10.20 p.m.
3rd S.A.I.,	10.30 p.m.
64th Field Coy. R.E. with Working Parties and Carriers detailed in Bde. Instrn. No.2, para 3, dated yesterday, (marching in a body in the following order) - 1st S.A.I., 4th S.A.I., and 2nd S.A.I.,) ~~passing the Starting Point at~~	10.40 p.m.
28th Bde. M.G. Coy. (less 6 M.G. with their teams),	10.50 p.m.
T.M. Battery.	10.55 p.m.
Bearer Section.	11.00 p.m.
Transport, under Transport Officer. (To march in same order as units)	11.15 p.m.

5. ADVANCE PARTIES. Advance parties will meet their units on "X" Route, just South of the BRAY-CORBIE Road, at K.18.d.8.8. The Officers with the Advance Parties will proceed from GROVETOWN VALLEY to-night with the 27th Brigade in order to ascertain where the various Infantry units of that Brigade are located in TRIGGER WOOD, BILLON WOOD and COPSE VALLEY. They should move with the unit whose camping site they take over in GROVETOWN VALLEY. They will rejoin their units in GROVETOWN VALLEY to-morrow, not later than 9 a.m.

6. BRIGADE HEADQUARTERS. Brigade Headquarters in GROVETOWN VALLEY will be about L.8.c.2.9.

Please acknowledge.

J.M.

J. Mitchell-Baker

Major.
Brigade Major.

Copy No.1 to	1st S. A. Inf.,	Copy No. 9 to	Bde. L.T.M. Batty.
2	2nd do	10	28th Coy. M.G. Corps.
x 3	3rd do	11	Bearer Sect. S.A.F.A.
4	4th do	12	Bde. Signal Section.
5	9th Division.	13	Bde. Transport Off.
6	51st Bde. R.F.A.	14	26th Inf. Brigade.
7	64th Field Co. R.E.	15	27th do do
8	107th Coy. A.S.C.	16	Office Copy.

102

Secret

B.M. 447/10/3

1st Regt. S.A.I.
2nd Regt. S.A.I.
3rd Regt. S.A.I.
4th Regt. S.A.I.

On May 28th and 31st at 6 p.m. a horse ambulance from 28th F.A. will parade at LE BIZET to follow battalions on march. On 29th sick will be collected in morning from BAILLEUL and NOOTBOOME by 27th F.A.

At STRAZEELE the 1st S.A.F.A. will come into touch with brigade and afford all medical attendance during march to EBNY ST JULIEN. At latter place S.A.F.A. will treat all sick not requiring evacuation during period of stay there.

Please communicate this to your Medical Officer.

M.O. [illegible]

[illegible]/5/16.

[illegible]

R. Pepper
Captain.
A/ Brigade Major.

102

"C" Form (Duplicate).
MESSAGES AND SIGNALS.

Army Form C. 2123.

No. of Message.............

Rec'd 5.50 pm

~~102~~

103

Charges to Pay. Office Stamp.

Service Instructions.

1 JUN 1916

Handed in at............ Office.......... m. Received ......3 0 p.m.

TO 3rd Regt

Sender's Number	Day of Month	In reply to Number	AAA
S/C 504	1st		

Reference billetting instructions Strazeele to rest area aaa please cancel those portions detailing where guides will meet their battalions on 2nd and [illegible] aaa You will be advised tonight for move to Steenbecque - Morbecque where you will be met

FROM Brigade

PLACE & TIME 2.40 pm

(108. 37,500 Pads. 11/15. McC. & Co., Ltd. Forms C 2123.

104

HEADQUARTERS,

1st S. A. INFANTRY BRIGADE.

Officer Commanding,
1st S. A. Infantry.
2nd do do
3rd do do
4th do do
1st S.A. Field Ambulance.

B.M.47/12. 1st June, 1916.

The Army Commander has expressed his wish to see the Brigade on the line of march, and the Brigade will in all probability pass him near BOORE, midway between STRAZEELE and HAZEBROUCK.

Major.

Brigade Major.

105

Billetting instructions for move from

STRAZEELE to REST AREA

Note. Map references given are taken from the following maps.

Map 36A move to STEENBECQUE, MORBECQUE and WITTERNESSE.

Map 5A move from WITTERNESSE to final REST AREA.

BRIGADE HEADQUARTERS, during Move and in REST AREA will be as follows :-

On the night of 2/3rd June at the Area Officer's Office, MORBECQUE.

On the night of 3/4th June at LES TOURNIERES

On the night of 4/5th June at Chateau Cappe de Baillon, ERNY ST. JULIEN. This will be BRIGADE HEADQUARTERS whilst in REST AREA.

Move from STRAZEELE to STEENBECQUE, MORBECQUE Area.

Billetting Officers will meet the Staff Captain at 5.pm., on Thursday, 1st June, at the Area Officer's Office, MORBECQUE, to be allotted billets.

Billetting guides will meet their regiments on 2nd June as follows :-

3rd Regt. At cross-roads beyond MORBECQUE (C.19.d.4.3.)
1st -do-) At cross road before entering MORBECQUE (C.20.a.5.9.)
2nd -do-)
4th -do- At cross road D.14.b.6.1[illegible].

Move from STEENBECQUE, MORBECQUE to WITTERNESSE Area.

Billetting Officers will meet the Staff Captain at the Mayor's house (an Estaminet) at WITTERNESSE at 4.pm, on 2nd June. Regiments will be advised later where their billetting guides will meet them on 3rd June.

Move from WITTERNESSE to ERNY ST. JULIEN Area.

Billetting Officers will proceed on 3rd June direct to their billetting areas as allotted below, with the exception of the Billetting Officers of the 1st Regiment and the S.A.Field Ambulance, who will meet the Staff Captain at 5.pm., on 3rd June at the Chateau de Baillon, ERNY ST. JULIEN.

3rd Regt. Villages of BON COURT, LE PLOUY and PIPPEMONT.
2nd -do- Village of FLECHIN.
1st -do- ERNY ST. JULIEN.
4th -do- ENGUINEGATTE.
S.A.F.A. ERNY ST. JULIEN.

Billetting guides will meet their respective regiments on 4th June as follows :-

3rd Regt. On the main road from CUHEM to FLECHIN; where village of FLECHIN starts.
2nd -do- Same as 3rd Regiment.
1st -do- On direct road from ENQUIN-LES-MINES to ERNY ST. JULIEN.
4th -do- At the cross roads (as shown on the map) from [illegible] to ENGUINEGATTE.
S.A.F.A. Same as 1st Regiment.

NOTE. These billetting instructions to be read in conjunction with the OPERATION ORDER re MOVE.

[signature] CAPTAIN,
STAFF CAPTAIN,
1st INF. BDE. S.A.O.E.F.

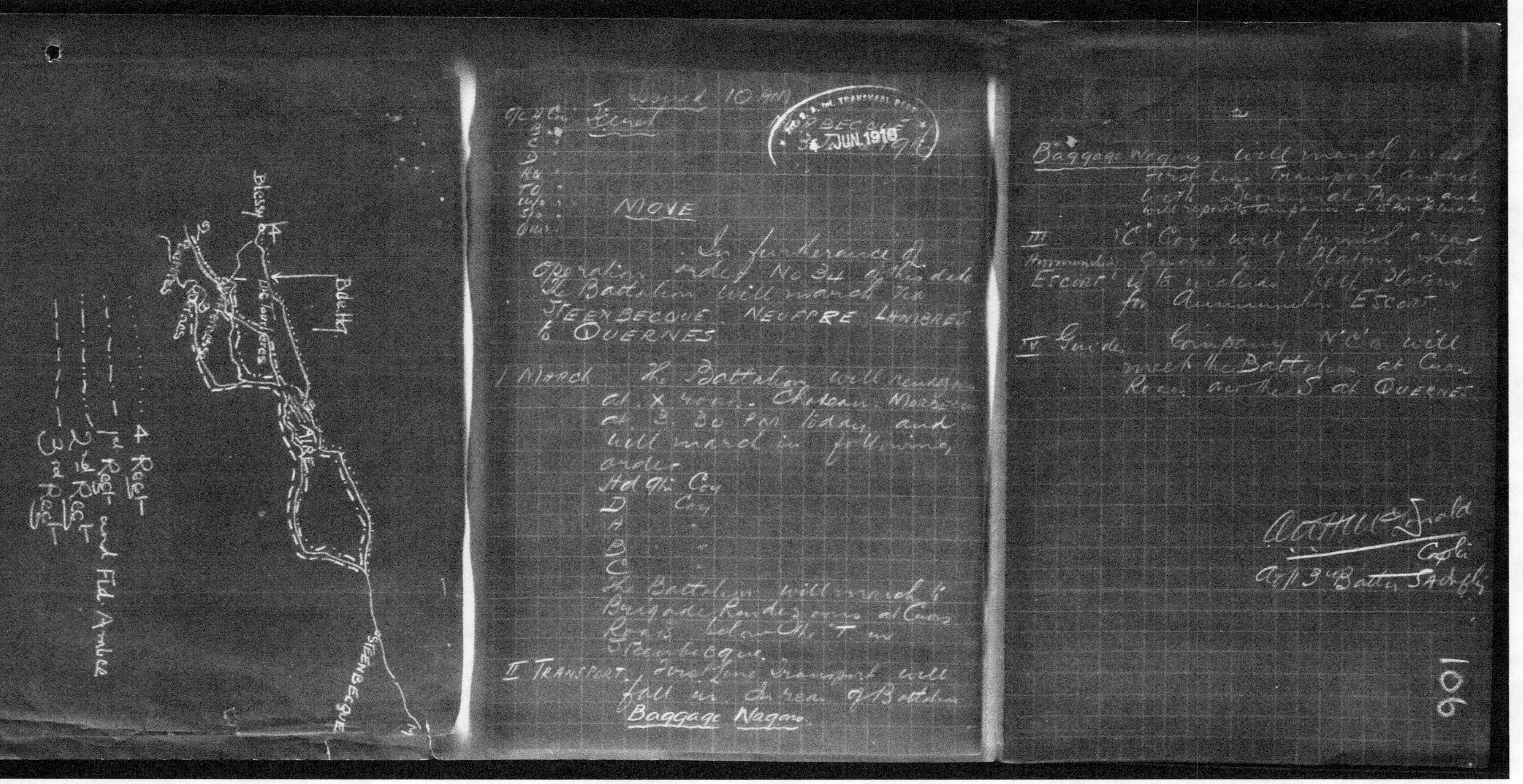

Issued 10 AM

O/C A Coy
B
C
D
HQ
TO
M/O
S/O
QM

Secret

MOVE

In furtherance of Operation order No 34 of this date the Battalion will march via STEENBECQUE. NEUFPRE LAMBRES to QUERNES

I March. The Battalion will rendezvous at X roads. Chateau. Marbecq at 3.30 PM today and will march in following order.
Hd Qr Coy
D Coy
A "
B "
C "
The Battalion will march to Brigade Rendezvous at Cross Roads below the T in Steenbecque.

II TRANSPORT. First Line Transport will fall in in rear of Battalion Baggage Wagons.

2

Baggage Wagons will march with First Line Transport and not with Divisional Train and will report to companies 2.15 PM for loading

III Ammunition Escort. "C" Coy will furnish a rear Guard of 1 Platoon which is to include half Platoon for Ammunition Escort.

IV Guides. Company N.C.O's will meet the Battalion at Cross Roads on the S at QUERNES

A.A. McDonald
Capt
A/Adj 3rd Battn S.A. Inf

106

107

— 1st ARMY. —
SPECIAL MANŒUVRE AREA.

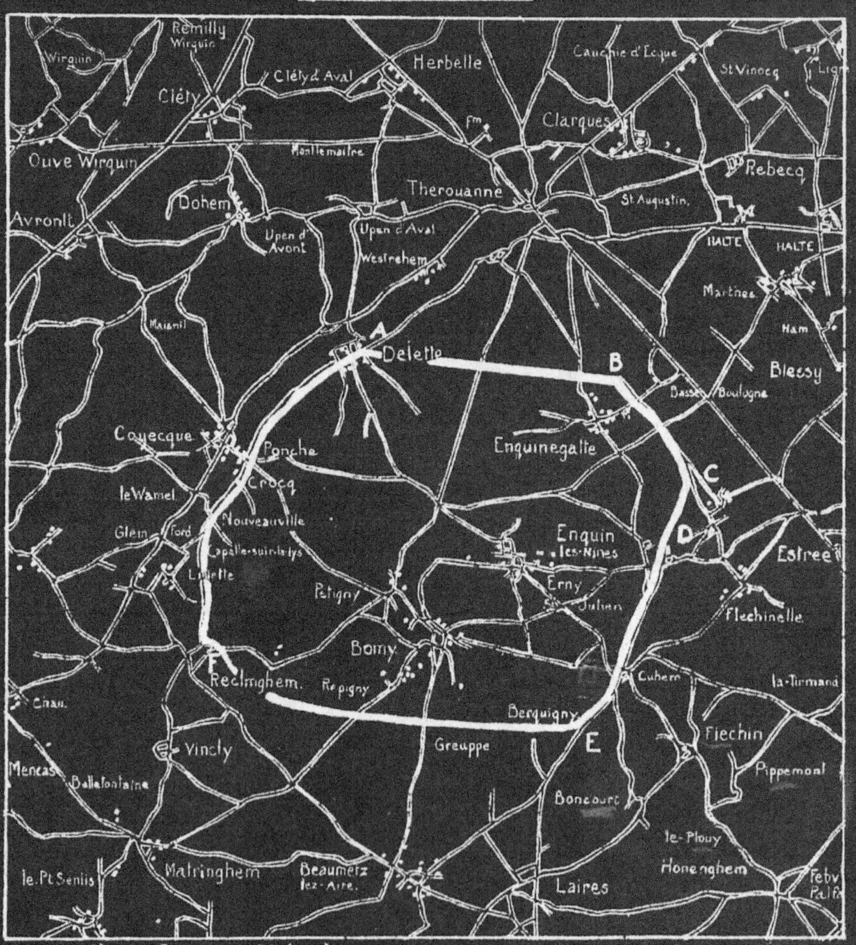

1st Army Printing Sec R.E. (878).

NOTE.

The boundary of the area between A and B, between C and D, and between E and F is marked by posts with white flags. Elsewhere the boundary is the road.

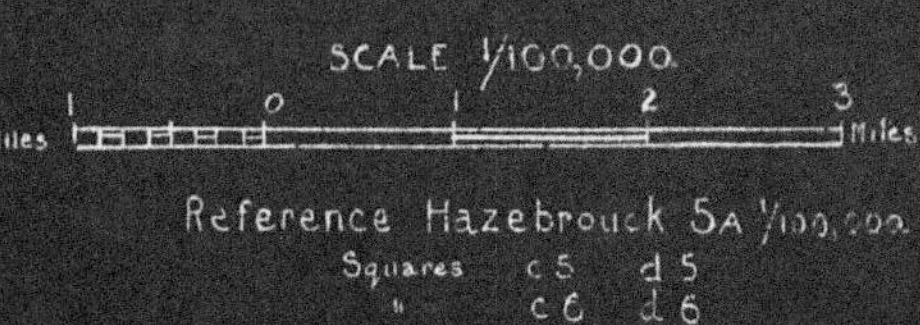

App 131 108

SECRET.

Copy No.......

HEADQUARTERS,

1st S. A. INFANTRY BRIGADE.

3rd June, 1918.

Map Reference:-
Hazebrouck.
1/100,000. S.A.

OPERATION ORDERS No. 35.

1. MARCH. The Brigade will march to-morrow, 4th inst., to billets in the Training Area as set forth below. Units will march independently, under orders of their own Commanders, but all must be clear of the WITTERNESSE Area by 6 p.m.

2. BILLETS IN THE TRAINING AREA. Brigade Headquarters will be billetted in the Training Area at ERNY St. JULIEN (Chateau Cappe de Baillon); 1st S. A. Infantry at ERNY St. JULIEN; 2nd S. A. Infantry at FLECHIN; 3rd S. A. Infantry at BONCOURT, le PLOUY and PIPPEMONT; 4th S. A. Infantry at ENGUINEGATTE; and 1st S. A. Field Ambulance at ERNY St. JULIEN.

3. GUIDES TO BILLETS. Billetting Officers will proceed to billetting areas at such an hour as will enable them to make the necessary arrangements before the arrival of their units, and to meet their units and lead them to their billets as they arrive in the vicinity thereof.

4. BRIGADE HEADQUARTERS. Brigade Headquarters will move to-morrow from LES TOURBIERES at 10 a.m. and open at ERNY St. JULIEN at noon.

Mitchell Baker
Major.

Brigade Major.

Copy No.1 to 1st S. A. I.,
2 2nd do
3 3rd do
4 4th do
5 9th Division.
6 107th Coy. A.S.C.,

Copy No.7 to O. i/c Brigade Sig. Sec.
8 1st S.A. Field Amb.,
9 G.O.C., the Brigade.
10 Brigade Major.
11 Staff Captain.
12 Office Copy.

Issued by Orderly at...10 pm...........

App 130

S E C R E T.

Copy No. 3 .....

109

HEADQUARTERS,

1st S. A. INFANTRY BRIGADE.

3rd June, 1916.

Map Reference --
Hazebrouck.
1/100,000 (S.A.)

OPERATION ORDERS No. 34.

1. MARCH. The Brigade will march this afternoon, 3rd inst., to the WITTERNESSE Area.

2. ROUTE TO BE FOLLOWED. All regiments will march on the main MORBECQUE-STEENBECQUE road as far as the Cross Roads below the "T" in STEENBECQUE, thereafter as shown on the plan attached.

3. ORDER OF MARCH & TIMETABLE. The order of march will be the same as yesterday. Brigade Headquarters will move off at 3.30 p.m.; the 4th Regiment following in rear immediately Brigade Headquarters is clear of their front; other units following in succession.

4. DISTANCES. The distances laid down in Operation Orders No.33 will be adhered to throughout the march to the Training Area.

5. BAGGAGE WAGONS. These will march with First Line Transport and not with the Train. This order will hold good during the remainder of the march to the Training Area.

6. GUIDES TO BILLETS. Billetting Officers of units will be instructed by Brigade Headquarters regarding the places at which they are to meet their units and lead them to their billets.

7. ORDERS FOR FOLLOWING DAY'S MARCH. An officer from each unit will report at Brigade Headquarters (at LES TOURBIERES) at 9 a.m. on the 4th inst., for orders for march that day to Training Area.

[signature]

Major.

Brigade Major.

Copy No.1 to	1st S. A. I.,		Copy No.7 to	O. i/c Bde Sig. Sec.
2	2nd do		8	1st S.A. Fd. Amblce.
✓ 3	3rd do		9	G.O.C. the Brigade.
4	4th do		10	Brigade Major.
5	9th Division.		11	Staff Captain.
6	107th Coy. A.S.C.,		12	Office Copy.

Issued ~~by Orderly~~ personally to officers at 9am 3/6/16 at.................

110

2 ROUGE CROIX

3 BOURT CROIX

MOOLENACKER

4 PRADELLES

BORRE

Bde Hq STRAZEELE

F/A

HAZEBROUCK

1st S.A.I. route to STARTING Pt

2nd " " "

3rd " " "

× STARTING POINT

5

HEADQUARTERS,

1st S. A. INFANTRY BRIGADE.

EXTRACTS FROM STANDING ORDERS for the Brigade

whilst on the march. (Issued in Egypt).

- - - - - - - - - - - - - - -

6. STRAGGLING. (a) Straggling on the line of march is strictly forbidden.

(b) Men wishing to fall out for any reason must first obtain the permission of an officer - if unable to reach an officer they must report to a N.C.O. before falling out.

7. PARTIES WITH TRANSPORT OR BAGGAGE. Men accompanying transport or baggage must march properly formed bodies under an officer or a N.C.O.

9. SMOKING. Smoking on line of march is forbidden, but men may smoke during halts in day time. Smoking on line of march by night is strictly forbidden.

111

War Diary App 137

112

SECRET

XIII Corps.
9th. Division.
C.R.E.
21st. Infantry Brigade.
27th. Infantry Brigade.
11th. Bn. Royal Scots.
6th. Bn. K.O.S. Borderers.
2nd. Bn. S. African Brigade.
3rd. Bn. S. African Brigade.
Signal Coy.
"Q".
Major Holland D.S.O.

G.733. 21st. June, 1916.

The following moves will take place:-

June			
22	21st. Bde.	1 battn. to BRAY	BRAY-CORBIE Road. Not to march E. of BOIS DES TAILLES before 10.30 p.m.
		1 battn to ETINEHEM CAMP) 2 battns to ETINEHEM)	River road. To pass ETINEHEM CHURCH by 2 p.m.
	11th. R. Scots	from BRAY to BOIS CELESTINS	By small detachments only, out of BRAY. To pass ETINEHEM CHURCH 7 pm.
	1 battn. S.A. Bde.	from ETINEHEM CAMP to BOIS CELESTINS.	By River road. No. of battn. to move will be published later. To pass ETINEHEM CHURCH 3 pm.
23	6th K.O.S.Bs.	from BRAY to BOIS CELESTINS	By small detachments only out of BRAY
	1 battn. S.A. Bde.	either to CELESTINS or remain at ETINEHEM CAMP	by River Road. Information awaited from 9th. Division.

Night 23/24th. Further orders will be published for movement of troops this night.

R.K. Ross Capt.
for Lieut. Colonel.
General Staff

30th. Division.

War Diary

Issued at 2.45 pm B102

28-6-16

To
O/C A Coy
B "
C "
D "
HQ "
TO "
Comm "
M/O "
S/O "

In Compliance with operation order No 30 of this date the Battalion will move tonight to GROVETOWN by X route.

1. Move. The 15 Battalion will parade at 10 PM tonight and will march past starting point at K34.b.9.7 at 10.30 pm.

2. Order of March } Hd Qrs Coy
B "
C "
D "
A "

For information the Brigade order

2

Order of march is
1st Regt
4th "
2nd "
3 "
64 Field RE with working pa[rty]

(3) Advance parties will meet [their] Units on X route just South [of] the BRAY CORBIE Road at K18. [...] The officer with the advance [party] will proceed from GROVETOWN Valley tonight with the 3rd [...] in order to ascertain the [...] locality in TRIGGER WOOD, [...] WOOD or CORSE VALLEY. This officer will rejoin his Unit in GROVETOWN Valley not later than 9 am tomorrow.

(4) Brigade Hd Qrs in GROVETOWN Valley will be about L 8.C.[...]

5. Marching Order } For this march Great[coats] will be rolled in Bando[liers]. Haversacks on order. [...] Tin. attached to Belt.

[signature]

War Diary

Issued at 2.45 pm B102

28-6-16

To

O/C A Coy [initials]
B " [initials]
C " [initials]
D " [initials]
HQ " [initials]
T/O " [initials]
Comn " [initials]
M/O " [initials]
S/O " [initials]

In compliance with Operation Order No 30 of this date the Battalion will move tonight to GROVETOWN by X route.

1 Move. The Battalion will parade at 10.15 PM tonight and will march past starting point at K34.c.9.7 at 10.30 pm.

2 Order of March } HdQrs Coy
B "
C "
D "
A "

For information the Brigade order

2

Order of March is
1st Regt
4th "
2nd "
3 "
64th Field RE with working parties

(3) Advance Parties will meet their units on X route just South of the BRAY CORBIE Road at K18 d 2.8. The officer with the advance party will proceed from GROVETOWN Valley tonight with the 2nd Brigade in order to ascertain the units locality in TRIGGER WOOD, BILLON WOOD or COPSE VALLEY. This man will rejoin his unit in GROVETOWN Valley not later than 9am tomorrow.

(4) Brigade HdQrs in GROVETOWN Valley will be about L8.c.2.9

5. Marching Order. For this march Great Coats will be rolled on Bandolier; Haversack on [illegible] with [illegible] Tin attached to Belt.

[signature]

3

Mvt Order Continued in compliance Operation No 30

6 TRANSPORT. Transport will be packed ready to move off under T/O to march on same day as units and to be at starting point at 11-15 PM tonight.

7 Baggage Ammunition Guard. A Coy will detail 1 platoon under a senior NCO as Baggage and Ammunition Guard to report at Quarters at 10.00 pm.

[signature]
Capt
Adjt 3rd Regt SAI

113

War Diary

R 4/83. 21/6/16 App 135

Orders re move tomorrow ~~21/6/16~~

The Battalion (less 4 officers 150 OR "B" Coy & 4 officers 150 OR "C" Coy (attached to 9th Div Artillery) will be ready to march from this camp at 2.30 pm sharp. 22/6/16

Order of March

H.Q. Pns. A. B. C. D. Transport

Machine Gunners to march behind "D" Coy.

Details of "B" & "C" Companies to be under the Command of 2 Lt. Ritchie during the absence from the Regt of these two Companies.

Two G.S. Wagons will be at this camp at 11 am to convey "Packs" of the fatigue men of "A" and "D" Companies to new camp.

These packs will be piled on road outside Guard room by 10.30 am. Companies concerned will detail 2 men each to accompany these wagons.

A EUC — Mach Gun
B [illegible] — Transport
C [illegible] — Quartermaster
D [illegible]

[signature] Capt & Adjutant

"A" Form. Army Form C. 2121.

MESSAGES AND SIGNALS. No. of Message

Prefix ... Code ... m. Words Charge

Office of Origin and Service Instructions. Sent At ... m. To ... By ...

This message is on a/c of: App 136 Service. (Signature of "Franking Officer.")

Recd. at ... m. Date ... From ... By ...

TO 3rd S.A. Battalion.

* Sender's Number.	Day of Month	In reply to Number	
G 789	21		AAA

Reference this office G 733 of today aaa 9th Division wire that 8 officers and 300 will be required for work under CRA 9th Division from tomorrow aaa CRA will send instructions and guides to your camp at 9 am tomorrow aaa These men will be split up among batteries of 9th Div and will remain with them for 2 or 3 days aaa Rations for tomorrow must be carried by the men. aaa Remainder are placed at disposal of H Signals 30th Div who will arrange that they cease work in time to reach BOIS CELESTINS Camp tomorrow evening aaa Acknowledge

From 30th Division.

Place

Time 9.35 pm.

The above may be forwarded as now corrected. (Z)

Censor. Signature of Addressor or person authorised to telegraph in his name.

* This line should be erased if not required.

(4198) Wt. W14013—M14. 300000 Pads. 12/15. Sir J. C. & S.

115

HEADQUARTERS,

1st S. A. INFANTRY BRIGADE

18th June, 1916.

B.M.47/26/2.

1st SOUTH AFRICAN INFANTRY BRIGADE.

Parties Visiting Trench Area.

The parties visiting the Trench Area will be sub-divided as follows:-

First party will visit GROVETOWN VALLEY; see the accomodation there for troops; follow "X" route from there forward into TRIGGER WOOD, BILLON WOOD and COPSE VALLEY, in which places they will see the accomodation for troops.

Second party will reconnoitre the best route forward from COPSE VALLEY, both over the open and by trench, to the road running from the S.E. corner of MARICOURT (Sheet 62c N.W. A.22.9.5.) westward for about a mile.

Third party will reconnoitre the best route forward from BILLON WOOD, both over the open and by trench, to the road running from the cross roads S. of CAFTET WOOD (Sheet 62d N.E. F.18.c.6.3.) eastward for about 1500 yards.

The senior officer with each ~~of these~~ day's party will arrange with the guides from the 30th Division - who will meet the parties at the Town Hall, BRAY,-at 11 a.m. - for one to go with each sub-party.

(Note. Officers may be required to guide their regiments over the sections reconnoitred by them).

J Mitchell Baker

Major.

Brigade Major .

HEADQUARTERS,

1st S. A. INFANTRY BRIGADE.

Officer Commanding,
1st S. A. Infantry.
2nd do do
3rd do do
4th do do

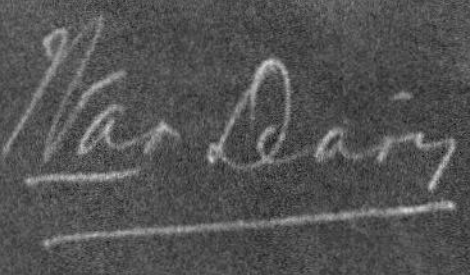

B.M.47/26/2. 18th June, 1916.

It is very desirable that as many regimental officers as possible should know

(1) The covered route which is marked "X" and runs from BOIS-LES-CELESTINE (Sheet 62d N.E. K.27, 33 and 34) forward to TRIGGER WOOD (Sheet 62d N.E. L.6.)

(2) The best routes forward from TRIGGER WOOD, BILLON WOOD (Sheet 62c N.W. A.19, 20, 25 and 26) and COPSE VALLEY (Sheet 62c N.W. A. 26)

Officers Commanding the 2nd and 3rd Battalions, S. A. Infantry, should accordingly arrange, as far as possible, for officers under their command to reconnoitre the ground mentioned, and report to this office any arrangements they have been able to make in this connection.

Parties visiting the Trench Area from AILLY-SUR-SOMME will, from to-morrow, be divided up as follows:-

First party will visit GROVETOWN VALLEY; see the accomodation there for troops; follow "X" route forward from there into TRIGGER WOOD, BILLON WOOD and COPSE VALLEY, in which places they will see the accomodation for troops.

Second party will reconnoitre the best route forward from COPSE VALLEY, both over the open and by trench, to the road running from the S.E. corner of MARICOURT (Sheet 62c N.W. A.22.9.5.) westwrd for about a mile.

Third party will reconnoitre the best route forward from BILLON WOOD, both over the open and by trench, to the road running from the cross roads S. of CAFTET WOOD (Sheet 62d N.E. F. 18.d.6.3.) eastward for about 1500 yards.

The Officers Commanding 1st and 4th S. A. Infantry will please detail the 5 Officers to accompany the party for the Trench Area to-morrow as follows:-

One for the first party referred to above.
Two for each of the second and third parties.

If more than 5 Officers are sent with the party from one unit, Commanding Officers will please detail the others to particular sub-parties.

Mitchell Baker

Major.
Brigade Major.

Instructions regarding War Diaries and Intelligence Summaries are contained in F. S. Regs., Part II. and the Staff Manual respectively. Title Pages will be prepared in manuscript.

Page 24

WAR DIARY
or
~~INTELLIGENCE SUMMARY~~
(Erase heading not required.)

3rd SAI
9
Vol 4

Army Form C. 2118

July

Place	Date 1916	Hour	Summary of Events and Information	Remarks and references to Appendices
GROVETOWN	July 1	6 am	In Camp. ~~Received~~ Brigade Operation Order No 40	App 143
	2	–	Supplied working party of 2 NCOs & 40 men for work on road at CARNOY	App 144
			Received Brigade Opn Order No 41	App 145
			Issued Battalion Move Order to COPSE VALLEY.	
		9.30pm	Battalion marched off.	
COPSE VALLEY	3	2am	Arrived here & took up position as instructed.	App 146
		7am	Working party 2 NCOs & 40 men returned from CARNOY	
	4	7am	"A" Coy detailed as working party on road at CARNOY	
		2.30pm	Received Bde Op Order No 42	App 147
		3.5pm	Issued Battn Move Order B10.	
		4.30pm	"A" Coy working party returned	
		"	Battalion moved to MARICOURT via STANLEY AVENUE	
		5.30pm	Arrived MARICOURT	
		8 pm	Battalion moved via STANLEY AVENUE to occupy old British Front Line Trenches – taken over from Col Poyntz, Bedford Regiment.	
		12.30	Relief completed.	
STANLEY AV & VICINITY.	5th	–	Intermittent Shelling – 3 men wounded by shell fire.	
	6th	–	Supplied working party of 80 men to work on Fire Trench to Briqueterie	App 148
			Re-organised position of Battalion in trenches	
			Received Operation Order No 43 – later cancelled	App 149

117

~~107~~

1875 Wt. W593/826 1,000,000 4/15 J.B.C. & A. A.D.S.S./Forms/C. 2118.

Instructions regarding War Diaries and Intelligence Summaries are contained in F. S. Regs., Part II. and the Staff Manual respectively. Title Pages will be prepared in manuscript.

Army Form C. 2118

25

WAR DIARY or ~~INTELLIGENCE~~ SUMMARY

(Erase heading not required.)

Place	Date 1916	Hour	Summary of Events and Information	Remarks and references to Appendices
STANLEY AV etc	July 7	–	In position in trenches. Intermittent Shelling of our position	
	8th	–	Supplied working party for BERNAFAY WOOD of 1 Platoon A Coy. This party suffered severely, casualties being 3 men killed, 11 wounded including 2/Lt Abel and 1 missing	App 150
			Received Bde Operation Order No 44 – later cancelled.	
			Received Preliminary Notice from HQrs to be ready to take up another position	
	9th		Position again heavily shelled during day. 1 Man killed 3 wounded.	
			Received phone order to carry out Operation Order No 44	
		12 pm	Completed move order + vacated trenches vicinity STANLEY AVENUE	
SILESIA + SUPPORT TRENCHES	10th	1 am	Took up position in SILESIA and SUPPORT TRENCHES	
			D Coy occupied GLATZ REDOUBT	
	11th		Positions generally shelled intermittently 5 Casualties.	
			12 NCOs + men reported to Lt Beverly, 2nd SAI for training as scouts.	
	12th		Desultory shelling. 2 Casualties.	
		5 30pm.	Working party detailed of 350 all ranks, in charge of Capt MacLachlan for work at BERNAFAY WOOD. Stayed there until about 3 am 13/7/16 + then returned. 3 Casualties.	App 151
	13th		Enemy's bombardment of our positions more severe.	App 152
		5 30pm	Received Battalion Move order and in accordance with same, vacated trenches + occupied position at TALUS BOIS.	

118

1875 Wt. W593/826 1,000,000 4/15 J.B.C. & A. A.D.S.S./Forms/C. 2118.

Instructions regarding War Diaries and Intelligence Summaries are contained in F. S. Regs., Part II. and the Staff Manual respectively. Title Pages will be prepared in manuscript.

WAR DIARY
or
~~INTELLIGENCE~~ SUMMARY
(Erase heading not required.)

Army Form C. 2118

Place	Date 1916	Hour	Summary of Events and Information	Remarks and references to Appendices
TALUS BOISE	July 14th	6 am	Received Order to hold ourselves in readiness to move	
		8 am	Received verbal instructions from G.O.C. re move, confirmed later by written Order BM 35.	App 153
		11 30am	Moved up S of MONTAUBAN as instructed. Remained there till 4 pm. Received verbal order from G.O.C. to move forward, regarding attack on DELVILLE WOOD from west in conjunction with 2nd Regt. (Confirmed by B.O. 48 Copy No 1).	
			Moved forward to MONTAUBAN about 5 pm. Heavily shelled. Halted in Village. Received verbal orders from G.O.C to occupy trench N of MONTAUBAN.	
	14/15th	Midnight	Received orders to carry out attack on DELVILLE WOOD from W.	App 154
	15th	1 am	Received orders & moved forward for this attack. Received orders to stand fast & verbal orders from G.O.C. cancelling previous order and to attack from S W of wood at 5 am (Confirmed by BM 45)	
		2 30am	Moved forward supported by 2nd S.A.I.	
DELVILLE WOOD		4 am	Arrived at support trench E of LONGUEVAL. Col Tanner (2nd SAI) and Col Thackeray (3rd SAI) pushed forward to consult O.Cs of A & S Highlanders Cameron Highlanders and Black Watch. As enemy held north of village and NW of wood, decided to attack from S.W. Occupied Southern half with 3rd Regt & then the north half with 2nd Regt. Formed up on BUCHANAN ST at 5.30 am. Attacked southern	

1875 Wt. W593/826 1,000,000 4/15 J.B.C. & A. A.D.S.S./Forms/C. 2118.

Instructions regarding War Diaries and Intelligence Summaries are contained in F. S. Regs., Part II. and the Staff Manual respectively. Title Pages will be prepared in manuscript.

27

WAR DIARY
or
~~INTELLIGENCE~~ SUMMARY

(Erase heading not required.)

Army Form C. 2118

Place	Date 1916	Hour	Summary of Events and Information	Remarks and references to Appendices
DELVILLE WOOD	July 15	–	half of wood between PRINCES ST and SOUTH ST from BUCHANAN STREET occupying as the advance was made, SOUTH ST (C Coy) PRINCES ST (D Coy) and eastern and NE. end of wood with A and B Coy. xxx D Coy pushed forward on NE of SOUTHERN HALF OF WOOD occupied by 3rd S.A.I. by 7am. Supported by 2nd Regt. x 2nd Regt attacked northwards. Occupied ~~perimeter~~ from left of ~~3rd~~ Regt on NE to point N of STRAND ST and S to junction STRAND ST and BUCHANAN ST. Both Regiments digging themselves in, which were joined up by strong points and gradually connected. All salients occupied by Lewis Guns. Enemy's fire steadily increased. Patrol D Coy (Capt Tomlinson) pushed out to enemy's trench N.E. Captured 2 Officers 35 men & 1 Machine Gun. Patrol B Coy (Capt Medlicott) pushed forward SE and captured 1 Officer and 100 men. Enemy reported in strength in trenches East of Sugar Refinery (WATERLOT), E towards GINCHY N and NW in direction of FLERS. One Coy Cameron Highlanders in small trench BUCHANAN STREET and small trench running E from village in PRINCES ST. Headquarters 2nd and 3rd Regts established in BUCHANAN STREET. Enemy opened heavy artillery, machine gun and rifle fire. The casualties increased. Capt MacLachlan (C. Coy) Killed. Capt Vivian (A Coy) Wounded. 2/Lt Hanks died of wounds.	

120

1875 Wt. W593/826 1,000,000 4/15 J.B.C. & A. A.D.S.S./Forms/C. 2118.

Army Form C. 2118

Instructions regarding War Diaries and Intelligence Summaries are contained in F. S. Regs., Part II. and the Staff Manual respectively. Title Pages will be prepared in manuscript.

No 28

WAR DIARY or ~~INTELLIGENCE~~ SUMMARY

(Erase heading not required.)

Place	Date 1916	Hour	Summary of Events and Information	Remarks and references to Appendices
D. WOOD	July 15		During night 15th/16th. Consolidated position, sent out patrols and replied to enemy's fire. Pushed forward Machine Guns to Strong points. Estimated casualties 140.	
	16th		Continued to consolidate positions all around perimeter under heavy artillery, M.G and rifle fire. Repulsed small attacks on perimeter. Received reinforcements 1 Coy 4th SAI. who were pushed out E and NE. 1 Coy 2nd SAI. supported SOUTH ST. 1st & 4th Regts carried out attack on N of village & NW of wood with a portion of 1SAI. under Major Burgess, and portion of 4th Regt under Major Hunt. This attack unable to penetrate. Was supported in STRAND STREET direction by 2nd Regt. Was informed other Brigades would attack wood towards E and N which would give relief to S.A Brigade	
	17th		Enemy's fire increased & enemy reinforced from GINCHY and FLERS. GOC 1st SAI. Bde and Bde Major visited BUCHANAN ST also Officers of Brigades to carry out attacks E and towards WATERLOT. Enemy's fire intense. Col Tanner wounded. Col Thackeray assumed command. Capt Jackson (2nd in Command 3rd SAI) reported for duty & was sent to A Coy. who were left without Officers. All available reinforcements pushed up to perimeter. Enemy penetrated at wood from NW. During night heavily attacked BUCHANAN STREET and PRINCES STREET	

121

1875 Wt. W593/826 1,000,000 4/15 J.B.C. & A. A.D.S.S./Forms/C. 2118.

Instructions regarding War Diaries and Intelligence Summaries are contained in F. S. Regs., Part II. and the Staff Manual respectively. Title Pages will be prepared in manuscript.

Army Form C. 2118

WAR DIARY
or
~~INTELLIGENCE~~ SUMMARY
(Erase heading not required.)

No 29

Place	Date 1916	Hour	Summary of Events and Information	Remarks and references to Appendices
	July 17th		with rifles and bombs. Gained entrance but were driven out with heavy loss. Enemy attacked perimeter N, NE, E and S but were repulsed. Casualties heavy. Enemy snipers numerous in wood.	
	18th		Major Gee & Major McLeod reported for duty. Enemy's artillery fire was intense. Coys reduced to a few men only. "A" Coy of Gordon Highlanders pushed forward & gained the orchard and NW of wood. Major Burgess 1st Regt pushed forward to support them. This Coy of Gordons was forced to retire - throwing open the left flank of the perimeter and exposing the 1st & 2nd Regts. Major Burgess was killed and Major McLeod returned to me wounded. Major Gee who moved forward to N was wounded and died. His Adjutant ~~went out~~ Lt. Tatham, went out with him and was wounded and has since been missing. Major McLeod again went out and was again twice wounded. The enemy penetrated behind our defensive line on the perimeter. The 7 Machine Guns with all their Officers were knocked out. Four Lewis Guns of 3rd Regt were knocked out and the few men left of the 1st 2nd, 3rd & 4th Regts holding the perimeter were either killed or wounded. Capt McDonald, Adjutant 3rd Regt was wounded but pushed back to LONGUEVAL for assistance when Lt Perkins	

1875 Wt. W593/826 1,000,000 4/15 J.B.C. & A. A.D.S.S./Forms/C. 2118.

Instructions regarding War Diaries and Intelligence Summaries are contained in F. S. Regs., Part II. and the Staff Manual respectively. Title Pages will be prepared in manuscript.

No 30

WAR DIARY
or
~~INTELLIGENCE~~ SUMMARY
(Erase heading not required.)

Army Form C. 2118

Place	Date 1916	Hour	Summary of Events and Information	Remarks and references to Appendices
	July 18th.		and Lt Beverley, 2nd Regt who were with me were wounded, also Lt Green of 2nd Regt on my right flank. I was left alone without any officer and only some few details in BUCHANAN and PRINCES ST. Lt Phillips arrived with some 200 details from 1st, 2nd, 3rd & 4th Regts attached to LTMB of 1st SAI Bde. Capt McDonald & Lt Green who were both wounded returned to Buchanan St. In the evening the enemy made three determined attacks in force with large bodies of infantry from three directions – NW, N & NE, on Buchanan St and Princes St but were repulsed with heavy loss. Lt Bell & Lt Cormack were Killed. Lt Creed wounded. Capt McDonald went back for further assistance but was detained by Medical authorities owing to his wounds. Capt Stiles was wounded in endeavouring to remove Capt Brown, Adjt 4th Regt who had been unable to evacuate. Lt Phillips was wounded during this period & I was left with only these two wounded officers to assist me. Sergt Major Thompson, 2nd Regt pluckily held on to Strong Point S of Buchanan St.	
	19th		On morning of the 19th July, the Norfolk Regt attacked the wood in a northerly direction W of Buchanan St, when we were able to bring a heavy flanking fire on the retreating	123

1875 Wt. W593/826 1,000,000 4/15 J.B.C. & A. A.D.S.S./Forms/C. 2118.

Instructions regarding War Diaries and Intelligence Summaries are contained in F. S. Regs., Part II. and the Staff Manual respectively. Title Pages will be prepared in manuscript.

Army Form C. 2118

No 31

WAR DIARY
or
~~INTELLIGENCE~~ SUMMARY
(Erase heading not required.)

124

Place	Date	Hour	Summary of Events and Information	Remarks and references to Appendices
	1916 July 19		Who however left many snipers in the wood. The Berkshire Regt attacked towards the NW and I was informed that attacks would take place by 76th Brigade towards N and E. The Royal Welsh Fusiliers formed up in the evening but the attack was not pushed forward. The RW Fusiliers entrenched in SW of Buchanan St. The DLI were ordered to relieve but this was not effected. Enemy resumed artillery bombardment, MG and sniping fire. Enemy prepared to attack but did not push home.	
	20th		Heavy shelling & sniping continued. In the evening the few details left with me in Buchanan St were relieved by the Suffolk Regt. These details consisted of 1st SAI. 9 OR. 2nd SAI 1 Off (Lt Green) 33 OR 3rd Regt 14 OR. 4th Regt 25 OR. LTMB. 1 Off (Lt Phillips) 59. OR. (Total 3 Officers 140 OR.)	
			3rd SAI. marched into DELVILLE WOOD on the 14/7/16 and on relief rejoining Brigade on 21st inst, mustered only 1 Officer (Col Thackeray) and 104. OR, 28 Officers + 749 OR. being Killed Wounded & missing. Every detachment of 3rd SAI. carried	

1875 Wt. W593/826 1,000,000 4/15 J.B.C. & A. A.D.S.S./Forms/C. 2118.

Instructions regarding War Diaries and Intelligence Summaries are contained in F. S. Regs., Part II. and the Staff Manual respectively. Title Pages will be prepared in manuscript.

Army Form C. 2118

WAR DIARY or ~~INTELLIGENCE~~ SUMMARY

(Erase heading not required.)

Page 32

Place	Date 1916	Hour	Summary of Events and Information	Remarks and references to Appendices
	July 21st.		Out instructions to hold on at all costs & not a single detachment retired from their positions, either in the perimeter of the wood or from the support trench. It is regretted that they were not strong enough to drive out the enemy on the perimeter, where they were all wiped out.	
	20th		Draft of 80 men arrived from BASE, and reported at HAPPY VALLEY	
	~~21st~~		Details of Regt left at TALUS BOISE and Others, with Capt Liebson. M.O & Lt Carding QMr proceeded to new area at HAPPY VALLEY	
	21st		2/Lt A.G. Money & 60 O.R. (details) arrived from Base.	
			Lt Col Thackeray 2/Lt Phillips & 35 O.R. reported at HAPPY VALLEY	
	22nd		In Camp.	
	23rd		Battalion marched to MERICOURT and entrained for	
			After detraining, marched to BOUCHON and occupied billets.	
	24th		In Billets at BOUCHON	
	24th		Received BM/17/12. Move Order.	App 155
	25th	6.30 am	Vacated area at BOUCHON and marched to LONGPRE STATION, entraining & departing at 7.41 am for new area at la THIEULOYE.	App 156
		3 pm	Arrived at occupied billets at la THIEULOYE.	
	26th		Received BM 17/12 Move Order and left la THIEULOYE at 1.30pm for FRESNICOURT. arriving about 5.30pm	App 157
	26th/31st.		In FRESNICOURT.	

[signature] Lt. Col.
Commanding 3rd. S. A. Infantry. (Transvaal Regt.)

125

W3875 Wt W593/826 1,000,000 4/15 J.B.C. & A. A.D.S.S./Forms/C. 2118.

2

their Carrier Platoons to take forward all Stores from BILLON WOOD to Battalion Camp. Transport will not go beyond BILLON WOOD, supplementary men to carry all Stores to be detailed under an Officer.

(4) TRANSPORT. Transport as detailed will accompany the Battalion to BILLON WOOD but all must be sent back to GROVETOWN VALLEY as soon as off loaded excepting Cookers and Water Carts. The animals for the Cookers will also return to GROVETOWN VALLEY the only animals remaining at BILLON WOOD being the animals for Water Carts

5 STARTING POINT | The Starting point will be at L.8.a.8.0.

6 INTERVALS Companies will march with an interval of 5 minutes.

A.W.H. McDonald Capt.
A/Adj 3rd Regt S.A. Infy

145
127

Issued at 7.55 PM B106

2.7.16

To O/C A Coy
B "
C "
D "
HQ "
LGO "
M/O
S/O
Qmr
T/O

App 145

I In compliance with Operation Order No 41. The Battalion will move by X route to BILLON WOOD VALLEY, TRIGGER WOOD VALLEY and COPSE VALLEY tonight, moving off at 9.30 PM
Companies will parade at 9.20 PM

II Order of MARCH
HQ Coy
C Coy
D "
A "
B "

(3) RE. STORES Companies will detail

SECRET.

Copy No. 3

128

1st SOUTH AFRICAN INFANTRY BRIGADE.

OPERATION ORDERS No. 41.

In the Field,
2nd July, 1916.

1. MOVE. The South African Brigade, 64th Field Company, R.E., and "B" Company, 9th Seaforths, will move by "X" Route to BILLON WOOD VALLEY, TRIGGER WOOD VALLEY and COPSE VALLEY ~~this after-noon~~ 1st day in relief of the 27th Brigade. Time of move will be notified later.

2. ORDER OF MARCH. The Brigade will march by Companies or similar formations in the following order:-

1st S. A. Infantry.
2nd do do
~~3rd~~ 4th do do
~~4th~~ 3rd do do
28th Bde. M.G. Company.
S. A. Bde. L.T.M. Battery.
64th Field Company, R.E.
"B" Company, 9th Seaforths.
Bearer Section, S.A.F.A.

3. STARTING POINT. The starting point will be at L.8.d.8.0.

4. INTERVAL. The leading Company of the 1st S. A. Infantry will pass the starting point at the starting hour, and each succeeding Company will follow its preceding Company at five minutes' interval. This interval will be maintained throughout the march.

5. TRANSPORT. Transport will march ~~by sections (to be decided by the Brigade Transport Officer)~~ in rear of ~~the Brigade, in the same order as~~ units.

Such First Line Transport as Commanding Officers desire to take may be taken as far as to BILLON WOOD, but all must be sent back to GROVETOWN VALLEY as soon as off-loaded, excepting cookers and water carts. The animals for the cookers will also be returned to GROVETOWN VALLEY, the only animals remaining at BILLON WOOD, being the animals for water carts.

6. CAMPING SITES. Units will occupy the camping sites taken over by their advance parties.

7. BRIGADE HEADQUARTERS. Brigade Headquarters will be in BILLON WOOD VALLEY at A.25.d.4.5.

Please acknowledge.

J. Mitchell Baker
Major.
Brigade Major.

Copy No. 1 to	1st S. A. Inf.		Copy No. 10 to	107th Company, A.S.C.
2	2nd do		11	O.C. Bearer Section.
x 3	3rd do		12	9th Division.
4	4th do		13	52nd Brigade, R.F.A.
5	64th Field Coy. R.E.		14	G. O. C.
6	O.C. "B" Coy, 9th Sea. Hrs.		15	Brigade Major.
7	O.C. 28th M.G. Coy.		16	Staff Captain.
8	O.C. L.T.M. Battery.		17	Office Copy.
9	O.C. Bde. Signal Sect.		18	War Diary.

Issued by Orderly at 6.10 pm

129

HEADQUARTERS,

1st S. A. Infantry Brigade.

1st July 1916.

B.M. 47/12/40

Officer Commanding,
1st S. A. Infantry,
2nd -do-
3rd -do-
4th -do-
Bde. M.G.Coy,
Bde. L.T.M.Battery.
64th Field Coy, R.E.,
Bearer Section, S.A.F.A.

With reference to No.1 of Bde Operation Order No.40 dated today; permission has now been given for the following transport to be taken by units as far as BILLON WOOD:

Infantry units:-	Cookers; water carts and 2 G.S. Limbers
M.G. Coy:-	1 G.S. Limber for each pair of guns; water cart and 1 G.S. Limber containing cooking utensils.
L.T.M. Battery:-	The transport provided for it at BOIS les CELESTINS.
64th Field Co. R.E.:-	Such transport as the C.O. considers essential.
Bearer Section, S.A.F.A.:-	1 water cart.

All G.S.Limbers will be returned to First Line Transport from BILLON WOOD as soon as they are off-loaded.

Cookers and water carts may remain at BILLON WOOD until units go forward from there, when they will be returned to First Line Transport.

[signature]

Major.
Brigade Major.

Q.M. WMC

T O ARC

Rec

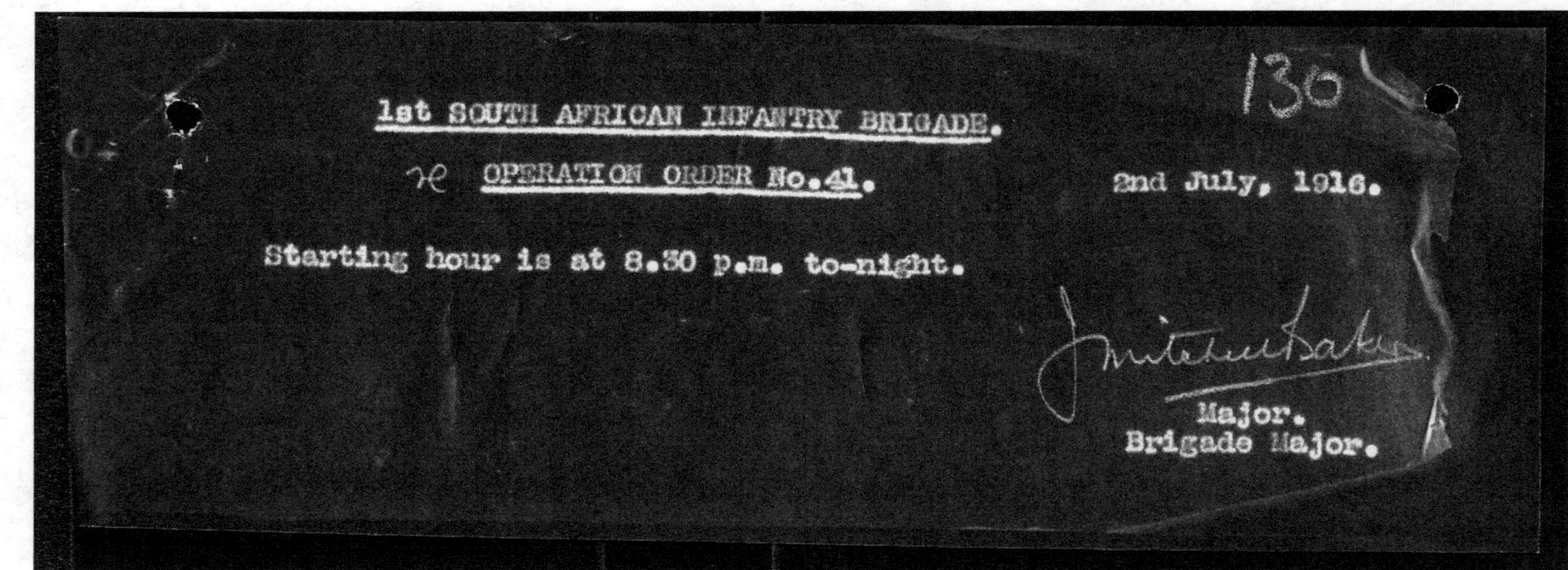

130

1st SOUTH AFRICAN INFANTRY BRIGADE.

OPERATION ORDER No.41. 2nd July, 1916.

Starting hour is at 8.30 p.m. to-night.

J Mitchell Baker

Major.
Brigade Major.

To
O.C.
3rd SAI

The Brigade (less the 4th SAI) and the SAFA: 64th Field Coy R.E. 28th M.G. Coy. L.T.M. Battery will entrain at MERICOURT tomorrow at 11.30 am.

The 4th SAI will entrain at 5.30 pm.

The S.A.F.A. will march to MERICOURT under the orders of its own C.O. but must be at MERICOURT STATION by 11am.

The 1st 2nd & 3rd SAI 64th Field Coy R.E. 28th M.G. Coy and L.T.M. Batty will parade at 8 am. ready to move off.

Further orders will be issued tomorrow morning to all excepting the S.A.F.A.

[illegible] Major
Bde Major

22.7.16
9.45 pm.

B.M. 47/10/10.

132

With reference to No. 1 of Operation Order No. 40 dd. today; permission has now been given for the following transport to be taken by Units as far as Billon Wood.

Infantry Units:– Cookers; water carts & 2 G.S. Limbers 1 G.S. Limber for each pair of Guns; water cart & 1 G.S. Limber containing cooking utensils.

All G.S. Limbers will be returned to First Line Transport from Billon Wood as soon as they are off loaded.

Cookers and water carts may remain at Billon Wood until units go forward from there, when they will be returned ~~from~~ to First Line Transport.

from Brigade Major.

[illegible] Capt.

1/7/16.

7 INTELLIGENCE Our troops reported in Dublin Trench, Dublin Redoubt, Casement Trench, Glatz Redoubt and Pommiers Trench.

French have retaken THEAUMONT FARM (VERDUN).

A.W. McDonald
Capt & Adjutant
3rd S.A. Infy

2/

4/ REPORTS & MESSAGES Unless a name is actually shewn on the MONTAUBAN 1/20000 sheet, all reference to positions in trenches will be described by co-ordinates.

5/ CAMPING SITES Coy Commanders will ensure that their lines are scrupulously clean on marching out.

The M.O & QMr. will inspect the site when the Battalion moves off & will render a written report signed by both officers to Brigade Headquarters as to the condition of the camp.

6/ ARMY COMMANDERS MESSAGE
In wishing all ranks good luck the Army Commander desires to impress on all infantry units the supreme importance of helping one another & holding on tight to every yard of ground gained. The accurate sustained fire of the Artillery during the bombardment should greatly assist the task of the Infantry

Issued at 9·45 am

B105
1/7/16

SECRET

To O/C A Coy
B "
C "
D "
H.Q "
T.O
M.O
Q.Mr
S.O

Extract from Brigade Operation Orders No 40
9·15 am

(1) MOVE The Battalion will hold itself in readiness to move at ten minutes notice and all ranks are confined to unit lines.

(2) TRANSPORT Transport will not move out with the Battalion.

(3) GREAT COATS These will be packed in bundles of twelve as previously instructed & stacked in the Coy lines until further instructions can be issued.

1. Cookers and water carts may remain at BILLON WOOD until units go forward from there when they will be returned to First Line Transport.
The Cookers of "A" "B" and D. Coy's will carry Camp Kettles Etc of "C" Coy and H.Q. the Coy.

A W McDonald
Capt & Adjt
2nd Regt SA Infty

O/C A Coy 8 PM Issued 3 Am
B "
C " 7 to PM
D " 80
HQ " 8/7
T/O
QM
M/CO of water

137

I

R/204
1-7-16

S I Wright

1. Move In furtherance of Brigade Orders re move to BILLON WOOD, the following transport is required to accompany the Battalion today at a time to be given later.

(a) Company Cookers
(b) Water Carts
(c) 7 G S Limbers to be loaded with Company RE Stores, Water etc.

1 Limber to report to O/C A and B Company

1 Limber to report to O/C C + D Coy to be loaded each half limber with half load tools 1/4 load water 1/4 load of coins.

All G S Limbers will return to First Line Transport from BILLON WOOD as soon as they are offloaded

138

War Diary

To 1st Brigade H.Q.

From Regiment Rec^d 9 pm

Please detail a working party of one Sergt and 20 privates to report at 9 am on July 30th to a Representative of 179 Coy R.E on Road P. 36 B 4.9 near GAUCHIN LEGAL. Tools not to be taken. Haversack rations to be taken.

Copy detail 28/7/16

P.D. Pepper Capt

Adj Capt

Detailed Field 28/7/16

HEADQUARTERS, 139

1st S. A. INFANTRY BRIGADE.

Officer Commanding,
1st S. A. Infantry.
2nd do do
3rd do do
4th do do
Brigade L.T.M. Battery.
28th Bde. M.G. Company.

App 157

B.M.12/12. 26th July, 1916.

The Brigade will move under the orders of unit Commanders, subject to the following conditions, as under:-

From.	To.	
MAGNICOURT.	FREVILLERS.	Brigade Headquarters, M.G. Company, L.T.M. Battery, and 1st S. A. Inf. To be clear of Magnicourt by 1.30 p.m.
LA THIEULOYE.	ESTREE CAUCHIE.	2nd S. A. Infantry. Not to enter Magnicourt before 1.30 p.m. and to be clear of La Thieuloye by that hour.
do	FRESNICOURT.	3rd S. A. Infantry. Not to enter Magnicourt before 2 p.m. To follow 2nd S. A. Inf., and to be clear of La Thieuloye by 2 p.m.
do	HERMIN.	4th S. A. Infantry. To follow 3rd S. A. Infatry, and to be clear of La Thieuloye by 2.30 p.m.

The 2nd, 3rd and 4th S. A. Infantry will march via FREVILLERS and HERMIN.

Billeting parties will precede their units in time to make billeting arrangements. Billeting parties of the 1st S. A. Inf., MG Company, and L.T.M. Battery will meet the Staff Captain at the Church in FREVILLERS at 10 a.m. to-morrow.

Two lorries will be allotted to each of the 2nd and 3rd S. A. Infantry to assist them in moving, and one to the 4th S. A. Infantry. If necessary, these lorries can make a double journey. The lorries will not report at the various Battalion Headquarters until 2.30 p.m. and the necessary loading parties must therefore remain behind.

Brigade Headquarters, from 2 p.m. to-morrow, will be at FREVILLERS.

Please acknowledge.

Mitchell Baker

Major.
Brigade Major.

HEADQUARTERS,

1st S. A. INFANTRY BRIGADE

App 156

Officer Commanding,
2nd S. A. Infantry.
3rd do do
4th do do

B.M.12/12. 25th July, 1916.

Your Battalion will be billeted in the new area at la Thieuloye, about six miles N.E., of St. Pol.

Brigade Headquarters will be at Magnicourt.

[signature] Baker

Major,
Brigade Major.

recd 6.30p.m. 25-7-16.

156

140

Copy No. 22.

141

INSTRUCTIONS No.3. for move of 9th (Scottish) Division.

1. 9th Division complete less Artillery, Mob.Vet.Sect. 104th Company A.S.C. and Motor Vehicles will entrain at LONGPRE and PONT REMY for IV Corps Area at times to be notified later but commencing night 24th/25th.

2. As at present arranged Entrainments take place from -

from PONT REMY.
- Div.H.Q. (Band, Salvage Coy. & Convl.Coy).
- 90th Field Coy R.E.
- 9th Seaforth Highrs.
- 27th Infantry Brigade.
- R.A.M.C. (including Sanitary Section).
- Divl. Train (less 104 Coy).

from - LONGPRE-LES-CORPS-SAINTES -
- 26th Infantry Brigade.
- S.A.Brigade.
- 63rd Field Coy.R.E.
- 64th Field Coy.R.E.

3. Troops to arrive at Entraining Stations one hour and Transport 3 hours before advertised time of departure of trains.

4. Motor Vehicles to be despatched in convoys on 25th and 26th under separate instructions issued.

5. D.A.A. & Q.M.G., 9th Division and Staff Captains, also 1 Officer 9th Seaforth Highrs., 1 Officer R.A.M.C. and 1 Officer R.E. will be prepared to proceed by Motor to new area tomorrow morning 24th instant at hour to be notified.
N.B. Map Sheet LENS II 1/100,000 suitable.

6. S.A.Infantry Brigade will be prepared to detail a working party of 100 men at LONGPRE and 27th Infantry Brigade a working party of 100 men at PONT REMY to report to R.T.Os. at those places 4 hours before advertised time of departure of first train.

7. Units will entrain with rations for day following the day of Entrainment unless otherwise ordered - O.C., 9th Divl.Train will supervise this arrangement and report instances where not practicable to Divisional Headquarters.

A. A. McHardy
Lieut.Colonel,
A.A. & Q.M.G.,
9th (Scottish) Division.

ISSUED at 23/7/16.

Copies to:-	26th Inf.Bde.	9th Div.Train.	G.
	27th Inf.Bde.	9th Signal Coy.	
	S.A.Bde.	A.D.M.S.	
	C.R.A.	A.D.V.S.	
	C.R.E.	A.P.M.	
	9th Seaforth Hrs.	Camp Comdt.	

departure of the train by which his unit will travel, namely, 10.21 a.m. on the 26th inst.,

Loading parties for transport and animals will be detailed by Commanding Officers.

J Mitchell Baker

Major.
Brigade Major.

Brigade HQuarters
24 7 16

C.O. 3rd Regiment SAI

The attached copy of instructions No 3 for move of 9th Division issued by Divisional Headquarters for your information.

Please note particularly paras 3 and 7.

Times of departure of trains will be notified as soon as the Brigadier is advised thereof.

OsC 1st and 2nd SAI will each be prepared to furnish a working party of 50 men at Longpre to comply with para 6 of the attached instructions.

Reference 17/17

Recd 1-30pm 24/7/16

J Mitchell Baker
Major
Brigade Major

24/7/16.

Recd: G.S.J.H. 24/7/16

143

HEADQUARTERS,

1st S. A. INFANTRY BRIGADE.

Officer Commanding,
1st S. A. Infantry.
2nd do do
3rd do do
4th do do
S.A. Bde. L.T.M. Battery.
28th Bde. M.G. Company.

App 155

B.M.12/12. 24th July, 1916.

B.M.12/12 of to-day, the Brigade and attached units will entrain at Longpre as follows:-

Unit.	Time.	Date.
Brigade Headquarters, 28th Bde M.G. Company, and L.T.M. Battery.	11.00 p.m.	25th July.
1st S. A. Infantry.	1.41 a.m.	26th July.
2nd do do	4.51 a.m.	do
3rd do do	7.41 a.m.	do
4th do do	10.21 a.m.	do

Transport (including the supply vehicles) will proceed with units. Loaded supply vehicles will reach units at station of entrainment in sufficient time to entrain with units.

The Officer Commanding, 4th S. A. Infantry, will detail an officer to be attached to the R.T.O., Longpre, during the period of entrainment of the Brigade. This officer will report to the R.T.O. at 8 p.m. to-morrow, 25th inst.,

Billeting officers have proceeded by motor to-day. Officers Commanding Infantry units will each detail a billeting party of 8, and the Officers Commanding M.G. Company and L.T.M. Battery each a billeting party of 2 to proceed by the 7.41 a.m. train to-morrow, 25th inst., from Longpre. These parties will report to the R.T.O. at Longpre, and will be met at the station of detrainment by the officers who have preceded them.

The Officers Commanding, 1st and 2nd S. A. Infantry, will each detail a working party of 50 men, under a senior N.C.O. and a suitable number of other N.C.O's to report to the R.T.O. at Longpre at 4 a.m. to-morrow 25th inst., These Commanding Officers will arrange for working parties of the strength mentioned being at the disposal of the R.T.O. until 7 p.m. on the 25th inst., when the working parties will be relieved by parties of similar strength, to be detailed by the Officers Commanding, 3rd and 4th S. A. Infantry.

The Officer Commanding, 3rd S. A. Infantry, will be responsible that a working party of the strength mentioned is furnished by the unit under his command and is at the disposal of the R.T.O. from 7 p.m. on the 25th inst., until the departure of the train by which his unit will travel, namely, 7.41 a.m. on the 26th inst., and the Officer Commanding, 4th S. A. Infantry, will be responsible that a working party of the strength mentioned is furnished by the unit under his command and is at the disposal of the R.T.O. from 7 p.m. on the 25th inst., until the

144

"A" Form. Army Form C. 2121.

MESSAGES AND SIGNALS. No. of Message..........

Prefix .... Code .... m.	Words	Charge	This message is on a/c of:	Recd. at .... m.
Office of Origin and Service Instructions.	Sent		.... Service.	Date ....
	At .... m.			From ....
	To			
	By		(Signature of "Franking Officer.")	By ....

TO S. Africans

Sender's Number.	Day of Month.	In reply to Number.	AAA
* Pi/203	19th		

The following is circulated for information AAA The 76th Bde. will attack tomorrow at 3.35 AM AAA No troops are to be North of PRINCES ST after 1 AM at which hour bombardment will start AAA All wire is to be removed from the area East of the STRAND from the Point where it joins PRINCES ST and Northwards AAA All ranks are to be warned that other troops will be passing through them during the night AAA For the last 30 minutes of bombardment all Vickers Guns will fire AAA From the hour of attack 53rd Bde. comes under 3rd Division
Acknowledge

From PINE
Place
Time 9.50 pm

The above may be forwarded as now corrected. (Z) [illegible] Capt

Censor. Signature of Addressor or person authorised to telegraph in his name.

* This line should be erased if not required.

225,000. W 14042—M 44. H. W. & V., Ld. 12/15.

To Lt PHILLIPS B.M. 11

You will move forward with your command and endeavour to regain touch with our Brigade in DELVILLE WOOD

You will move with all precautionary measures

When you gain touch with our Brigade in the wood you will place yourself under the senior officer there informing him that the Brigade is being relieved in the wood tonight.

You will endeavour to keep me informed of your progress and movements

of any of our other troops on your right or left

You will enter DELVILLE WOOD by the S.W. corner and move north till you gain touch with our Brigade on the northern edge of the wood.

It is not certain whether or not there are enemy in the wood & your primary duty will be to clear up the situation

[illegible]

18 7.30 pm [illegible]

3rd SAI. 4/5 7-16. relieving XXX Divn

A Co. 4 Platoons in New Trench
1 " " No 1 S Point
1 " " " 5 "
B Co 2 " " " Old Front Line Left on Head St
1 " " No 6 S. Point
1 " " " 4 " (GLATZ)
C Co 2 " " Old Front Line Rt on Head St
1 " " No 2 S. Point
1 " " " 1 " (GLATZ)
D Co 3 " " CASEMENT TRENCH
1 " " ALT TRENCH

Hd Qrs 3 LG & Sigs

✱ = Strong Point No [illegible] MONTAUBAN.
▬ = Platoon.
MG not known
LG = ▬

OLD GERMAN FRONT
GLATZ
DUBLIN
Brickstacks
ALT
CASEMENT
D Co
NEW TRENCH
FAVIERE SUPPORT
FAVIER
OLD BRITISH FRONT TRENCH
HEAD ST
2 Platoons C Co
2 Platoons B Co
BTN HQ
Sig
3 LG

N.
APPROX 1/20000

5.
7.
16.

S. J. Strachan Lt Col
Comdg. 3rd SAI

147

War Diary File

1745 pm. 6-7-16

The attached Sketch and distribution of Battalion for retention

A. W. H. McDonald Capt
a/Adjt 3rd Reg^t S A Infy

148

Urgent

O/c 3rd + 4th Regiment SAI

The O/c 3rd Regt SAI will concentrate his regiment in the area contained ~~almost~~ roughly in 10 a. b. south of a line running east & west through GERMAN'S WOOD (to include the new trench running from the South east corner of that wood & eastwards) 10 c and d and the northern half of 16 a and b. (MONTAUBAN sheet). He will report to Brigade Headquarters as soon as possible his new dispositions.

The O/c 4th SAT will on the withdrawal from CASEMENT trench of the 3rd SAI occupy that trench.

5. 7/16

J Mitchell Baker
Major
Brigade Major

Head Street – No Communication Trenches used as such are to be occupied.

(c) "C" Coy – will withdraw from S.P. Nos 1 and 2. into the Old BRITISH TRENCHES retaining those already occupied with right on HEAD STREET excluding Communication Trenches.

(d) "D" Coy will withdraw from CASEMENT and HALT TRENCHES to old FAVIERE SUPPORT and FIRE TRENCH.

O.C. Companies withdrawing from strong points will hand over same to Regiments occupying the adjacent Trenches.

LEWIS GUNS will be withdrawn with their Companies.

This withdrawal is to be carried out as soon as possible without exposure and only in small parties, well extended.

A.W.H. McDonald Capt.
Adjt 3rd Regt S.A.I.

S E C R E T.

Cy No. 3.

150

1st SOUTH AFRICAN INFNTRY BRIGADE.

OPERATION ORDER No. 43.

In the Field,

6th July, 1916

1. RELIEF. The 1st S. A. Infantry will come out of the front line to-night - with the exception of the strong points in the area at present occupied by that unit - to make room for other troops.

The relief of that portion of the 1st S. A. Infantry in the BRIQUETERIE will take place at 8 p.m.; the remainder of the relief will take place at 10 p.m. On coming out of the front line the 1st S. A. Infantry will be accommodated in portions of the British original front line trenches.

2. OFFICERS TO TAKE OVER NEW TRENCH AREA. The Officer Commanding 1st S. A. Infantry will send whatever number of officers he considers necessary to report to the Staff Captain at the Headquarters of the 2nd S. A. Infantry (CAMBRIDGE COPSE) this afternoon at 5 p.m. in order that they may be shown the trenches to be occupied by their unit to-night. These officers will return to their unit to lead it to its new quarters.

3. STRONG POINTS TO REMAIN GARRISONED. The Officer Commanding 1st S. A. Infantry will leave a garrison of one platoon in each of these strong ponits within the area now occupied by him.

Machine Guns at present in these strong points will also be left there.

4. NEW FRONT LINE OF S. A. BRIGADE. On the withdrawal from the front line of the 1st S. A. Infantry the South African Brigade will hold the line from the point on the BRIQUETERIE-MONTAUBAN Road, where there is a screen. This point is at the end of the hedge running, roughly, East and West, and from the other end of which a communication trench runs back to GLATZ REDOUBT, as shown in sketch plan attached.

The 4th S. A. Infantry will hold the line from that point (inclusive of the communication trench from the hedge to GLATZ REDOUBT) to the left of the French.

5. COMPLETION OF RELIEF. The Officer Commanding 1st S. A. Infantry will report to Brigade Headquarters

1. Completion of relief.
2. When his unit has arrived at its new quarters, stating where he has taken up his Headquarters.

6. TOOLS. All tools belonging to the Brigade now on charge to the 1st S. A. Infantry will be brought out of the trenches, excepting such as may be required to be left in the strong points. Tools which were drawn from the Brigade will be collected and dumped at A.4.c.1.9. by 8 p.m. and a guard placed over them. This point is where the MONTAUBAN-MARICOURT Road cuts GLATZ REDOUBT. They will be removed from there to the Brigade Dump by the Brigade Transport Officer.

7. STORES. Receipts for stores, etc., handed over will be obtained in duplicate in the usual way.

RATION RENDEZVOUS. The rendezvous for rations for the 1st S. A.

151

War Diary

10/45 Am. B/110

To O/C A Coy 6-7-16
B "
C "
D "
L.G.O "

MOVE

1. Company Commanders will withdraw their Companies to fresh positions as hereunder stated in area allotted to the Battalion

(a) "A" Coy will maintain NEW TRENCH and No (1) FAVIER. Strong POINT but will withdraw No 5 Strong POINT
"A" Coy will take over from "B" Coy No 6. S.P. at A.10.a 5.3

(b) 'B' Company will withdraw from No 4 and No 6. S. Points and Concentrate in the Old BRITISH TRENCHES including those already occupied with their LEFT on HEAD STREET.

Infantry to-night will be at FOUR WILLOWS, East of MACHINE GUN WOOD.

9. BRIGADE HEADQUARTERS. Brigade Headquarters is now in "B" COPSE, South of PERONNE Road.

Please acknowledge.

Jmitchell Baker
Major.
Brigade Major.

Copy No.	To	Copy No.	To
1	1st S. A. Infantry.	11	O.C. Bearer Sect.
2.	2nd do do	12	9th Division.
×3	3rd do do	13	52nd Brigade, R.F.A.
4	4th do do	14	G.O.C.
5	64th Field Coy. R.E.	15	Brigade Major.
6	O.C. "B" Coy. 9th S.H.	16	Staff Captain.
7	O.C. 28th Bde. M.G. Coy.	17	Office Copy.
8	O.C. Bde. L.T.M. Batty.	18	War Diary.
9	O.C. Bde. Signal Section.	19	21st Inf. Brigade.
10	107th Coy. A. S. C.	20	27th do do

Recd 5/25pm

Issued by Orderly at ...3. 30 pm...

HEADQUARTERS.

1st S. A. INFANTRY BRIGADE. 153

3rd S A Infantry

....

App 149

OPERATION ORDER No.43.

With reference to above, the whole arrangements are postponed for 24 hours.

The Order will come into force to-morrow, 7th inst., and will be carried out without further orders, unless further postponement is advised.

Recd 8pm

J Mitchell Baker
Major.
Brigade Major.

To OC 3 S.A.I.

X 35/35

Division report it is believed that enemy are attacking French on our right. Be prepared please

6.7.16
7.40pm

J Mitchell Baker Major
BM 1 Bgde

154

Issued at 3/20

To B112

O/Commdg [illegible] Coy 6-7-16

B [illegible]

C " [illegible]

Working Party

The O/Commdg "B" and "C" Companies will each furnish a platoon of not less than 40 men to report to O/C 4th Regt at 9 pm today for work in improving and completing Fire Trench leading from DUBLIN TRENCH to BRIQUETERIE

A. McDonald
Capt
Adjt
3rd Regt S A Infy

for signature by C/C.

155

"A" Form. Army Form C. 2121.

MESSAGES AND SIGNALS. No. of Message..........

Prefix..........Code..........m. | Words | Charge | *This message is on a/c of:* ....*Service.* (Signature of "Franking Officer.") | Recd. at..........m. Date.......... From.......... By..........

Office of Origin and Service Instructions.

Sent At..........m. To.......... By..........

TO O/C A.B.C.D Coy B Coy
WALTER C [illegible]

Sender's Number.	Day of Month.	In reply to Number.	AAA
* C 5	fifth		

Companies will furnish working parties today report as hereunder but it is to be clearly understood that Platoons must not be taken from Strong Points where work must be carried on AAA Detail "A" Coy will find 1 Platoon for carrying at A 10. C. 2.7 to report at 9.30 pm No tools required AAA B Coy will detail one platoon to report for work on Fire Trench from Point "1" A 10. c. 2.7 at 9.30 pm D Company will furnish to report same point one platoon (both platoons to carry proportion 2 shovels to one pick AAA C Coy to find 2 Platoons to report for work on H. Support at A16. a. 2.5 at 9 pm tools as above to be obtained from dump: at

From Adjutant
Place A16.
Time 3/30 pm

The above may be forwarded as now corrected. (Z) [signature]

Censor. Signature of Addressor or person authorised to telegraph in his name.

* This line should be erased if not required.

225,000. W 14042—M 44. H. W & V., Ld. 12/15.

All Companies will take tools with Coy

156

War Diary

"C" Form.

Army Form C. 2121

MESSAGES AND SIGNALS

July 5th

No. of Message

Prefix Code m. | Words | Charge | This message is on a/c of: | Recd. at m.

Office of Origin and Service Instructions.

Sent At m. To By 11.15 PM

Urgent

(Signature of "Franking Officer.")

Date

From

By

TO O.C. 3rd S.A.I.

Sender's Number.	Day of Month	In reply to Number	AAA
*			

Please detail working parties as under to [illegible] meet an R.E. Officer at point where Maricourt–Montauban road crosses German front line at 10.30 pm tonight.

(1) 1 Company to work on partly constructed fire trench running from Dublin Trench towards Briqueterie

(2) 2 Platoons to work on "H" Strong Point

These parties are to be provided with tools, which are to be drawn from Brigade Dump at A.16.a.4.8.

From

Place

The above may be forwarded as now corrected. (Z)

Censor. Signature of Addressor or person authorised to telegraph in his name.

* This line should be erased if not required.

W14069—M44. 250,000 Pads. 12/15. S. & J. C. & S.

157

"C" Form (Original).

MESSAGES AND SIGNALS.

Army Form C. 2123.
(In books of 50's in duplicate.)
No. of Message

Prefix ... Code ... Words ... Received ... From ... By ...
Charges to collect
Service Instructions. Vc
Sent, or sent out: At ... m. To ... By ...
Office Stamp.

Handed in at ... Office 8.20a m. Received 8.32a m.

TO Walter

*Sender's Number	Day of Month	In reply to Number	AAA
BM 61	6th		

Please send out at once two platoons of not less than 40 men each to report to O C 4th Regt for work in improving and completing the fire trench leading from DUBLIN Trench to BRIQUETERIE aaa Two platoons similar strength to parade at 9 pm today for same work aaa acknowledge addsd WALTER repeated JOHN for information

Detailed B Coy C Coy 8/30 9/30

FROM
PLACE & TIME Venice 8.20 am

* This line should be erased if not required.

Wt. 492—M437 530,000 Pads. H W V 5/16 Forms C.2123.

3/10 pm

HEADQUARTERS,

1st S. A. INFANTRY BRIGADE.

Officer Commanding,
1st S. A. Infantry.
3rd do do
4th do do
64th Field Coy. R.E. (for information).

App 148

158

BM.47/28/19/ 5th July, 1916.

Working parties, under R.E., will be detailed by regiments as follows:-

1st REGIMENT.

(a) For work on Strong Point "B" and Communication Trench to West. Tools to be taken - 2 shovels to one pick.
2 platoons, From 2 p.m. to 8 p.m.
2 platoons, " 9 p.m. to 2 a.m.

(b) For work on Point "C". Tools as above.
1 platoon, From 2 p.m. to 8 p.m.
1 platoon, " 9 p.m. to 2 a.m.

(c) Carrying for R.E., at A.10.c.2.7. Will be met by representative of R.E., there. No tools required.
2 platoons, At 9 p.m.

3 rd REGIMENT.

B (a) For work on Communication Trench, GLATZ REDOUBT, N.E. corner towrds BRIQUETERIE. Tools to be taken - 2 shovels to 1 pick.
1 platoon, At 2 p.m.

(b) For work on Fire Trench from Point "I", A.10.c.2.7. Tools as above.
2 platoons, At 9.30 p.m.

"A" For Carrying at A.10.c.2.7. No tools required.
1 platoon, rendezvous At 9.30 p.m.

(c) For work on "H" Support at A.12.a.2.5. Tools as above.
2 platoons, At 9 p.m.

4th REGIMENT.

(a) For work on GLATZ REDOUBT. Tools to be taken - 2 shovels to 1 pick.
2 platoons, From 2 p.m. to 8 p.m.
2 platoons, " 9 p.m. to 2 a.m.

(b) Forework on Strong Point, corner of Casement Trench and and Glatz Trench. Tools as above.
1 platoon, From 2 p.m. to 8 p.m.
* 1 platoon, " 9 p.m. to 2 a.m.
(* To be engaged on wiring - no tools required).

(c) For work on Strong Point "E". Tools as above.
1 platoon, From 2 p.m. to 8 p.m.
1 platoon, " 9 p.m. to 2 a.m.

Acknowledged 5/7/16
4/15/5.

Please acknowledge

[signature]
Lieut.
for Brigade Major.

Issued 3/30 pm

2 platoons 9pm C. Coy A.16.a.2/5
1 Platoon 9/30 B "
" " 9/30 A "

159

Issued 3/40 pm. CB/109
4.7.16

To O/C Hq Coy A.P.
A "
B "RFA"
C "RMA"
D "LWT"

Transport Notification has been received from Brigade Hd Qrs that Batt. Transport will be at a point A 20. B 9. 7 near PERONNE AVENUE at 7. 30 pm tonight. Companies will detail an offloading party each of sufficient NCOs and men to carry Company Rations to billets. An Officer of D Coy will be detailed to accompany the party who will report to Batt. Hd Qrs on completion of the duty.

A. McDonald Capt.
3rd Reg. S A I. Adjt.

160

Issued at 3/5 PM. B/105
4-7-16

To O/C "A" Coy
3rd Regt CARNOY

1 Move The Battalion has received orders to move to MARICOURT and will leave by 4.30 pm today.
You will return to COPSE VALLEY and pick up all R.E. Stores, Etc, and will move off to join Battalion via STANLEY AVENUE.
The Battalion will be billeted in Maricourt and Great Coats should be taken.
A Regimental Dump has been organised to remain at COPSE VALLEY under a guard. And all surplus Equipment Etc. must be dumped under their charge.

[illegible] Capt
3rd Regt S.A.I.

161

Urgent

HEADQUARTERS,

1st S. A. INFANTRY BRIGADE,

Officer Commanding,
3rd S. A. Infantry.

B.M.X24/42. 4th July, 1916.

Your Battalion will move via ~~SUPPORT TRENCH~~ STANLEY AVENUE to MARICOURT this afternoon. Billeting party to be at the entrance to MARICOURT (22.a.1.5.) at 3.30 p.m., where it will be met by an officer detailed by the 89th Brigade.

Your Battalion will be billeted in MARICOURT, and must be clear of COPSE VALLEY - excepting, possibly, the one company now at CARNOY - by 5.30 p.m. The above will be included in an Operation Order to be issued later.

The Brigade Transport Officer will be round to see you regarding transport arrangements which may be possible.

[signature]
Major.
Brigade Major

Head more

161

162

War Diary

War Diary. Issued at 2/55 pm B 107

4-7-16

To

O/C A Coy

B " [illegible]

C " [illegible]

D " [illegible]

HQ " [illegible]

1 MOVE. A billetting party of 2 Officers with 2 other ranks from each Company to parade at Bn Head Qrs at ~~[illegible]~~ once.

B Coy Lieut. Rose

C " " Thompson

The Billetting party to be at the entrance to MARICOURT 22. a. 1. 5.) at 3/30 pm where it will be met by an Officer detailed by the 89th Brigade.

A W McDonald Capt
Adjt
3rd Reg SA Infty

163

The cookers and water carts of the 1st and 4th S. A. Infantry will be sent to 16.a.centre, North of MARICOURT, where Carriers from these units will be provided to carry forward the dixies from the cookers - the water carts being retained at the Bde. Forward Dump.

3. BRIGADE DUMP. The Brigade Dump will be North of MARICOURT at 16.a.4.8.

4. TOOLS. The regimental tools (mobilisation stores) at present in the Brigade Dump will be sent up to the 2nd and 3rd S. A. Inf. under Brigade arrangements. These tools will be off-loaded and the wagons sent back to the First Line Transport.

The regimental tools (mobilisation stores) of the 1st and 4th S. A. Infantry will be taken under Brigade arrangements to North of MARICOURT at 16.a.centre, where the tools will be taken over by regiments.

5. BRIGADE HEADQUARTERS. Brigade Headquarters will be North of COPSE "C", approximately 21.b.1.4.

6. COMPLETION OF RELIEF & UNIT HEADQUARTERS. Officers Commanding units will report without delay when they have taken over, and where they have taken up their Headquarters.

7. COMMAND. On completion of relief, the command of the portion of the line at present held by the 89th Brigade and of the Trench Area at present occupied by the 21st Brigade will pass to the G.O.C., South African Brigade.

8. DIVISIONAL RESERVE. The 3rd S. A. Infantry will be in Divisional Reserve.

9. BATTALIONS IN RESERVE. The Officers Commanding 2nd and 3rd S. A. Inf. will reconnoitre routes to the front line held by both the 1st and 4th S. A. Infantry, so as to be able to lead their commands to reinforce any part of the line.

Please acknowledge.

[signature]
Major.
Brigade Major.

Copy No.	To	Copy No.	To
1	to 1st S. A. Inf.	10	to 107th Coy. A.S.C.
2	2nd do	11	O.C. Bearer Sect. Fd. Am
X 3	3rd do	12	9th Division.
4	4th do	13	52nd Brigade, R.F.A.
5	64th Field Coy. R.E.	14	G. O. C.
6	O.C. "B" Coy. 9th S.H.	15	Brigade Major.
7	O.C. 28th Bde. M.G. Coy.	16	Staff Captain.
8	O.C. Bde. L.T.M. Batty.	17	Office Copy.
9	O.C. Bde. Signal Sect.,	18	War Diary.
		19	21st Inf. Brigade.
		20	89th Inf. Brigade.
		21	26th Inf. Brigade.

Recd 8/45 PM

Issued by Orderly at.................

SECRET. 147 3. Copy No. 3....

164

1st SOUTH AFRICAN INFANTRY BRIGADE.

OPERATION ORDERS No. 42.

App 147

In the Field,

4th July, 1916.

1. MOVE. The 1st S. A. Infantry Brigade will relieve the 21st and 89th Brigades to-day, as follows:-

2nd S. A. Infantry will relieve the 21st Brigade in the Trench Area in the vicinity of TALUS BOISE. This Battalion will move by platoons under regimental arrangements, but must be clear of BILLON VALLEY by 6 p.m.. An officer detailed by the 21st Brigade will meet the O.C. 2nd S. A. Infantry at the North West corner of CAMBRIDGE COPSE at 5 p.m. An officer will be detailed by the O.C. 2nd S.A. Infantry to report to the Headquarters of the 21st Brigade in COPSE "B" at 4 p.m. to take over stores, etc.,

3rd S. A. Infantry will relieve that portion of the 89th Brigade at present quartered in MARICOURT. This Battalion will move by platoons under regimental arrangements, but must be clear of COPSE VALLEY by 5.30 p.m.

Billeting party from 3rd S. A. Infantry will be met by an officer of the 89th Brigade at the entrance to MARICOURT (22.a.1.5.) at 3.30 p.m.

1st and 4th S. A. Infantry will relieve to-night the units of the 89 th Brigade in the line.

These Battalions will move by platoons under regimental arrangements, but must not cross the PERONNE ROAD before 9.30 p.m. They must be clear of their present billeting areas by 10.30 p.m.

The 64th Field Coy, R.E., "B" Coy, 9th Seaforths, 28th Brigade M.G. Coy, Brigade L.T.M. Battery and Bearer Section, S.A.F.A. will each move under the orders of its Commanding Officer, and, with the exception of the Bearer Section, will move into portions of the line. They will send an officer to Brigade Headquarters to receive information regarding these portions.

The Bearer Section will be accomodated in MARICOURT, and an officer will report at Brigade Headquarters for instructio-ns.

2. TRANSPORT. The Brigade Transport Officer will arrange for regimental transport to be sent to each unit this afternoon. The Officers Commanding 2nd and 3rd S. A. Infantry will arrange for guides to meet their transport on the BRONFAY FARM - MARICOURT Road at point 20.b.7.7. at 7.30 this evening.
The Officers Commanding 1st and 4th S. A. Infantry and the O.C. L.T.M. Battery will arrange for the necessary Carriers to meet their transport on the MONTAUBAN Road, North of MARICOURT, at 16.a. centre, at 11 p.m.

The transport of the 64th Field Coy. R.E., and 28th Bde. M.G. Coy. will move under orders of the Officers Commanding these units, but must not proceed beyond MARICOURT before dark.

Cookers, water carts, mess cart and Maltese cart of the 2nd and 3rd S. A. Infantry will be sent to their respective units.

146
165

B.M.9
3.7.1916
App 146

O.C.
3rd S.A.I.

A Working Party of one Company is required for work on the road at CARNOY, to report ~~[illegible]~~ tomorrow to

Lieut. Anderson
'B' Coy 9th Seaforths
R.E. Dump. CARNOY.

at 8 a.m.

Please detail this Company from the unit under your command and report to this office their ~~[illegible]~~ departure tomorrow morning.

Haversack ~~[illegible]~~ rations should be taken.

J Mitchell Baker
Major
Bde Major.

166

War Diary

Issued at 9.30 PM

B 107.

3-7-16

To O/C. 'A' Coy.

WORKING PARTY.

In Compliance with Brigade Instructions BMq of this date your Company is detailed as a working party to turn out as strong as possible to work on the road at CARNOY to report tomorrow to Lieut. Anderson B Coy. 9th Seaforths R.E. Dump CARNOY at 8 am. ~~[illegible]~~ 4.7.16.

HAVERSACK Rations to be carried.

The Company to parade under Company arrangements in Full Marching Order to report at time stated.

Greatcoats to be rolled in bundles of 12 and left at Company Dump.

[illegible]

A. McDonald
Capt.
Adjt 9 SHS Bn

167

Amount of Trench accommodation which will be allotted to Companies

A. McDonald
Captn
3rd Reg S A Inf Bn

168

Re 17/7/

SECRET.

B.M. 36.

13th July 1916

Officer Commanding
3rd S.A. Infantry.

The 9th Division will take part in an attack on the enemy's second line tomorrow at 3.25 am.

The S.A. Brigade is in reserve and all units must be ready to move any time after the hour mentioned. It must be understood, however, that in the case of emergency they may be called on during the night at short notice, and arrangements must be made accordingly.

J. Mitchell Baker
Major
Bde Major.

114

169

"A" Form.

Army Form C. 2121.

MESSAGES AND SIGNALS.

No. of Message

Prefix ...... Code ...... m.	Words	Charge	This message is on a/c of:	Recd. at ...... m.
Office of Origin and Service Instructions.	Sent		...... Service.	Date
	At ...... m.			From
	To			
	By		(Signature of "Franking Officer.")	By

TO { VENICE

Sender's Number.	Day of Month	In reply to Number	
* 115	Thirteenth		AAA

Battalion Head Quarters at
Pumping Station TALUS BOIS aaa
will you issue instructions for
Transport to bring rations to this
point aaa [illegible] [illegible]
Battalion now in new area

From WALTER
Place TALUS BOIS. H.Q.
Time 7-15 pm

The above may be forwarded as now corrected. (Z) [illegible signature] Captn

Censor. Signature of Addressor or person authorised to telegraph in his name.

* This line should be erased if not required.

(774-5) —McC. & Co. Ltd., London.— W 1789/1402. 150,000. 8/15. Forms C 2121/10.

Y 9th

[illegible] to [illegible] under
Company arrangements from
R.E. Dump at A.16.a.4.6

Captain McLachlan will
report to 13th [illegible]
at Bgd Head Quarters at
1 am to receive definite
orders of the work to be
performed

A.H. [illegible]
Capt.
3rd Regt [illegible]

152
171

1. 1 98/2 Issued 5/10
No. 076 A Coy A Coy 8UV D 118
B " B " ANV 13. 7. 16
~~C~~
~~D~~
HQ
IGO
T/O
M/O

App 152

1. MOVE The Battalion will move in accordance with Brigade Instructions and take over position West of TALUS BOISE.
Companies will move off as follows commencing 5/30 pm
~~[illegible]~~
C Coy
Head Quarters
B Coy
A "
D "

2. Grenades 4 Grenades per Company will report at Btn Head Qrs 5/30 pm

3 Cover Companies will move from present area - as far as possible under cover to TALUS BOISE. It is understood there is a certain

172

Issued at 7 am R[illegible]

To O/C B Coy 12.7.16
" " C "

WORKING PARTY

The O/C [illegible] "B" and "C" Companies will find working party as [illegible] [illegible] [illegible] [illegible] [illegible] [illegible] [illegible] [illegible] [illegible] to a [illegible] taken [illegible] R.E. [illegible] [illegible] [illegible] [illegible] [illegible] [illegible] [illegible] [illegible] [illegible] [illegible] [illegible] to be not less than 350 all ranks

II Carriers 1 Platoon of each Company to be detailed as Carrier Platoons under the R E

(3). Tools. All Company Picks & Shovels to be taken. [illegible] Carrier Platoons will not carry tools but the remainder [illegible] [illegible] each carry 1 Shovel per man & a pick [illegible] every [illegible] [illegible]

Any Tools required to Comp[illegible]

173

(In pads of 50 dupls.) "C" Form (Duplicate). Army Form C. 2123.

MESSAGES AND SIGNALS. No. of Message

Recd 7.10pm 92 VC Kapel

Charges to Pay. £ s. d.

Office Stamp. 12/7/16

Service Instructions. Priority

Handed in at VC Office 6.50p m. Received 7.0p m.

TO WALTER Wurdlary

Sender's Number	Day of Month	In reply to Number	AAA
BM 171	12.7.16		

Two companies approximately 350 other ranks with officers will report to engineer officers at A4C14 at 9.30 tonight aaa Two platoons will be carrying material and will therefore NOT carry tools aaa remainder of the two companies will carry a shovel per man and a pick for every two men aaa Any tools required by you in addition to what you have should be drawn now from engineer Dump at A16A4.6 aaa Officer to Command party should report here as

FROM VENICE

TIME

51. 75,000 Pads. McC. & Co., Ltd., London. 1/16. Forms/C.2123.

151

174

"A" Form.

Army Form C. 2121.

MESSAGES AND SIGNALS.

No. of Message ....

Prefix .... Code .... m.

Office of Origin and Service Instructions.

Words | Charge

This message is on a/c of: .... Service.

(Signature of "Franking Officer.")

Sent
At .... m.
To ....
By ....

Recd. at .... m.
Date ....
From ....
By ....

TO [illegible]

Sender's Number. | Day of Month. | In reply to Number. | AAA

Brigade Headquarters notify Germans again in occupation of Trones Wood aaa You are to hold yourself and Company [illegible] to reinforce [illegible] at Bernafay Wood and [illegible] Artillery [illegible] to signal [illegible] you move forward aaa the signal [illegible] Bernafay [illegible] 2 [illegible] rockets meaning that reinforcements [illegible] required and on which signal you must act aaa 5 red rockets if sent up means Artillery barrage. [illegible] may [illegible] Keen look out and must be kept / acknowledge

x for you to reinforce

From Adjutant WALTER

Place [illegible] ESIA TRENCH

Time 12.35 pm 11/12

The above may be forwarded as now corrected.

(Z)

Censor.

Signature of Addressor or person authorised to telegraph in his name.

* This line should be erased if not required.

000 W 14042—M 44. H. W. & V., Ld. 12/15.

175

"C" Form (Duplicate). Army Form C. 2123.

MESSAGES AND SIGNALS. No. of Message

Charges to Pay.	Office Stamp.
£ s. d.	

Service Instructions.

Handed in at Office m. Received m.

(2)

TO

Sender's Number	Day of Month	In reply to Number	AAA

soon as possible for instruct[illegible]

FROM Venace

PLACE & TIME 6. 25 pm

W 15680—M 151 75,000 Pads. H & S 2/16 Forms/C.2123. (5656)

176

War Diary

HEADQUARTERS,

1st S. A. INFANTRY BRIGADE.

Officer Commanding,
3rd S. A. infantry.

B.M.X31/85. 9th July, 1916.

You will be ready with your Battalion to move into the area of which you were advised yesterday, i.e., to the North West of your present lines, any time after 9.30 to-night, when you will be relieved by a Battalion of the 89th Brigade.

Please have guides at the corner of NAPIER'S REDOUBT (where the main MARICOURT Road cuts the PERONNE Road) at 9.30 p.m.

Please report when your Battalion is in its new camping site, and the map reference of your Headquarters.

Acknowledge, please.

Received.

Recd. 8/5 pm

Major.
Brigade Major

176

177
3

Copy No........

[S.] AFRICAN INFANTRY BRIGADE

[OP]ERATION ORDER No. 46.

In the Field,
10th July 1916

[1.] RELIEF. The O.C.4th S.A.I. will detail two Companies to relieve the 2nd S.A.I. to-night in BERNAFAY WOOD. Relief to commence at 10.pm.
Headquarters,4th S.A.I. to take over from Headquarters, 2nd S.A.I.

O.C., 28th M.G.Company will detail two machine guns with their teams and two fresh teams to replace those in BERNAFAY WOOD to report to the O.C., 4th S.A.I., at Headquarters of the 4th S.A.I., GLATZ REDOUBT at 9.pm.
These 4 machine guns will be disposed as ordered by the O.C., 4th S.A.I.
Separate orders will be issued to the O.C., 4th S.A.I., regarding his dispositions in BERNAFAY WOOD and the holding of LONGUEVAL ALLEY.

The 2nd and 4th S.A.I., will move to and from BERNAFAY WOOD via MONTAUBAN-MARICOURT ROAD and CHIMNEY TRENCH VALLEY to avoid clashing with the reliefs which are taking place of troops of the 30th Division.

The 2nd S.A.I., will return to their original Camping site in the vicinity of CAMBRIDGE COPSE.

2. MOVES. Those portion of the S.A.Brigade which are at present outside the S.A.Brigade area will move into that area to-night.

The remainder of the 4th S.A.I., will occupy that portion of the S.A.I. Brigade area within NORD and TRAIN ALLEYS (both inclusive).

The O.C. 4th S.A.I., will leave one Company in DUBLIN ALLEY and down DUBLIN TRENCH connecting with the left of the French until relieved by 30th Division troops. This relief will probably take place about midnight.

The O.C.,3rd S.A.I., will detail a garrison for GLATZ REDOUBT and will take over from the O.C., 1st S.A.I., the strong points within the S.A.Brigade area.
Four guides from the 1st S.A.I., will report to the O.C. 3rd S.A.I. at 9 o'clock to-night where the MONTAUBAN-MARICOURT Road cuts the GLATZ REDOUBT.

Recd 12/B.G.Bn
11/7/16

[signature]
Major.
Brigade Major

178

The dividing line between the [illegible] Div

areas will be
a line from Trench junction S.23.c.27.1. [illegible]
Corner of orchard S.28.c.7.6 – SE Corner of
orchard S.28.c.3.3. Railway line A.4.a.0.6
thence along Railway to A.14.b.6.6 thence
Southwards to the [illegible] Rd at A.14.d.4.1

The [illegible] Inf Bde will be prepared to relieve
the 30th Division in the Northern portion of
Trones Wood as soon as possible after its occupation
by the 30th Division on receipt of orders which
will be issued later.

179

"C" Form (Duplicate). Army Form C. 2123.

MESSAGES AND SIGNALS. No. of Message

Ia 63 IC

Service Instructions.

Charges to Pay. £ s. d.

Office Stamp.

Handed in at IC Office 11-5 m. Received 11-10 pm.

TO Walter urgent

Sender's Number	Day of Month	In reply to Number	AAA
BM 136	9.7.16		

You will hold your regiment in readiness to take over the trenches at present held by JOHN aaa You will carry out the move already ordered however aaa JOHNS trenches are (1) from BRIQUETERIE to DUBLIN TRENCH which is a new trench called DUBLIN ALLEY (2) DUBLIN TRENCH (3) GLATZ REDOUBT (4) GLATZ ALLEY aaa acknowledge

Issued 11.30 pm ack

FROM Venice

PLACE & TIME

(25696) M.R.Co.,Ltd. Wt.W.4303/2049. 50,000 Pads -6/15. Forms/C.2123.

SA Bde H.Q.

8th July 1916

O/C 3rd & 4th SAI

180

Recd/ 4.15

The 30th Division will relieve the 3rd & 4th SAI in the areas at present occupied by them as early as possible after operations today.

These units will therefore be ready to move at shortest notice.

The area into which the 4th SAI will move includes NORD ALLEY and GLATZ REDOUBT & the area to the west of these trenches as far as the Railway line which is the western boundary of this Brigade Area.

The area which the 3rd SAI will move into is bounded as follows:- on the north by a line drawn from the Southern point of GLATZ REDOUBT due west to the Railway. On the west by the Railway, on the south east by a line from Breslau point to the point where SILESIA trench cuts the MONTAUBAN-MARICOURT road, & on the east by the MONTAUBAN-MARICOURT Road.

Some portions of units will undoubtedly have to bivouac in the open as it is unlikely that there will be sufficient trench accommodation for all.

Mr Pirie detailed — Os C. 3rd & 4th SAI will send representatives now to select the places within the areas defined above in which they will place their units.

done — A map shewing the areas referred to above is being sent by ~~Runner~~ Bearer for perusal by Commanding Officers. The map should be returned by the Runner. Battalion Commanders will report as soon as possible where they have taken up their Headquarters.

J. Mitchell Baker
Major
Brigade Major

War Diary

SECRET. Copy No. 3

181

1st SOUTH AFRICAN INFANTRY BRIGADE.

OPERATION ORDER No.44.

In the Field,
8th July 1916.

1. RELIEF. The Headquarters and two Companies of the 2nd S.A. Infantry, with two Machine Guns with teams to be detailed by the O.C., 28th Brigade M.G.Company, will relieve portions of the 12th Royal Scots and 6th K.O.S.Borderers this afternoon in BERNAFAY WOOD.

2. GUIDES. The 27th Infantry Brigade will arrange for guides to be at the junction of CHIMNEY TRENCH and NORD ALLEY at 3.pm. to lead above units to positions.

3. REPORTS. Situation reports will be sent to Brigade Headquarters every clock half hour after position is taken over.
Completion of relief to be reported to Brigade Headquarters, at the same time giving map reference of Battalion Headquarters.

4. BATTALION HEADQUARTERS. The Headquarters of the 2nd S.A.Infantry will take over the Headquarters of the 12th Royal Scots.

Please acknowledge.

J Mitchell Baker
Major.
Brigade Major.

Copy No.	to	Copy No.	to
1	1st S.A.Inf.	11	Bearer Coy. S.A.F.A.
2	2nd -do-	12	9th Division
3	3rd -do-	13	52nd Brigade R.F.A.
4	4th -do-	14	G.O.C.
5	64th Field Co.R.E.,	15	Brigade Major
6	"B" Co. 9th Seaforths	16	Staff Captain
7	28th Bde.M.G.Coy.	17	Office Copy
8	BDe. L.T.M.Battery	18	War Diary
9	Brigade Signal Section	19	27th Inf.Brigade
10	107th Co. A.S.C.,	20	

Issued by Orderly at 2.15 pm

Recd 4/55 PM.

182

Com memo 12-45 am

Have occupied Glatz Redoubt + Glatz Alley

Signature LW Tomlinson Capt

No. 13 Date 9-7-16

From OC D Coy To Adjt

Place FAVIERE Place A16

Despatch h. 2 m. 30 a.M Receipt h. m. M

night
Issued 12/25 Am 8th and 9th

To 96 D 115

D Coy.

WALTER.

1. MOVE

Enemy heavily Counter attacking TRONES WOOD
You will send at once 2 Platoons to relieve JOHN in GLATZ ALLEY and 2 Platoons to GLATZ Redoubt and report to John
You will move forward to effect this relief at once and report when completed

A. W. Hill Ingals Capt.
Adjt 3rd Regt S A Infty

183

150

184

Issued 2pm D114
8/7/16

96

A Coy

WORKING PARTY App 150

Please detail a working party of one Platoon to Rendezvous at 3pm to day at A 10 C 2.7.
No Tools to be taken.
RE representative will meet party who will probably be out till midnight.

AWHMcDonald Captn
Adjt 3 Regt SAI

185

(In pads of 50 dupls.) "C" Form (Duplicate). Army Form C. 2123.

MESSAGES AND SIGNALS.

No. of Message

Charges to Pay. £

Office Stamp. 8.VII.16

Service Instructions.

Handed in at ... Office ... m. Received ... m.

TO WALTER — War Diary

Sender's Number	Day of Month	In reply to Number	AAA
B.O. 109	8.7.16		

Enemy heavily counter attacking TRONES WOOD aaa Send at once two platoons to relieve JOHN in GLATZ ALLEY and two platoons to GLATZ REDOUBT aaa Report to JOHN aaa Have remainder your Regt ready to move at short notice addressed WALTER repeated JOHN

Recd 12/25 am See D 115

D Company

FROM VENICE

PLACE & TIME 11.45 am to O.C. Company

W 15660 M/151. 75,000 Pads. McC. & Co., Ltd., London. 1/16. Forms/C.2123.

186

A Coy. 2 Platoons in NEW TRENCH
1 " in No 1 Strong Point.
1 " " No 5 Strong Point.

B Coy. 2 Platoons in old Front line with left on HEAD ST.
1 Platoon in No 6 Strong Point
1 Platoon in No 4 Strong Point GLATZ

C Coy. 2 Platoons in old Front Line with Right on HEAD ST.
1 Platoon in No 2 Strong Point
1 Platoon in No 1 S.P. GLATZ

D Coy. 3 Platoons in CASEMENT TRENCH
1 " in ALT TRENCH.

49

No. Date 1-7-16 Time 9.15 am Place

To Place **App 144**

Operation orders No 40

1 Readiness to move. All details will be confined to their own unit lines, & Units will be ready to move at 10 minutes notice. Transport does not move with unit. It is not expected however that the Brigade will be required to move today.

2 Reports & Messages. Unless a name is actually shown on the Montauban 1/20 000 sheet [illegible] all reference to positions & trenches will be described by Co-ordinates.

3 Inspection of Camping Sites. O.C. Inf Units will detail their Q master & M.O. to inspect Camping sites which have been occupied by their unit. A written report signed by these two officers will be forwarded in each instance to Bgde H.Q. O.C. other units in the Brigade will arrange for their Camping sites to be [illegible] inspected by an

From 35

No. Date Time Place

To Place

an officer & written written report to Bgde HQ in each instance.

4 Army Commanders Message. In wishing all Ranks Good Luck the A.C. desires to impress on all Inf Units the supreme importance of helping one another, & holding on tight to every yard of ground gained. The accurate sustained fire of the Artillery during the Bombardment should greatly assist the task of the Inf.

Intelligence.

Our Troops reported in Dublin Trench, Dublin Redoubt, [illegible] Trench, Glatz Redoubt, Pommiers Trench. [illegible] have retaken [illegible] Farm (Verdun)

[illegible]

From 36

144

187

188

Appx 143

Urgent BM2

To O.C. 1st S.A.I.
2nd ..
3rd ..

War Diary

The following working parties will be detailed as stated

Unit and strength	To report to	Hour to report	Will be kept for
(1st S.A.I.) 2 NCO 40 men	Sgt. FRASER, 9th SEAFORTH'S at BRONFAY FARM	as early as possible tonight	6 hours
(2nd S.A.I.) — do —	— do —	8 am 2nd inst	— do —
(3rd S.A.I.) — do	— do — left at 1pm	2 pm 2nd inst	— do —

Please report to Bde. Hq. the departure of the party detailed by 9pm.

1. 7. 16, 7pm

J Mitchell Baker Major
Bde Major

9D

189

3rd South African Regiment

AUUGST

1 9 1)6

==========================

Instructions regarding War Diaries and Intelligence Summaries are contained in F. S. Regs., Part II. and the Staff Manual respectively. Title Pages will be prepared in manuscript.

No 33

WAR DIARY
or
~~INTELLIGENCE SUMMARY~~
(Erase heading not required.)

Army Form C. 2118.

3RD S. A. INF (TRANSVAAL R...)

Vol. 5

Place	Date 1916	Hour	Summary of Events and Information	Remarks and references to Appendices
~~Aug~~ FRESNICOURT	Aug 1		In Billets and HUTS. Training under Company arrangements, no area available for Battalion training. Periodical inspection of Battalion by O.C. On 5th Aug 1916, Battalion marched to field NE of FREVILLIERS where it was inspected - together with other battalions of the South African Brigade - by Commander of 1st Army Corps.	
do	Aug 13th			
do	Aug 13th		Received B.O.O. No 49. (attached)	App 158
do	14th		Training under Company arrangements. Inspection by O.C.	
do	15th		Issued Battalion Move Order to GUOY SERVINS (attached)	App 159
-		4 pm	Vacated FRESNICOURT.	
GUOY SERVINS	-	6 pm	Arrived GUOY SERVINS and occupied billets. Training under Company arrangements. Various working parties supplied (1) daily on public road and (2) for Royal Artillery. On 20th August 1916, No 1221 Pte M. LEVIN killed by premature shell burst, while with R.A. working party.	
do	20th			App 160
do	20th		Received preliminary notice from South African Brigade re taking up position in trenches. (attached)	App 161
do	21st		Received B.O.O No 50 (attached)	App 162
			Major Young 2nd in command with Capts Langdale & Montgomery and Lieuts Mallett & Croft also 12 N.C.Os visited sector of trenches to be taken over.	App 163

190

1875 Wt. W593/826 1,000,000 4/15 J.B.C. & A. A.D.S.S./Forms/C. 2118.

Instructions regarding War Diaries and Intelligence Summaries are contained in F. S. Regs., Part II. and the Staff Manual respectively. Title Pages will be prepared in manuscript.

WAR DIARY
or
~~INTELLIGENCE SUMMARY~~

(Erase heading not required.)

No 34

Army Form C. 2118.

Place	Date 1916	Hour	Summary of Events and Information	Remarks and references to Appendices
GUOY SERVINS	Aug 22		C.O proceeded on leave. Major Young took over command with Major Hemming as 2nd in Command.	
			Issued Battalion Move Order for relief of section of trenches occupied by 5th Cameron Highlanders. (attached)	App 164
	23rd	9am	Battalion paraded and Leading platoon left. Total Marching Out 18 Officers 647 O.R. Quartermaster, Transport Officer and com[illegible] of 1st Line Transport billeted at PETIT SERVINS.	
FRONT LINE TRENCH	23rd	6.30pm	BERTHONVAL Section of trench line taken over from 5th Cameron Hrs, and relief completed. Headquarters notified accordingly.	
	23rd to 30th		During occupation of trenches, position generally has been quiet but at times our lines were heavily shelled. The enemy made frequent use of trench mortars. Patrols were sent out nightly to gather what information they could, paying particular attention to the enemy wire and also whether his line was strongly held. Snipers were fairly active and the usual machine gun fire was kept up. Our casualties during occupation of front line 2 Men Killed, 1 Wounded & Missing, 21 Wounded (3 accidentally) and including Major H S Lamond Hemming (slightly to duty). Patrol Reports & Daily Intelligence Summary attached.	App 165
	29th		Received Bde Operation Order No 51 (attached)	App 166

161

1875 Wt. W593/826 1,000,000 4/15 J.B.C. & A. A.D.S.S./Forms/C. 2118.

Army Form C. 2118

3RD S. A. INF.
TRANSVAAL RGT

Instructions regarding War Diaries and Intelligence Summaries are contained in F. S. Regs., Part II. and the Staff Manual respectively. Title Pages will be prepared in manuscript.

35

WAR DIARY
or
~~INTELLIGENCE SUMMARY~~
(Erase heading not required.)

Place 1-	Date 1916	Hour	Summary of Events and Information	Remarks and references to Appendices
TRENCHES	Aug 30	7am	Vacated BERTHONVAL II Sub Section being relieved by 1st South African Infantry. Took up position in support trenches	
	31		In Support trenches. – CABARET ROUGE	

B. Young Major
3 SAI

192

1875 Wt. W593/826 1,000,000 4/15 J.B.C. & A. A.D.S.S./Forms/C. 2118.

wire as he proceeded & steadying it taut when he arrived within 20 or 25 yards of the Germans trenches where he was to find a suitable place to conceal himself. while holding the wire taut & the other 7 men were to get over at 9pm. the bombing sap on the extreme right extend forward to within 20 yards of the German wire calculated at 10 yards interval & then work down parallel to the German wire until they reached the plain wire strand. As a further guide to direction arrangements were made for a VERY light to be sent up at regular intervals, from GRANBY AVENUE. the extreme left of the sector. in a direction at right angles to the line of the advance. Everything was carried out as arranged & the ground was thoroughly searched the German

wire being reached at 10 pm. the first man of the patrol returning through the gap in the wire on the left at 1 pm. & 3 others following at intervals of 3 minutes. Up to time of writing the other 3 had not arrived.

No signs of the enemy patrols or working parties were seen or of any work done by the enemy.

1.20 am.
26/8/16

Capt
E.C. A Coy

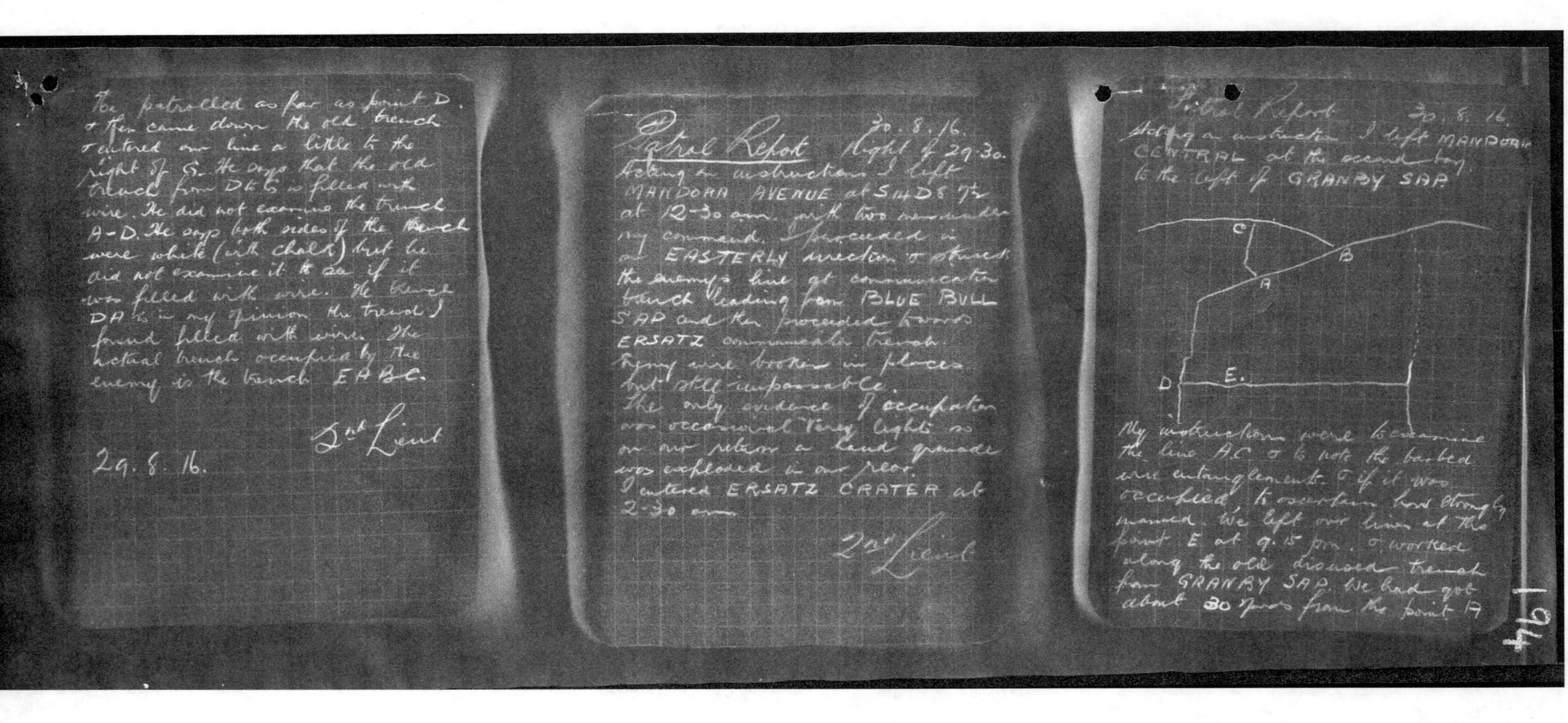

He patrolled as far as point D & then came down the old trench & entered our line a little to the right of G. He says that the old trench from D to G is filled with wire. He did not examine the trench A–D. He says both sides of the trench were white (with chalk) but he did not examine it to see if it was filled with wire. The trench DA is in my opinion the trench I found filled with wire. The actual trench occupied by the enemy is the trench EABC.

2nd Lieut

29.8.16.

Patrol Report 30.8.16.
Night of 29-30.

Acting on instructions I left MANDORA AVENUE at S14D8 7½ at 12-30 am with two men under my command. I proceeded in an EASTERLY direction & struck the enemy's line of communication trench leading from BLUE BULL SAP and then proceeded towards ERSATZ communication trench.
Enemy wire broken in places but still impassable.
The only evidence of occupation was occasional Very lights & on our return a hand grenade was exploded in our rear.
I entered ERSATZ CRATER at 2-30 am.

2nd Lieut

Patrol Report 29.8.16.

Acting on instructions I left MANDORA CENTRAL at the second bay to the left of GRANBY SAP.

My instructions were to examine the line A.C & to note the barbed wire entanglements & if it was occupied, to ascertain how strongly manned. We left our lines at the point E at 9.15 pm & worked along the old disused trench from GRANBY SAP. We had got about 30 yards from the point A

194

intention of striking the German wire where it met the continuation of INTERNATIONAL AVE. Striking it at this point & finding it impossible to get through there I followed it along to the NORTH and after going some 40 yards I found myself in between two rows of barbed wire with a clear path down the centre running NORTH. Finding it was impossible to get through the wire on our right to the enemy's trench the parapet of which could be seen about 15 yards on the other side we tried to get through the wire on our left as we could see the two lines of wire met just ahead. In attempting to get through we evidently alarmed the enemy who commenced throwing bombs at us. About 6 bombs were thrown (3 of which failed to explode.)

I regret to say that PTE MALCOLM who was following close behind me was hit. Pte Boothman and I lay still for a time and no more bombs were thrown for two or three minutes. We examined PTE MALCOLM & found that he had been hit in the face and was unconscious and was breathing with difficulty. More bombs were then thrown at us and being surrounded with barbed wire we found it quite impossible to bring him through being a heavy man. We managed to force our way through the wire without being hit but had no option but to leave the wounded man between the rows of wire where he had fallen. We eventually reached our own lines at 11-45 pm. The enemy continued bombing the spot where MALCOLM fell fully an hour after my return.

2-30 AM.
28. 8. 16.

2nd Lieut

P.S. When I attempted to get through the enemy wire, there was apparently no trench filled with barbed wire such as I struck last night between it and the occupied trench. I estimate the spot where I went through the wire last night to be some 30 yards to the left.

196

7. OFFICERS' KITS &c. Officers' kits and any other baggage which requires to be transported to the line will be taken up at night with the rations.

8. DEFENCE SCHEMES PHOTOGRAPHS ETC All air photographs, panorama photographs and reproduction of panorama photos, also all copies of sunprints (scale 1/5,000) of German trenches in BERTHONVAL Section, and copies of Defence Schemes in possession of Units being relieved will be taken over by relieving units.

9. GUIDES. Officers Commanding units will detail 4 N.C.Os. to report with leading platoons to the Staff Officer who will be on duty at CARENCY at point X.16.c.4.3.

10. BILLETS. The 102nd (Tyneside Scottish) Brigade will relieve the 1st SAI Brigade in the CHATEAU de la HAIE area on the afternoon of the 23rd instant. Billetting areas will be taken over by Advance Billetting parties, and units of the SAI Brigade need not leave parties in their billets to hand these over formally.

11. BRIGADE HEADQUARTERS. Brigade Headquarters will be at Battle Headquarters, CABARET ROUGE. The Staff Captain will be at VILLA D'ACQ.

Only matters connected with Operations eg. Situation reports, Intelligence reports, work reports etc., will be sent to CABARET ROUGE. All other matters, including Daily States, Indents, Returns, &c., &c., will be sent to VILLA D'ACQ.

Acknowledge.

J. Mitchell Baker
Major,
Brigade Major.

Copy No.	to	Copy No.	to
1	1st S.A.Infantry	11	9th Division
2	2nd do	12	26th Inf.Brigade
3	3rd do	13	27th Inf.Brigade
4	4th do	14	Brigadier-General
5	28th M.G.Company	15	Brigade Major
6	L.T.M.Battery	16	Staff Captain
7	64th Field Co., R. E.,	17	Office Copy
8	Bde.Signal Section	18	War Diary
9	107th Co., A. S. C.,	19	
10	S.A.F.Ambulance	20	

Issued by Orderly at 9.30.pm 21st August 1916

SECRET Copy No. 3

1st SOUTH AFRICAN INFANTRY BRIGADE

OPERATION ORDER No. 40

Map reference -
Sheet 36B 1/40,000

In the Field,
13th August 1916.

1. MOVE. The 1st South African Infantry Brigade, less the 2nd S.A.Inf. will march as under to the Reserve Brigade area in the relief of the 102nd and 103rd Composite Infantry Brigade, in Divisional Reserve, CHATEAU LA HAIE area.

Units will march under regimental arrangements. They must arrive, however, in their new billets by 6.30.pm, and not earlier than 5.pm.

1st S.A.Infantry	to CAMBLAIN L'ABBE
3rd do	to GUOY SERVINS
4th do	to MESNIL BOUCHE
28th M.G.Coy.,	to CAMBLAIN L'ABBE
T.M.Battery	to GUOY SERVINS

The 2nd S.A.Infantry will remain at ESTREE CAUCHIE for the present.

2. BILLETTING PARTIES. On the night of the 14/15th instant units of the 27th Inf. Brigade are marching out of the billets to be occupied by units of this Brigade in the above places, and units of the 102nd and 103rd Composite Brigade will move into these billets on the same night.

Officers in charge of Billetting Parties must therefore be warned accordingly.

Billetting Parties, as follows, will proceed in advance of their units by at least 6 hours.

Infantry Battalions	1 Off.&	5 O.R.	with Interpreter
28th M.G.Company	1 "	2 "	
T.M.Battery	1 "	2 "	

Officers in charge of BILLETTING Parties proceeding to CAMBLAIN L'ABBE and GUOY SERVINS will report to the Town Majors there.

3. TRANSPORT. First line transport will march with units.

Brigade Headquarters will arrange transport to carry the guns and equipment of the Trench Mortar Battery.

4. COMPLETION OF MOVE. Units will report without delay to Brigade Headquarters (CHATEAU de la HAIE) when they are complete in their new billets, stating the number, if any, who fell out during the march.

5. BRIGADE HEAD QUARTERS. Brigade Headquarters will close at FREVILLERS at 6.pm. on the 15th instant and will open at CHATEAU de la HAIE at the same hour.

Acknowledge.

J Mitchell Baker
Major,
Brigade Major.

Copy No.1 to 1st S.A.Infantry		Copy No.11 to 9th Division	
2	2nd do	12	26th Inf.Brigade
3	3rd do	13	27th do
4	4th do	14	Brigadier-General
5	28th M.G.Company	15	Brigade Major
6	L.T.M.Battery	16	Staff Captain
7	64th Field Co., R.E.	17	Office copy
8	Brigade Signal Section	18	War Diary
9	107th Co., A.S.C.	19	
10	S.A.F.Ambulance	20	

Issued by Orderly at 5 pm 13.8.16

Map Ref.
[illegible] 36 B.
S.E. 1/20,000.

Copy No. 3. App 166

1.98

1st South African Infantry Brigade
Operation Order 51.

In the Field 29/8/16.

1. Reliefs. The 1st S.A.I. will relieve the 3rd S.A.I. in the BERTHONVAL II sub-section on the 30th instant.

The 2nd S.A.I. will relieve the 4th S.A.I. in BERTHONVAL I sub-section on 31st inst.

Units relieved will occupy the trenches and billets at present occupied by the units relieving them. O's C. Machine Gun Company and L.T.M. Batty will arrange for the relief of their personnel during the afternoon of 30th inst.

Movement. Movement will be by bodies not larger than platoons with 10 min interval between platoons.

Routes. IN — CARENCY-MAESTRE LINE — POINT "G" — CABARET ROAD — ERSATZ AVENUE.

OUT For the Companies to occupy the MAESTRE Line:— CENTRAL AVENUE and DUCK WALK.

For all others:— WORTLEY AVENUE - BOYAU 123.

Time Reliefs to commence. The first platoon of each of the relieving Battalions will reach the head of ERSATZ AVENUE by 7 am. on the day they are relieving. All details of relief will be arranged between unit commanders.

Completion of relief. Completion of reliefs will be reported by wire to Brigade Headquarters.

Acknowledge.

[illegible]
Major
Brigade Major.

Copy No. 1 1st S.A. Infantry
2 2nd do.
3 3rd do.
4 4th do.
5 28th M.G. Coy.
6 S.A. L.T.M. Bty.
7 64th Field Co. R.E.
8 Brigade Signal Section.

Copy No. 9 107th Coy A.S.C.
10 S.A. Field Amb.
11 9th Division
12 26th Inf. Bde
13 27th Inf. Bde
14 Brig. General
15 Bde Major
16 Staff Captain
17 Office Copy
18 War Diary

} For Information

Issued by orderly at 5.30 pm 29th August 1916.

S E C R E T

Copy No. 3

199

1st SOUTH AFRICAN INFANTRY BRIGADE

Operation Order No. 50

Map ref.
Sheet 36B S.E.
1/20,000

In the Field,
21st August 1916.

App 162

1. RELIEF. The 1st S.A. Inf. Brigade will relieve the 26th Inf. Brigade in the BERTHONVAL Section on 23rd August 1916. The relief will be carried out as follows:-

The 4th SAI will relieve the 8th Black Watch in the right sub-section of the line.

The 3rd SAI will relieve the 5th Cameron Highlanders in the left sub-section of the line.

The 1st SAI will relieve the 7th Seaforth Highlanders in the Support Trenches.

The 2nd SAI will be billetted in CAMBLAIN L'ABBE as the Battalion in Reserve.

The S.A. Bde. M.G. Company will relieve all guns of the 26th Inf. Bde in the line

S.A. Bde. T.M. Battery will take over Trench Mortars from the 26th Inf. Bde - the exchange of mortars being arranged between the Officers commanding Batteries.

(Note. The working parties of the 2nd SAI in the MAESTRE LINE on the morning of the 23rd August will remain there until further orders.)

2. TIME-TABLE. Reliefs will be carried out in accordance with the attached time-table.

3. FORMATION OF MARCH AND MARCH ROUTE. Battalions will move by platoons at 500 yards distance, the necessary connecting files being put out to avoid congestion.
Units will move forward from point W.18.a. central by the new road which runs east therefrom and just south of the railway line; through CARENCY to point X.16.d.2.3., where they will enter the trench as directed by the Staff Officer who will be on duty at CARENCY.

4. RESERVE MACHINE GUNNERS & T.M. BATTERY PERSONNEL The Reserve Machine Gunners and Reserve T.M. Battery personnel will be billetted at PETIT SERVINS.

5. TRANSPORT. Bde., H.Q. Transport will be at VILLA D'ACQ, W.30.b.2.4. Regimental Transport will remain at PETIT SERVINS, where Quartermasters and Transport Officers will remain.

6. SURPLUS OFFICERS. Surplus Officers of the 1st, 3rd and 4th SAI will be accommodated at PETIT SERVINS.

App 166 26. 8. 16

200

Acting under instructions I went
over the parapet with two men opposite
the right gap of the wire of
MANDORA CENTRAL at 9-30 p.m.
My instructions were to ascertain
the state of the German wire
opposite & if possible to find
how it was held at night
without alarming the enemy
but to miss no opportunity of
capturing a prisoner. A
prearranged signal to enable
me to locate my position
was 3 rifle shots followed by
a Verey light fired at intervals
of half an hour from the
centre bay (10) of the Company
section. This signal worked
successfully. Keeping my
direction & finding my way
back. After passing the gap
[illegible] I made an exact
[illegible] estimate I struck
for the enemy [illegible] yards to the left
of a [illegible]

SECRET

MOVE ORDERS by Lt Colonel
E. F. Thackeray CMG Commanding
3rd South African Infantry

App 159

In the Field
15/8/1916.

In terms of S.A. Brigade Operation Order No 49, the Battalion will move to GUOY SERVINS today.

PARADE The Battalion will parade at 3.30 pm (~~[illegible]~~) on Battalion Parade Ground.

Dress Full Marching Order.

Water Bottles to be filled before leaving.

Baggage All baggage (except "A" Coy) will be deposited at a spot in "D" Coys lines at present occupied by the guard and piled in Companies. "D" Coy will provide a guard of 1 NCO & 3 men for this baggage

2

"A" Coy will pile their baggage at side of road near their lines, and place a guard over same.

SPARE KIT etc All spare kit etc must be collected & not left in huts and O.C. Coys will be held responsible for this being done.

LINES All lines and huts must be left in a thorough state of cleanliness and the Orderly Officer of the day will report to this effect, after inspection.

Advance Party.
The Q.M. with advance party will take over billets at 12 noon 15.8.16 [illegible] accompany this party.

[illegible]

[illegible]
Capt. & Adjutant,
3rd. S. A. Infantry (Transvaal Regt.)

S.A. Brigade HQ

App 160

3rd Regiment

Please detail a working party of one Sergt two Corporals or Lance Corporals and 25 [illegible] to report at 9 a[illegible] tomorrow 17th at [illegible] Stone Depot on [illegible] between GRAND SERVIN and PT. SERVINS Q 34 B [illegible] to load slag on [illegible] wagons which will report at [illegible] same. [illegible] wagons will make several trips and will work till 3.0 pm. Shovels to be taken [illegible] Haversack rations should also be taken

[illegible] Capt
[illegible] Capt

16/8/16

201

App 164

SECRET

MOVE ORDERS by Major B. Young Temp: Commanding 3rd South African Infantry

In the Field
22.8.16

In the terms of S.A. Brigade Operation Order No 30, the Battalion will relieve the 5th Cameron Highlanders in the left sub-section of the line in the BERTHONVAL - Section

The Battalion will parade at 8.45 a.m. 23rd on Battalion parade ground

Dress. - Full marching order
Water Bottles - To be filled before leaving.

The Battalion will move off as follows:
Hd. Qr. Coy
A Coy
B Coy
C Coy
D Coy.

The Companies will move by platoons at 500 yds distance. The necessary connecting files being put out to avoid congestion

Officers kit or any other baggage which requires to be transported to the line will be taken up at night with the rations.

All air photographs etc. of German trenches & copies of Defence Schemes in possession of Units being relieved will be taken over by relieving units.

Bgde. Hd. Qrs will be at Battle Hd. Qrs CABARET ROUGE. The Staff Captain will be at VILLA D'ACQ.

Coy: Commanders will detail 1 N.C.O. per Coy to march with Hd. Qr. Coy to be used as guides later

22-8-16

B. Young - Major
Temp: Commanding 3rd S.A.I.

A
B
C
D

App 165

PATROLS

[illegible] patrol consisting of 9 men was selected for the night of 25th. Their instructions were to thoroughly search NO MAN'S LAND MANDORA CENTRAL looking especially for a sign of work done by the [illegible] the way of saps [illegible] enfiring posts. [illegible] of a thing of the sort [illegible] working parties [illegible] all possible [illegible] to be gathered if [illegible] alarming the [illegible] arrangements were as follows: [illegible] two men were to go over [illegible] the wire on the left of the [illegible] carrying a [illegible] of 80 yards of plain wire [illegible] of them was instructed to remain in the [illegible] holding one end of the wire while the other [illegible] his way towards the [illegible] wire uncoiling the

202

(NORTH) of INTERNATIONAL AVE.
(continuation of) I found no
difficulty of crossing through the
wire at this point. Close up
to the wire runs a trench which
does not seem to be occupied.
On looking over the parapet
nothing was to be seen
but by the light of a Verey light
sent up apparently by the enemy
from a point some 40 yards to
our right front was a trench
about 8 feet across & 5 feet deep
& filled up to 4 feet with
rolls of barbed wire. I went
back through the wire in the
trench & followed it some 30
yards to our left (NORTH)
& again went through it to the
trench. By the help of another
Verey light I saw it was similarly
filled up with wire. I tried
again at another point still
further NORTH with the same results

and found it quite impossible to cross
the trench. The wire in front appeared
to run parallel with the trench
a few yards in front of it.
The wire in front of the first trench
appeared to be neglected & could
be got through without difficulty
& evidently had not been attended
to for some time. The enemy
evidently relying on the wire trenches
to act as the principal obstacle
as it would be unexpected & would
hold up any attacking force
who were unaware of it & had not
provided themselves with bridges
or material for crossing.
Being unable to cross this obstacle
& hearing no sign of any movement
in the trenches behind [illegible] lines
getting through our wire at the centre
gap & over the parapet at Bay 10
where the signals had been fixed from
I returned at 11 pm.
1230 am. 27.8.16 2nd Lieut.

28.5.16.
Report on patrol from MANDORA
CENTRAL.
Acting under instructions I went
over with a patrol consisting of
four men and two Lewis gunners
with a Lewis gun at 9.30 p.m.
My instructions were to select a
suitable spot in NO MANS LAND
and leave the Lewis gun there
with the gunners and two bombers
to await an opportunity of
bringing the gun into action on
an enemy patrol or working
party, wh[illegible] I myself with
two bomb[illegible] went forward to
ascertain the extent of the
unoccupied trench, filled with
barbed wire reported on last
night [illegible] Lewis gun patrol
return[illegible] pm without
having [illegible] or seen any-
thing. Leaving left the Lewis
gun as instructed I went
forw[illegible] with two men with the

203

Daily Intelligence Report
Unit Rowlock.

From 4.30 pm 25/8/16 to 4 30 pm 26/8/16.

Part I.

Trench Mortars. The enemy put over 20 to 30 rifle grenades and Minnies between 8.15 pm + 9 pm. Further the enemy are at present 2.45 pm sending over rifle grenades + Minnies between WORTLEY + ERSATZ. AVES

Machine Guns Very intermittent burst of fire at night

New Work Enemy observed to have made new Snipers hole opposite Blue Bull Sap

General The general disposition of the Enemy seems to be very quiet, only occasional sniping taking place

Part II

Trench Mortars Our trench Mortars put over about 10. Medium Mortars registering shots on enemys wire at about 6.15 pm we also retaliated to enemys fire between the hours of 9.15 pm + 10 pm.

Patrols A patrol went out a portion of whom visited German front line trenches + found same unoccupied. It was also found that the wiring of their front line trenches was very defective

Sniping A Sniper was observed from ERSATZ Crater who was fired upon + believed to be hit

Major
Tempy Cmdg

Daily Intelligence Report
Unit ROWLOCK

From 4.30 pm 26/8/16 to 4.30 pm 27.8.16

Part I

Artillery at 6 pm two 5.9 fell in the vicinity of ERSATZ AV 8.30 AM six shells calibre unknown came over ridge S.W. of ZOUAVE VAL at 2.30 pm four 5.9.

ZOUAVE VALLEY –

Trench mortars Six minnies fell in the vicinity of ERSATZ AVE + GUBRON AVE at about 3.15 pm

Machine Guns Very intermittent during night

Working parties A working party was observed at 8.40 pm left of Blue Bull Sap

Lights one Red Very light was put up at 9.15 pm no result.

General The general disposition of the enemy is very inactive

Part II

Artillery Our 18 pdrs sent over several rounds registering on Enemy's front line wire

Trench Mortars Our MTMBRA Sent over 73 Mortars on enemy's wire + front line two of these apparently exploded the bomb others in enemy's line further 36 Stokes Mortar fired on enemys wire in front line trenches good results being observed

Our Machine guns opened fire about 8.40 pm on working party who were observed to disperse

Patrols A patrol left our front line trenches at 9 pm visiting the enemy's trenches they found them to be about 4 (four) feet deep of barbed wire, observation was made in three separate places – They were unoccupied This patrol returned at 10.30 pm

Another patrol left at 9 pm this party was unable to get through Enemy's wire + returned at 12 30 AM having nothing to report

Sign Major
Tempy Cmdg

204

3

Enemy's Artillery Contd.

At 2.45 pm 9 77MM were fired at MOTOR CAR CORNER.

Between 3 pm and 3.30 pm 10 77MM 9 - 10 cm and 11 HE were fired at RESERVE, DESPIERRE, and GUINNERS FARM.

At 5.10 pm he fired 5 rounds of H.E near SEVEN TREES REDOUBT.

MACHINE GUN & RIFLE FIRE

During the day a few bursts of machine gun fire was directed at a working party in the Right Sector, during the evening there was more activity.

Rifle fire has been considerably quieter than usual which is accounted for by the accurate shooting of our snipers on their plates.

Bombing At 10.30 pm enemy fired 4 Rifle grenades into T 96.3. No damage was done.

4

Movements in rear

A man was seen walking up a trench which runs from a building at HALTE to BLANCHISSERIE WOOD near C.A.[illegible]

ENEMYS DEFENCES

Front Support Lines

At C.4.d.2.5½ water has been pumped out new earth thrown on parapet and duckboard work progressing, it is thought that new duck boards are being put down.

WORKING PARTIES

At 9.15 a.m. a few men were seen carrying bundles of straw in front trench opposite T 95.

Between 7.30 and 9 a.m. pick & shovel work was carried on opposite T. 97.

205

Daily Intelligence Summary
Unit ROWLOCK
24/8/16

Artillery at about 11-30 AM today the enemy put about 11 (eleven) 4.2 about ERSATZ AVE which did not do any damage. Further about [illegible] 30 pm, 6 H.E. shells which fell S.W of ridge outside our Sector

Machine Gun a couple of machine Gun fire bursts took place during the night no damage or casualties taking place.

Sniping Very inactive, only one sniper being heard during the night.

General. General disposition of enemy very quiet

General Statement No action on this side to report for past 24 hours

Sgd B Young
Major
Tempy Comdg

Daily Intelligence Report
Unit ROWLOCK

From 4.30 pm 24 8.16 to 4.30 pm 25.8.16

Part I

Artillery at about 6 pm the enemy put about 6 (six) 5.9 in the direction of ERSATZ AVE. These were observed to burst in the valley causing no damage. During a bombardment which took place from 11 pm to 11.55 pm the enemy put over a considerable number of 4.2 & 5.9 in the valley between Battn HQ & ERSATZ AVE. Today about 11 AM the enemy again put about 6 (six) 5.9 towards the road near CARENCY

TRENCHMORTARS The enemy used a considerable number of HTMB Minnies during the bombardment from 11 pm to 12 noon.

Machine Guns Only sudden bursts of M.G. fire was heard which did not cause no any casualties.

General The enemy was very active during the bombardment from 11 pm to 11.55 pm otherwise during the remaining portion of the 24 hours seemed very inactive.

PART II

Operations At 5.20 pm our Stokes Guns opened fire on enemy trenches with very good Effect no retaliation was received from enemy again at 11 pm. our M.T.M.B RA opened fire on the enemy front line the effect of this action has not as yet been ascertained

A patrol went out at ERSATZ AVE at 9.30 pm. same returning without any casualties.

Major
Tempy Commdg

206

SECRET

124

Intelligence Report

Our Operations — from 12 noon 24th to 12 noon 25th

Artillery

Last night 8.25 p.m. our 18 pdrs fired 3 times on Westhoek [illegible] at 9.20 [illegible] our [illegible] Howitzers fired about 15 rounds [illegible] near the rear of BLANCHISSERIE WOOD.

Between noon and 3 pm our artillery were very active. Our 12 in Howitzer fired about 47 rounds on BLANCHISSERIE WOOD and DURIEZ.

7 Shrapnel over enemy support line at C 4 a 7.3

12 H.E. Shrapnel just enemy support lines opposite Gap C.1

8 4.2 shell over C 4 b 1.9

5 18 pdr in LE TOQUET

Between 4.30 and 5.15

4.5 and 18 pdr were fired upon enemy front & support line at C 4 a 8.6, C 4 b 8.5, C 4 d 8.8. The parapet was damaged in several places and a periscope. Firing reports seem [illegible] the enemy on the line as a result of our fire.

Bombing. During the afternoon we fired 88 bombs into enemy trenches opposite T 96 & 97 and also 97 Rifle Grenades.

Patrolling. Our patrol went out last night. They report the enemy trench opposite T 96 is a gap of 50 to 60 yds

207

4

At 1 p.m. he fired about forty rounds of shrapnel in vicinity of Badajos Walk and Reserve Farm

Between 4.20 and 6 p.m. he fired twenty five 10.5 cm at GLASGOW REDOUBT and RESERVE FARM

6) Sniping
Snipers were less active than usual.

7) Movements in rear.
A party was seen to be working on what appears to be a new communication trench at C.5.c 2.3.8 and new wire seems to have been erected at C.4.d.7.3. Another party was seen working between 8 and 9 a.m. at C.4.c.10.18

8) Identifications.
What appeared to be an enemy officer was seen walking in a communication trench opposite T.97, wearing a cap with a black shiny peak and dull red band.

Miscellaneous:
Smoke was seen issuing from a house during the afternoon at C.11.a 9½.4½.

[signature]
Lt. Col.
Commanding 3rd S. A. Infantry.
(Transvaal Regt.)

208

(2)

(3) Sniping

During the evening our snipers shot one of the enemy who shewed himself opposite T102/7

Another hit claimed from trees 600 yards E of 98 by our snipers.

(4) Enemy Activity

Attitude – Normal

Artillery Between 12 Noon and 1 pm enemy fired 18 77 mm at RESERVE FARM and DESPIERRE FARM.
About 3.30 pm he again fired 3 Shrapnel and 2 High Explosive shells but with little effect.
Between 4 pm and 4.30 pm the enemy shelled LUKER'S HOUSE with 32 10 cm C-10-C9.95

(3)

2 pm to 4 pm forty heavy shells were fired at Le Bizet – came from direction SE of Sector 98

(5) Bombing

Between 4.30 pm and 6.15 pm the enemy fired about 50 T.M. Bombs and 45 Rifle Grenades in the vicinity of T95/98 and Reserve Trenches
6 pm to 7 pm enemy fired five T.M. Shells and twenty Rifle Grenades into GLASGOW REDOUBT

(6) Sniping

Snipers were moderately active during the day but most energetic after 8 pm

4

till midnight.

(7) Miscellaneous

Smoke was seen issuing from a house at C4D9.2½

[signature]
....................Lt. Col.
Commanding 3rd S. A. Infantry
(Transvaal Regt.)

209

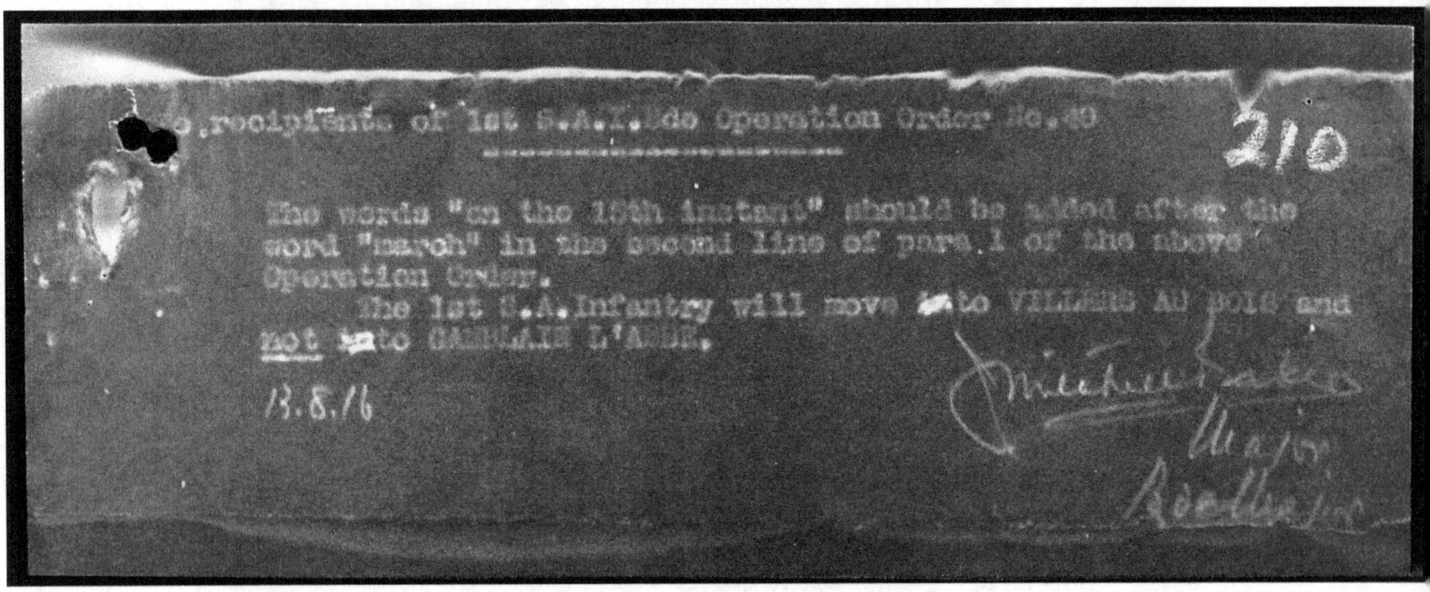

210

o.recipients of 1st S.A.I.Bde Operation Order No.40

The words "on the 15th instant" should be added after the word "march" in the second line of para.1 of the above Operation Order.

The 1st S.A.Infantry will move to VILLERS AU BOIS and <u>not</u> to CAMBLAIN L'ABBE.

13.8.16

Major

[illegible]

To: O.C. A - Coy
B "
C "
D "

SECRET M 10/3

(2)
App 160.

Please detail from your commands the following:—
A Coy - 1 Subaltern & 59 O.R.
B Coy - 1 Subaltern & 57 O.R.
C Coy - 1 Subaltern & 57 O.R.
D Coy - 1 Subaltern & 57 O.R.
to parade outside orderly room at 8 p.m. tonight. These are required so as to furnish the following working parties:—
(1) Three officers & 200 men to 51st Bgde H. Bn. R.A.
(2) One officer & 30 men to 53rd Bgde H. Bn. R.A.

"D" Coy Officer & 30 men of "D" Coy will form No 2 party.
The remainder, No I party.
Guides will be at Orderly Room at 8.30 p.m. for these parties.

N.C.Os & men must be rationed up to & including 18th.
Cooking utensils are to be taken.
A proportion of N.C.O. will be detailed

Draft men should be taken in these parties as far as possible.

Coy. Commanders must not detail any N.C.O. or man, whose name had been forwarded for a course.

Please inform the officer detailed by your Coy that he must report at Hd. Qr. mess at 8 p.m., as the Commanding Officer wishes to see the officers of these parties.

Dress Full marching order, packs not to worn, but brought on parade, & will be stacked in limbers, which will accompany each party.

A.J. Murray
Lt.

Issued 7 pm

Secret

To O.C. 3rd SAI   BM 47/26

App 161

This Brigade will relieve the 26th Inf Bde in the line (BERTHONVAL SECTION) on the night of 23/24th instant.
Detailed orders [illegible] later.
The 4th will be on the right and the 2nd on left of line; the 1st in support and the 3rd in reserve.

20.VIII.16   [illegible]

211

TO: ROWLOCK.

Measuring Patrol
Ref S14D 8 7"2

I attach statement of Cpl Middleton viz:—

"Proceeding at 10.5 pm from above point I went due EAST by compass. I reached enemy's wire & was just about penetrate same when a Verey light went up from enemy's trench immediately in front of me. I lay still for 10 minutes & heard conversation being carried on in the enemy's trench. I paced distance to enemy's trench to be 30 yards. The wire seemed to be thrown on in coils round stakes. It did not appear to be damaged to any extent & consider ~~[illegible]~~ that unless further demolished the wire would be strong obstacle".

Cpl Middleton was anchored to wire and amount paid out was exactly 30 yards. Total distance therefore 30 yards. Patrol returned at 11 pm.

29.8.16

O.C.
B. Coy.

29.8.16

Patrol Report

Acting under instructions I left MANDORA CENTRAL on patrol at about the centre of the trench. I had 6 men with me. My instructions were to see what damage by our artillery to the enemy wire & get any information possible. My plan was to make straight across to the enemy's line & then we were to divide. One party of 3 men under Cpl Hughes was to go N. My party was to go S. We struck the German line at the point A. & proceeded SOUTH. The wire SOUTH of point A was impenetrable. We proceeded as far as point B. & returned to our lines. Cpl. Hughes reports that after the party split up at point A he proceeded SOUTH WARDS along enemy wire. The wire was bad & could be penetrated about every 10 yards

212

Rowing
Lewis Gun Patrol. Appx [illegible]

I attach statement of Pte Rogers in charge of above stationary aggressive patrol:-

"Leaving fire bay stop 37 at 12 midnight I went straight into NO MANS LAND about 2/3rds way across taking up position in shell hole. I remained out till 2 am (29th) and during the time I was out I saw nothing. I did not fire during the time I was out.

Above patrol moved to point on left of old communication trench leading into BLUE BULL SAP

Capt
O.C. B Coy

28.8.16

Patrol Report

29. 8. 16
12.5 AM

Acting on instructions received I conducted a patrol from MANDORA NORTH which left at 9.55 pm. This patrol consisted of two men under myself & two others working in conjunction. My own party left the first line trench at a point NORTH OF GRANBY SAP where there is a break in our own wire. The other party left from BAY, 37 SOUTH of ERSATZ CRATER. Both parties then proceeded due EAST until in touch with enemys wire entanglements, they then turned due NORTH and SOUTH respectively and joined at a communication trench which is a continuation of BLUE BULL SAP. Turning due WEST we proceeded to the sap head and entered the first line trench.

Both parties report that the wire of the enemy though broken is still impassable & I myself found portions of broken wire about and also parts of standards. The only evidence of enemy occupation was that two lights were fired from each flank of the patrol* & my party was sniped from the salient in the enemy lines opposite GRANBY SAP. The patrol arrived back at 11-45 pm.

2nd Lieut.

* i.e. from enemys first line trench due EAST of GRANBY SAP and EASATZ CRATER.

213

214

3rd Regiment BM 190

With reference to Reliefs Operation Order 57 of today's date and to subsequent reliefs during the Brigade's term of duty in the trenches, Battalions will take over the working and carrying party duties found by the unit they relieve or are relieved by.

A list of these working and carrying parties with full particulars regarding strength and place of reporting, will be handed over by Battalion Commanders.

[illegible]

Mitchell Baker
Major
Brigade Major

29/8/16

Patrol Report In the field 29. 8. 16.

On instructions from my Coy. Commander I proceeded from the trench at a point S14 b10.2½ accompanied by C.S.M. Luker to examine the enemy wire entanglements from that point to Sap 3. We went along what appeared to be an old communication trench leading to the German trenches, but on the NORTHERN TIP of the ERSATZ CRATER. On getting within a few feet of the German wire I turned to the NORTH and found that the low and trip wires was blown away. A few yards further on we struck an old trench running N.N.W. which I was under the impression ran from the CRATER to SAP 3. I got through this old trench which strikes the German wire & again got just against the German wire.

I was then bombed from the rear, apparently from the old trench referred to above, and sniped from the enemy parapet.
This sketch may help in explanation.

ENEMY LINE
ERATZ CRATER
No3 SAP.
A
A. Route taken.

We stayed in a shell hole for 15 minutes & then attempted again to get on our left, but were again sniped at & bombed as we had evidently been observed. I returned by the same route more or less.

I don't think the wire is sufficiently destroyed to enable an assaulting force to get through without being impeded. Where I got on the German wire is 70 yards from our line & the distance I examined was on a front of 50 yds. the furthest point being perhaps 100 yards from our line.
I went out at 9-45 pm and got back to our lines at 11-30 pm.

2nd Lieut

215

B.M. 47/26

H.Q., S.A.Bde.

216

20th August 1916.

App 163

Officer Commanding,

3rd S.A.I.

Please arrange for a party consisting of not more than five and not less than two Officers and 12 N.C.Os to report at 10 am., on the 21st instant at point G, Map reference X.23.A.50, Hospital road, CARENCY.(Map 36B.SE.Edit.6) Guides will meet the party there and conduct them to their portion of the line, to be taken over by your battalion.

Officers should note the exact area to be taken over, accommodation available for men, and ~~such~~ obtain all such information as may prove useful.

Your battalion will take over that portion of the line at present occupied by *the Argylls* and a guide from *the Seaforths* will meet your party at Point G, A Similar party will be detailed by you for the following day and the instructions herein, followed.

Your Quartermaster must be included in one of the parties, and you will yourself, unless you have already done so, visit the trenches with one or other of the parties.

QM to take 4 C.Q.M.S.

Parties will *on their way forward* report at Brigade Headquarters, Chateau de LA HAIE at 8.30 am., each morning and will return to their respective units in the evening.

Wm Maclean

Lieutenant

for Brigade Major.

21st Major Young 2 i/c
Capt. Langdale D
Capt. Montgomery C
Lt. Mallet D
2nd Lt. Croft B.

12 N.C.O. 3 A.B.C.D. Co.

4

walls. Smoke or steam has been seen issuing from the rear of the house.

On the evening of the 20th it was thought that the field gun was being fired from the rear of the house.

Bombing The enemy fired 4 T.M. bombs during the evening into 98 S.T.

Enemy Defences

Working Parties From 7–9 am and at 3.45 p.m. a small working party were observed throwing earth out of trench at C.4.d 2.5. Another party was seen throwing earth out of a new trench at C.4.d 6.2.

At C.4.d 3.5 a few men were seen carrying 3" piping about 20 ft lengths

5

Communications

Pigeons At 3 p.m. two pigeons were seen flying from Blanchisserie in the direction of LE BIZET.

At 3.30 p.m. three carrier pigeons were seen flying from the direction of DEULEMONT to BAILLEUL.

At 4 p.m. on the 21st inst. uncommon buzzing noises were heard on receivers of telephone both in front line and battalion headquarters.

Miscellaneous From 8 to 8.20 a.m. the throbbing of an engine was heard and sounded like a dynamo or petrol gas engine in rear of enemy lines. This throbbing was also thought to be audible yesterday, but was thought to be an aeroplane engine.

F. A. Heal[illegible] — Lt. Col.
Commanding 3rd S. A. Infantry
(Transvaal Regt.)

217

Instructions regarding War Diaries and Intelligence Summaries are contained in F. S. Regs., Part II. and the Staff Manual respectively. Title pages will be prepared in manuscript.

WAR DIARY or ~~INTELLIGENCE SUMMARY.~~

(Erase heading not required.)

Army Form C. 2118.

3RD S. A. INF. (TRANSVAAL RGT.) Vol 6

Place	Date	Hour	Summary of Events and Information	Remarks and references to Appendices
Cabaret-Rouge Trenches	1/9/16		Return from Leave of Lt. Col. E. F. Thackeray. CMG. resumed Command. Continuous Rain. Trenches in bad state, much repair work necessary. No shelling of this Sector of Support Trenches.	
"	2/9/16	P.M. 1.0	Operation Order No. 52. 1st S.A.I.B. received at 1. P.M. ordering Regiment into Reserve at Villier au Bois. Rainy weather.	Appendix 167.
"	3/9/16	3.0.PM	One Casualty from distant Rifle fire at 3. A.M. The Regt. vacated Cabaret Rouge Support Trenches moving by Bodies of One Platoon at 10 minutes interval, via Communication Trenches to Villier au Bois, being relieved at Cabaret Rouge by 7th Seaforth Highlanders. Weather rainy.	Move Order. App: 168.
Villier au Bois.	4/9/16		Major H.S.J.L. Hemming appointed Acting-Adjutant. 2nd Lieut A.G. Money. app: Transport Officer. Day spent in Organizing the Regt. to enable it to march out for action in 30 minutes. Operation Order No. 53. 1st S.A.I.B. (App: 169) received, detailing Regt. as Reserve to Carency Sector.	App: 169.
"	5/9/16		Weather rainy.	
"	6/9/16		Draft of 74 other ranks taken on strength.	
"	7/9/16		Weather rainy. Orders issued to Regt. that in future every O.R. to carry 2 Mills Bombs in Bandolier when proceeding to Trenches or Action.	

218

Instructions regarding War Diaries and Intelligence Summaries are contained in F. S. Regs., Part II, and the Staff Manual respectively. Title Pages will be prepared in manuscript.

WAR DIARY
or
~~INTELLIGENCE SUMMARY~~
(Erase heading not required.)

Army Form C. 2118

3RD S. A. INF. [TRAN]SVAAL [REGT.]

Place	Date	Hour	Summary of Events and Information	Remarks and references to Appendices
Villier au Bois	8.9.16		Weather Clear. Congratulatory message received by the Regt: from Lt-Genl. Smuts in East Africa through the High Commissioner, who says: "I have now received a message, dated 20/8/16 from General Smuts, Wami River, in the following terms. "Convey to O/C. 3. S.A.I. my congratulations on their achievements, and my deep grief at their losses." Permit me to associate myself entirely with this message". Schreiner. High Commissioner for South Africa.	
"	9.9.16		Weather Fair.	
"	10.9.16		Weather Fair.	
"	11.9.16		Weather Fair.	
"	12.9.16		Regt. called upon to find Working Parties numbering 5 Officers, and about 500 O.R. for Front Line Trenches. Weather Fine.	
"	13.9.16		Lieut H.P. Ellis joined for duty from II Reserve Regt. S.A.I. Working Parties of about 450 furnished for front line trenches. Weather Fine.	
"	14.9.16		Orders issued to Regt. All ranks to wear both Gas Helmets at all times. Working Parties of about 450 furnished for front line Trenches. Weather Fine.	
"	15.9.16		Operation Order No 54. 1st S.A.I.B. received. III S.A.I. to move to Gouy-Servins on the 18/9/16. Weather Fair.	App. 170.
"	16.9.16		The following N.C.Os and men promoted to Commissioned rank in this Regt. 7022. C/S/M/ THOMAS. W.F.G. 4972. Sgt. UYS. D.C. 345 Sgt. LEE. F.C. 8650 Sgt. MEDLICOTT. G.H.	
		6.15 P.M.	7437. Cpl. COOK. R.C. 68. Cpl. HYDE. R.K. Weather Fine. 6.15. P.M. Wire from 1st S.A.I.B. to the effect that Operation Order 54 suspended.	App. 171.
		7.30	7.30 p.m. Wire from 1st S.A.I.B. cancelling Operation Order 54, giving detail of Move to Front Line Trenches.	App. 172.

1875 Wt. W593/826 1,000,000 4/15 J.B.C. & A. A.D.S.S./Forms/C. 2118.

Instructions regarding War Diaries and Intelligence Summaries are contained in F. S. Regs., Part II. and the Staff Manual respectively. Title Pages will be prepared in manuscript.

WAR DIARY
or
~~INTELLIGENCE SUMMARY~~
(~~Erase heading not required.~~)

Army Form C. 2118

3RD S. A. INF. (TRANSVAAL RGT.)

Place	Date	Hour	Summary of Events and Information	Remarks and references to Appendices
Villier au Bois	16/9/16.	11.10 P.M.	Operation Order 55 - 1st S.A.I.B. received - III S.A.I. to relieve 1st S.A.I. in front line Trenches, at Carency No. 2 - by Platoons at 6 minutes interval, via Communication Trenches. First Platoon	
		P.M. 12.30.	to reach F. Line by 12.30. p.m 17/9/16. Regimental Move Order in accordance with this was issued	
		P.M. 11.30	at 11.30 pm.	App. 172A
"	17/9/16	9.0 P.M	Additional Regt. Move Order issued at 8. am. Relief completed by 9. P.M. Weather Rainy. Carency No 2. Sector. Trenches in bad state of repair, owing to Enemy's Artillery, rain, and previous neglect, and portions of front line Trenches destroyed and useless, thus isolating Centre Picquet from Right Picquet, and Left from Centre Picquet, the latter being completely isolated by day. Marching in Strength of Regt. 20 Officers. 480. OR. when total Garrison required to hold Sector is about 750. Position so serious that O/c III S.A.I. made	App. 173.
		P.M. 10.30.	urgent representations to G.O.C. 1st S.A.I.B. in letter ET.79. (10.30 P.M.) requesting that 300 men of this Regt. detached to tunnelling Companies R.E. etc might be returned. Weather very bad.	App. 174.
Carency - II. Trenches	18/9/16		Every available man employed on repair and maintainance of Front Line, Communication and Support Trenches. The continual fall of rain destroys the Trenches as fast as they are built up. The G.O.C. 1st S.A.I.B. inspected the Trenches in company with C/O. One Sergt. was killed during the night while on patrol. Enemy fairly active during day - with Trench Mortars, Bombs, and also 77. MM. H.E. Shell.	
"	19/9/16		Rain falling continuously, and weather cold. Trenches in places 2 feet - deep in water. Scarcely any shelter for men who are suffering from considerable hardships, sleep out of the question. 100. OR. who had been attached to R.E. as Working Party returned for duty with the Regt. which lightened the duties of all ranks considerably. Considerable enemy Trench Mortar and Artillery activity on this Sector. During the day one OR killed. 2 wounded. C/O was informed that should weather conditions remain so severe G.O.C. would relieve the Battalion at an early date.	

1875 Wt. W593/826 1,000,000 4/15 J.B.C. & A. A.D.S.S./Forms/C. 2118.

Instructions regarding War Diaries and Intelligence Summaries are contained in F. S. Regs., Part II. and the Staff Manual respectively. Title Pages will be prepared in manuscript.

WAR DIARY
or
~~INTELLIGENCE SUMMARY~~
(Erase heading not required.)

Army Form C. 2118

3RD S. A. INF. (TRANSVAAL RGT.)

221

Place	Date	Hour	Summary of Events and Information	Remarks and references to Appendices
Carency No. 2	20.9.16		Weather conditions remain severe. Most of the men have had no opportunity of sleeping since entering the Sector. One O.R. wounded by Shell in Left Picquet. All ranks employed on repair of Trenches. Enemy Trench Mortars and Artillery active. Several cases of Trench Feet reported. O/C informed by the Brigade Major that should weather conditions not improve the Regt will be relieved tomorrow on receipt by wire of Code word "ROWLOCK".	
"	21.9.16	A.M. 8.30.	Weather conditions still severe. O/C despatched Telegram "ROWLOCK" to Brigade H/Quarters. Telegram	
		A.M. 9.45	from Brigade H/Quarters to effect that III S.A.I. will be relieved by 1ST S.A.I. Relief commencing	App. 175.
Villers au Bois			about noon. Regt Move Order. Leading Platoon (1ST S.A.I.) marched in at 1.30. P.M.	App. 176.
			Relief completed by 5. P.M. except for one Platoon in isolated left Picquet. This Platoon	
		P.M. 9.0.	relieved at 9.0. P.M. During Relief enemy Trench Mortars very active, and enemy threw a considerable number of H.E. shells into BERTHORNAL ALLEY. Regt took over Billets of	
		P.M. 9.30	1ST S.A.I. at Villers au Bois. At 9.30. P.M. Telegram received from B.H/Qtrs. calling on Regt.	App. 177.
			to send forward Billeting Party to Estree Cauchie on 22nd inst.	App. 177.A.
"	22.9.16	A.M. 7.0	Operation Order 58 (1ST S.A.I.B.) ordering III S.A.I. to move to Estree Cauchie on 23.9.16. Weather	App. 178.
		A.M. 10.40	good. Telegram from Bgd. ordering III S.A.I. send forward Billeting Party to Chelers. Regt	App. 179.
			Move Order.	App. 180.
Estree Cauchie	23.9.16		In accordance with Operation Order 59. Regt proceeded by March Route to Estree Cauchie and took up Billets for the night. One man fell out en route.	App. 181.
CHELLERS	24.9.16		In accordance with Operation Order 59. Regt moved forward to Chelers and went into Billets for the night. Regtl Move Order. App. 182. Capt Lickson. M.C. S.A.M.C. proceeded to Abberville, struck off strength of this Regt. Lieut Stackpool R.A.M.C. taken on strength as Regtl M.O.	App. 182.

Instructions regarding War Diaries and Intelligence Summaries are contained in F. S. Regs., Part II. and the Staff Manual respectively. Title Pages will be prepared in manuscript.

Army Form C. 2118

WAR DIARY

or

~~INTELLIGENCE SUMMARY~~

~~(Erase heading not required.)~~

3RD S. A. INF. (TRANSVAAL RGT.)

Place	Date	Hour	Summary of Events and Information	Remarks and references to Appendices
Magnicourt sur Canche	25. 9/16		Weather Fine. In accordance with Operation Order 59. S.A.I.B. The Regt marched to Magnicourt sur Canche. Regt. Operation Order APP 183. Billets were found to be dirty & Verminous, Owing to inhabitants having gathered in their Crops, very few Billets could contain the number of men allotted on the Billeting Notice Boards. The inhabitants showed a very unfriendly disposition.	App. 181. App. 183.
"	26. 9/16		Health of the Regt very good. Only 5 men developed serious foot trouble during recent marching mostly owing to incipient "Trench feet," due to recent tour in the Trenches. By order of A.D.M.S. all men over 42 years of age were medically examined as to their fitness for service in the Front Line. Out of 51 men only 14 were found unfit and were marked for Permanent Base. Weather very good.	
"	27. 9/16		Weather fine and Sunny.	
"	28. 9/16	PM 7.0.	Operation Order 60. S.A.I.B. received at 7.0. P.M. Ordering Regt to move tomorrow at 10.0. A.M. to Grand Rullecourt. Billeting Parties were sent forward at 8.30. P.M.	App. 184
Grand Rullecourt	29. 9/16		Regt vacated Magnicourt and marched to Grand Rullecourt. No men fell out en route. Billets found good. Weather fine. Regtl. Move Order APP 185. A Draft of one Officer (Lt Elliott) and 21. OR. arrived here and were taken on Strength.	App. 185.
"	30. 9/16		Weather fine and Sunny.	

P. J. [illegible] ....Lt. Col.
Commanding 3rd. S. A. Infantry,
(Transvaal Regt.)

Office Copy

9th. Div. No.X.5/1826.

TRAINING.

AP 186

223.
END

1. It is impossible to say how long or short a time we shall be given in the Training Area

We must calculate on it being short when making out programmes of training.

2. I want Infantry Brigadiers and subordinate Commanders to work on the following lines.

Train the individual soldier to be quick on his feet and quick with his arms; accurate with his bomb throwing, fierce with his bayonet work, brisk with his loading, steady with his aiming. Dont keep men too long at the same job.

3. Train the Officers and N.C.O.'s to be wide awake, quick sighte nimble with their wits, and clear and practical in their orders.

4. This can only be done by Commanders of Companies, Platoons and Fighting Sections being constantly given imaginary tactical situations on the ground by their superior Officers, asked for quick solutions and informed how their solutions might be bettered

It is not necessary to have the men of the Fighting Section present at these exercises.

5. Each Company Commander should spend at least an hour daily teaching his platoon Commanders and Sergeants in this manner, and each Platoon Commander should a similar hour daily with the N.C.O.s of his Fighting Sections.

6. These exercises should embrace forming up for attack, moving in attack and taking full advantage of the lie of the ground, spotting likely places for enemy machine guns, rounding them up, assisting neighbouring troops by flanking fire or other attack, tactical use of rifle, bayonet, hand grenade, rifle grenade, smoke rifle grenad grenade, Lewis gun, Vickers machine gun, Stokes and 2" Mortars, movements through woods, orchards, villages, siting of trenches, covering parties, writing of messages.

7. Later in the week, small tactical exercises for, say, 3Platoons against one, or three Companies against one, should be arranged, sufficient umpires provided and previously coached by the Director as to how and when they are to hold up some portion of the attack and point the tactical position to the senior Officr or N.C.O. present.

8. Machine guns should be used by both sides in these exercises rattles or drums being utilised to show when they are in action against a visible target.

Stokes Mortars will also be used in these sham fights.

9. Brigadiers and Brigade Majors will pay special attention to the training of their machine gun Companies. The power of these Companies, if boldly and cleverly handled, can scarcely be exaggerated.

10. All the tactical teaching must drive home the fact that we are now on the top and that the way to stop there is by unflagging energy in the attack, a spirit ~~in the~~ of adventurous aggressiveness that will impel all ranks to go beyond their given objective rather than be stopped short of it, however strong the opposition encountered.

With such a spirit we shall be able to out-do any of our past performances, and that will mean good fighting

21st. September, 1916.

(Signed) P. STEWART.
Lieut.Col.
for MAJOR-GENERAL.
Commanding 9th. (Scottish) Dv

Page 13

Army Form C. 2118.

Instructions regarding War Diaries and Intelligence Summaries are contained in F. S. Regs., Part II. and the Staff Manual respectively. Title pages will be prepared in manuscript.

WAR DIARY
or
~~INTELLIGENCE SUMMARY.~~
(Erase heading not required.)

FROM EGYPT

DELTA & WESTERN FORCE

Hour	Date	Place	Summary of Events and Information	
2.0 pm	3.4.16	SOLUM	"C" & "D" Coys. left on trawlers "JERICHO" & "VERESIS" for AL[illegible]	
3.30 pm	4.4.16	do.	Hqrs. & "A" & "B" Coys. left on HMS. "MALLOW" for ALEXAND[illegible]	
8.0 pm	do.	ALEXANDRIA	"C" & "D" Coys. arrived at SIDI BISHR Camp.	
5.0 pm	5.4.16	do.	Hqrs. & "A" & "B" Coys. arrived at SIDI BISHR Camp.	
2.30 pm	6.4.16	do.	Orders received re disposal of transport, animals, supplies [illegible] view of approaching embarkation of S.A. Bde. for FRANC[E]	
4.0 pm	10.4.16	do	Brigade inspected at SIDI BISHR camp by G.O.C. [illegible] Expeditionary Force.	
2.30 pm	11.4.16	do	Orders received re embarkation of stores & baggage [illegible]	
11.30 pm	do	do	Orders received for embarkation of Brigade.	
6.0 am	12.4.16	do.	Order [illegible] for embarkation	appx 102
3.0 pm	12.4.16	do	Battalion (less transport section & 60 details) embarked on H.M.T. MEGANTIC.	" 103
12 noon	15.4.16	do	H.M.T. MEGANTIC left port.	
2 am.	20.4.16	H.M.T. MEGANTIC	H.M.T. MEGANTIC arrived MARSEILLES.	
2 pm.	-do-	MARSEILLES	Battalion disembarked.	
7.30 pm	-do-	-do-	Battalion entrained & left for STEENWERCK.	
4.30 am	23.4.16	STEENWERCK	Battalion arrived STEENWERCK & went into billets.	
12.30 pm	24.4.16	-do-	Orders received re parties of all ranks proceeding to trenches for instruction.	
4.0 pm	-do-	-do-	Orders issued re above.	
8.30 am	25.4.16	-do-	12 Officers and 120 N.C.Os & senior soldiers proceeded to the trenches.	

1

Page 13

Instructions regarding War Diaries and Intelligence Summaries are contained in F. S. Regs., Part II. and the Staff Manual respectively. Title pages will be prepared in manuscript.

WAR DIARY

~~or INTELLIGENCE SUMMARY.~~

(*Erase heading not required.*)

Hour, Date, Place			Summary of Events and Information	
2.0 pm	3.4.16	SOLUM	"C" & "D" Coys. left on trawlers "JERICHO" & "VERESIS" for ALEXANDRIA.	
3.30 pm	4.4.16	do.	Hqrs. & "A" & "B" Coys. left on H.M.S. "MALLOW" for ALEXANDRIA.	
8.0 pm	do.	ALEXANDRIA	"C" & "D" Coys. arrived at SIDI BISHR Camp.	
5.0 pm	5.4.16	do.	Hqrs. & "A" & "B" Coys. arrived at SIDI BISHR Camp.	
2.30 pm	6.4.16	do.	Orders received re disposal of transport, animals, surplus S.A.A. &c. in view of approaching embarkation of S.A. Bde. for FRANCE.	App. 99,100
4.0 pm	10.4.16	do	Brigade inspected at SIDI BISHR camp by G.O.C in chief Egyptian Expeditionary Force.	
2.30 pm	11.4.16	do	Orders received re embarkation of stores & baggage.	
11.30 pm	do	do	Orders received for embarkation of Brigade.	app 101
6.0	12.4.16	do.	Order issued for embarkation.	app 102
3.0 pm	12.4.16	do	Battalion (less transport section & 60 details) embarked on H.M.T MEGANTIC.	" 103
12 noon	15.4.16	do	H.M.T. MEGANTIC left port.	
2 am.	20.4.16	H.M.T MEGANTIC.	H.M.T MEGANTIC arrived MARSEILLES.	
2 pm.	- do -	MARSEILLES	Battalion disembarked.	
7-30 pm	- do.	- do.	Battalion entrained & left for STEENWERCK.	
4-30 am	23.4.16	STEENWERCK.	Battalion arrived STEENWERCK & went into billets.	
12-30 pm	24.4.16	- do.	Orders received re parties of all ranks proceeding to trenches for instruction.	
4.0 pm	- do -	- do.	Orders issued re above.	
8-30 am	25.4.16	- do.	12 Officers and 120 N.C.Os + senior soldiers proceeded to the trenches.	

(73989) W — 463. 400,000. 9/14. H.&J.Ltd. Forms/C. 2118/10.

www.ingramcontent.com/pod-product-compliance
Lightning Source LLC
Chambersburg PA
CBHW082010220426
43670CB00014B/2591
* 9 7 8 1 4 7 4 5 0 7 7 8 3 *